Shakespeare in His Time and Ours

Paul N. Siegel is Chairman of the English Department at Long Island University, Zeckendorf Campus. He received his B.S. degree from City College of New York, and his M.A. and Ph.D. from Harvard University. Previous books include *Shakespearean Tragedy and the Elizabethan Compromise*, and *His Infinite Variety: Major Shakespearean Criticism Since Johnson*. Journals in which his articles often appear are *SP*, *SQ*, *PMLA*, and *RES*.

Drawings by Rainey Bennett

SHAKESPEARE
IN HIS TIME
AND OURS

Paul N. Siegel

UNIVERSITY OF NOTRE DAME PRESS

Notre Dame   London

Library of Congress Catalog Card Number: 68–12294

MANUFACTURED IN THE UNITED STATES OF AMERICA

To My Wife

Acknowledgments

Earlier versions of three of these chapters were tried out on my colleagues of the Columbia University Seminar in the Renaissance and two of them on Professor Victor Harris, who, fortunately for me, happened to be working at the British Museum Library at the same time that I was. The questions raised at each of these occasions I found helpful. The staffs of the British Museum Library, the Long Island University Library, the Columbia University Library and the New York Public Library have been patient and courteous in ministering to my needs. So too has been my editor, Mrs. Anne Kozak, in working on the manuscript at a time when the author has been more than usually harried and preoccupied with other matters. Long Island University has furnished me with grants of time that have aided in the writing of the book. Ginn and Company has graciously granted me permission to quote from the George Lyman Kittredge edition of *The Complete Works of Shakespeare*. To each of these I extend my thanks.

Contents

Preface

The essays in this book are united by an underlying thread: the belief that the better we come to understand the Elizabethan Shakespeare, the greater the meaning he has for our time. We must try as best we can—we can never completely succeed—to understand how the intelligent and sensitive spectator of the audience for whom Shakespeare wrote responded to him. Only in so doing will we be true to Shakespeare and will the relevance we find in him be genuine, not factitious.

It is sometimes implied that we need not know the Elizabethan Shakespeare because Shakespeare changes with each age and we need to know only the Shakespeare of our own time. So Martin Esslin tells us in his introduction to Jan Kott's *Shakespeare Our Contemporary*, advancing Kott's candidacy as the creator of the twentieth-century Shakespeare, that "the angle of vision changes with the place, as well as the time, from which the great, the autonomous work of art is seen."[1] The trick is to stand at the vantage point from which Shakespeare can be seen anew, thus reinterpreting him for one's age.

[1] New York, 1964, p. xi.

1

It is true that every age has its own angle of vision as well as its own mode of analysis in interpreting Shakespeare. But critics not only react against their predecessors; they assimilate them. The critics who have allowed themselves to be assimilated, who have had a lasting influence, are those who have entered into the plays instead of using them as the occasion for presenting their own views on life, society and art. Voltaire and Goethe on *Hamlet* are interesting as illustrations of French classicism and German romanticism, but they are historical curiosities, as Hazlitt on *Othello* is not. Different angles of vision reveal new patterns hitherto only partially or dimly perceived, but the critic has to look steadily at the dramas to make sure that he is not imposing a pattern on them that is not there. Such a superimposed pattern can only blur their richness and complexity. And in analyzing this richness and complexity, we can profit from the results of the close scrutiny of any keen and sensitive observer, regardless of his angle of vision or mode of analysis.

Historical scholarship is only an aid to criticism, but it is virtually indispensable to it, lighting up the work so that we may examine it more thoroughly. "The great poets," R. W. Chambers has said, "speak to all time only through the language, conventions, and beliefs of their own age."[2] It follows that in order to hear them properly we must understand their language, conventions and beliefs and not confuse them with our own. The beliefs of an age expressed in a great work of art are generally implicit in it. They subtly shape it rather than being stuck into it like raisins.

It used to be generally said of Shakespeare, and still is frequently said of him, that he transcends any system of ideas.

[2] *Man's Unconquerable Mind* (London, 1939), p. 279.

2

He simply presents life in its vastness without expressing any view so that those of all times and places can respond to him as they respond to life itself. Thus Esslin states: "It is one of the roots of Shakespeare's universality that his work seems totally free of any ideological position . . ." (p. xvii). But art in imposing order on life shapes it in accordance with some design, and Shakespeare's art is no exception. That design springs from the way of looking at life that he acquired from his time.

The converse of the statement that Shakespeare has no ideological position is the assigning to him of an ideological position of one's own time, usually the critic's. Sometimes, the statement that Shakespeare has no ideological position turns out to be really the obverse of the statement that his position is one's own, as when Esslin hails Kott's discovery that Shakespeare was an existentialist—at least as far as the twentieth century is concerned, which is, after all, what counts for us. But Shakespeare is not our contemporary; he is an Elizabethan. His significance for us is not his ideological position, but the emotional experience he gives us through his plays.

That significance I have tried to spell out in the lead essay of this book, "Shakespeare and Our Time's Malaise," which in its discussion of the tragedies and the comedies gives an over-all view of the other essays and states the belief that underlies them. For us the significance of the plays is determined in part by the fact that our response to the experience they afford us must to some degree be affected by our experience living in our own time. Some aspects of Shakespeare have special reverberations for our time, and those who are most keenly aware of what our time is are best able to perceive these reverberations. He who lives on the placid surface of things in suburban United States and isolates himself from the violence and turmoil of our times will not sense them. This is the core of truth in Esslin's introduction to Kott and gives Kott's book what value it has. Kott is able to write eloquently of the *Macbeth* nightmare in connection with "the Auschwitz experience," but he finally distorts the play by making Macbeth's concluding vision of life the total impression gained from it. To be true to Shakespeare, we must not transform him into a twentieth-century man; we must know him as an Elizabethan and respond to him as twentieth-century men. By so doing, we shall find that he enables us better to know ourselves and our time.

Although it is the experience communicated to us by the dramas, not the ideological position that lies behind them, that is significant for us, an understanding of that ideological position helps us to come to grips with the experience. "The Chief Controversy in Shakespearean Criticism Today" attempts to show that the tragedies are an expression of a Christian outlook on life. One reason that the question has been so debated is that the ideas of Christianity remain alive even in our secularized age although not quite in the same form and not in conjunction with the same ideas as in the Elizabethan period. It arouses, therefore, feelings of belief or disbelief for many on the basis of their own philosophy. If the Elizabethans, however, could accept imaginatively Romeo and Juliet as occupying places in the paradise of lovers of the religion of love, as I argue in "Christianity and the Religion of Love in *Romeo and Juliet*," non-Christians today should be able to accept imaginatively the Christian afterlife adumbrated in Shakespeare's four great tragedies.

"Shakespeare's Kneeling-Resurrection Pattern and the Meaning of *King Lear*" seeks to demonstrate that such an

4

afterlife is suggested at the end of the tragedy. It is an interpretation that, it must be admitted, a modern director could not possibly convey to an audience lacking in knowledge of Elizabethan thought. Its acceptance by him, however, would determine the entire way in which he presents the play. In Kott's essay not a sentence is given to Cordelia, a feat almost as difficult to accomplish as discussing *Hamlet* without mentioning the Prince. Peter Brook's production of *Lear*, inspired by Kott, accordingly presented a completely bleak world devoid of meaning. To do so, Brook had to do such things as omit the commiseration of Gloucester by Cornwall's servants and make them instead thrust him brutally off the stage—kindliness and human fellowship being out of place in this world. A production governed by my interpretation would make Cordelia's life and death have significance and that significance would make possible the tragic meaning denied to *Lear* by Brook. The analysis of the ideological position, therefore, helps us to perceive the aesthetic pattern, and the perception of the aesthetic pattern provides us with an experience that makes us more fully conscious of the potentialities of life. This is the tacit assumption of all the essays.

"Shakespeare and the Neo-chivalric Cult of Honor," which bridges the group of essays concerned with tragedy and the group of essays concerned with comedy, demonstrates the contemporaneousness for Elizabethans of five plays with varied foreign settings. An understanding of how Shakespeare presents the destructiveness of the Elizabethan cult of personal honor at any price—we can compare it to our concept of a national honor governed by the consideration "My country, right or wrong"—clears up much that has been baffling in these plays. "Shakespearean Comedy and the Elizabethan Compromise" seeks to view the development of Shakespearean comedy as an expression of the dominant ideology of the Elizabethan period and in relation to the changing climate of feeling produced by a changing society. "The Turns of the Dance" analyzes the structure of *Much Ado About Nothing* in relation to the dominating idea found in the previous essay to lie behind the romantic comedies, the idea of a universal harmony or a cosmic dance. "*A Midsummer Night's Dream* and the Wedding Guests" attempts to recapture something of the experience of its first-performance audience of wedding guests by bearing the occasion in mind while observing the structure of the play.

In the final essay, the question of the relevance of a Shakespeare reconstructed by historical scholarship is sharply and explicitly posed. Must we, if we are to live with *The Merchant of Venice*, change Shylock from the hateful figure conforming to the medieval stereotype of the Jew established by historical scholarship into a character with whom we can feel sympathy? How can a man of the twentieth century who has lived through the Nazis' mass murder of millions of Jews respond to the play? The answer made is that through an understanding of Shylock's meaning for Shakespeare's contemporaries—one which we cannot accept—we can arrive at a meaning for us today without doing violence to Shakespeare's great work. This meaning I hold to be of the greatest significance.

I

Shakespeare and Our Time's Malaise*

In Aldous Huxley's satiric novel *Brave New World*, it will be remembered, the Savage, who has been brought up on an Indian reservation, one of the few isolated remnants of previous civilization in the world of the future, gets the opportunity to visit this world of Our Ford 600. He looks forward rapturously to seeing it and, having managed to acquire as a child one of the few surviving copies of the work of a curious old writer named Shakespeare, on which he has nurtured himself, exclaims in the words of Miranda when she sees human beings for the first time on Prospero's island, "O brave new world that has such people in it." He finds this new world to be a hierarchical society of stand-

* Reprinted by permission and with some alterations from *Teachers College Record*, vol. 65, No. 7, April 1964.

ardized human beings, each, conditioned from childhood to be satisfied with his place in it and to want only the same superficial pleasures, without individuality or depth of feeling. The very idea of expecting these people to understand Shakespeare is ridiculous.

Huxley's gauge of the ability to respond to Shakespeare as the measure of a civilization is a good one, and today, some thirty years after *Brave New World*, shortly after the four-hundredth anniversary celebration of Shakespeare's birth, with its tributes and its festivals, it may seem as if we come off very well indeed. A cynic may, however, wonder how many members of the theatre audience attending a Shakespeare performance (too frequently a theatrical occasion rather than a genuine performance) are making a ritualistic obeisance to culture and how many are involved in a genuine emotional experience. If the members of the theatre audience probably correspond mainly to the Beta Plusses of Huxley's class society, the members of the television audience predominantly correspond to the Deltas, and here we are told as a matter for self-congratulation that more people saw a Shakespeare play in a single television performance than in all previous performances put together. Our cynic may, however, ask how many persons went to the refrigerator for a beer while the set was on and with what degree of attention they watched the play after they returned—if, indeed, they did return.

We should indeed not be too complacent about the statistics of Shakespeare productions and Shakespeare editions. True, there are fine performances of Shakespeare which evoke a deep audience response, not merely the reverently unreceptive reaction of which Alfred Harbage has complained, and young students coming to Shakespeare do find their minds and emotions stirred. But if we are not yet living in Huxley's Brave New World, his society is a satiric extension of our own. Although Shakespeare has not been banned by us, as he is in Huxley's rigorously logical system, he may be said to be a kind of subversive counter-force, acting against the dehumanizing forces in our civilization.

As Lionel Trilling has said, "It is simply not possible for a work of literature that comes within the borders of greatness not to ask for more energy and fineness of life, and, by its own communication of awareness, bring these qualities into being."[1] This is true regardless of the beliefs expressed by the artist. We cannot today subscribe to such notions as the divinely appointed function of kings, one of the key ideas in the world view dominant in Shakespeare's time, but we need only accept them provisionally to participate in an emotional experience which, in moving us, affects the way in which we respond to life, a process which in the largest sense we can call educational. To say this is not to say that Shakespeare was the didactic artist Samuel Johnson wanted him to be and some Victorian critics made him out to be.

We can best examine this "educational" process by returning to *Brave New World* to observe how the life depicted there is similar to that which such a social diagnostician as Erich Fromm has described in analyzing the malaise of our own society, and then by looking at Shakespearean tragedy (we shall look at Shakespearean comedy later) to see how it communicates an experience that works against such a kind of life. "Expecting Deltas to know what liberty is!" laughs the World-Controller at the Savage's attempt to free the Deltas from their unthinking servitude to their machines and from their addiction to soma, the Brave New World equivalent to tranquilizers. "And now expecting them to understand *Othello!* My good boy!" Freedom and receptivity to *Othello* are indeed related.

[1] *Beyond Culture* (New York, 1965), p. 168.

In Brave New World there are, as the World-Controller tells the listening schoolboys, no pains spared "to preserve you, so far as that is possible, from having emotions at all." No one feels deeply about anything or any one. Sexual relationships are casual and superficial. The slogan which everyone has learned from childhood is "Every one belongs to every one else." This slogan does not express a genuine relatedness between individuals but the feelingless union of automatons. Occasionally, someone feels some small irritation or even gets some obscure sense of emptiness, but then there are always the distractions of electromagnetic golf and the holiday from reality of soma.

This is not too far different from the state of affairs described by Fromm as characterizing our own time:

> Human relations are essentially those of alienated automatons, each basing his security on staying close to the herd and not being different in thought, feeling or action. While everybody tries to be as close as possible to the rest, everybody remains utterly alone, pervaded by the deep sense of insecurity, anxiety, and guilt which always results when human separateness cannot be overcome. Our civilization offers many palliatives which help people to be consciously unaware of this aloneness: . . . the strict routine of bureaucratized, mechanical work . . . the routine of amusement, the passive consumption of sounds and sights offered by the amusement industry.[2]

In Shakespeare's tragic universe, however, the heroes are no "alienated automatons": they feel intensely and cause us to feel intensely. In fact, we may say that it is the capacity for suffering which is the mark of the tragic hero. He is superior precisely because he can suffer more—not mere animal pain, not superficial irritation, but the deeply human suffering that comes when

[2] *The Art of Loving* (New York, 1963), pp. 72–73.

a man of fine sensibility for whom things matter encounters calamity. Such a person is capable of a more exquisite joy as well as of a more exquisite pain than an automatized being. "O my soul's joy!" exclaims Othello when he rejoins Desdemona at Cyprus, "My soul hath her content so absolute/ That not another comfort like to this/ Succeeds in unknown fate" (II. 1. 186–194).* But just because Othello feels so deeply and because Desdemona means so much to him, he becomes a tragic hero. Iago tells him that in Venice all wives are unfaithful, but Othello is not one to accommodate himself to the behavior of the group. Desdemona is for him the ideal "where I have garner'd up my heart,/ Where either I must live, or bear no life" (IV. 11. 57–58). He is profoundly committed; he cannot "play it cool" or "take it easy."

Shakespeare's tragic hero does not follow the rules of ordinary worldly prudence. No marriage counselor would approve of the conduct of Romeo and Juliet, who fall in love at first sight, immediately get married despite their short acquaintance, incur grave dangers and then commit suicide. But Shakespeare, of course, was not writing a guide to marriage; he was writing tragedy, which gives a heightened sense of life. Although the reckless abandon of the lovers contributes to their disaster, their love is presented as glorious in the completeness with which two persons give themselves to each other, even to the giving up of their lives. Juliet does have a counselor, the nurse—worldly, practical, down-to-earth, to say nothing of earthy—whose advice to Juliet to forget her secret marriage to Romeo and to accept Paris as her new husband is in contrast to the unselfishness and intensity of Juliet's devotion. For the nurse, marriage merely entails

* George Lyman Kittredge, ed., *The Complete Works of Shakespeare* (Boston: Ginn and Co., 1957). All subsequent references are to this edition.

the satisfaction of sexual desire and the gaining of social position. One source of reconciliation at the close of the tragedy comes from our perception that the experience of Romeo and Juliet, brief as it was, was richer than anything that such crude natures as the nurse or such limited ones as Lady Capulet could have had in their entire lives. "Come what sorrow can," Romeo exclaims just before Friar Laurence joins him and Juliet in marriage, "It cannot countervail the exchange of joy/ That one short minute gives me in her sight" (III. vi. 3–5). Another source of reconciliation is the perception that their love triumphs over the hate of their parents, that through them the proper bonds that hold together men in human society are restored to Verona. Behind *Romeo and Juliet* lies the Renaissance concept of sexual love as a manifestation of the all-pervading love of God through which the universe is governed, and this concept is an expression of the realization of man's need to liberate himself, as Fromm says, from his alienation "from himself, from his fellow men, and from nature."[3]

In *Brave New World*, Helmholtz Watson, the propaganda technician who becomes conscious of latent powers untapped within him (or, we may say, the Madison Avenue advertising man who should have been a poet), can only laugh despite his admiration for Shakespeare's use of language when the Savage reads *Romeo and Juliet* aloud to him. "Getting into such a state about having a girl—it seemed rather ridiculous." But because "every one belongs to every one else," because there are no deep emotions, Watson has nothing about which to write.

Today, Fromm has pointed out, there is not only prevalent the idea of the 1920's that all that is needed in sexual relationships is a knowledge of technique, which will solve every prob-

---

[3] *Beyond the Chains of Illusion* (New York, 1963), p. 48.

lem in the same way as in industrial production, but there is prevalent also the "team" idea of marriage:

> In any number of articles on happy marriage, the ideal described is that of the smoothly functioning team. . . . All this kind of relationship amounts to is the well-oiled relationship between two persons who remain strangers all their lives, who never arrive at a "central relationship," but who treat each other with courtesy and who attempt to make each other feel better.[4]

In their brief marriage, Romeo and Juliet came closer together than ever do two such cogs in the social machine.

Automatons cannot feel, cannot love, cannot suffer. Shakespeare's tragic hero suffers as he does because he is in a sense more fully human than most human beings, a figure convincingly lifelike yet greater than life size, with stronger passions than most men command. He may be a great leader of men like Othello, with his emotions superbly held in check so that he seems incapable of losing control of himself; but underneath his self-control is a strength of feeling which can erupt and destroy him. It can destroy him because, as Elizabethans were fond of reiterating, passion not subject to reason leads to ruination; yet this strength of feeling springs from a force of character which makes him a titan.

If Shakespeare's tragic hero is a magnification of ordinary humanity in the intensity of his emotion, an intensity which makes him, in the words of Walter Pater, burn with a "hard, gemlike flame," his villain, while the creature of his master passion, serves that master passion with the "cold fire" of the fanatic. The fanatic, says Fromm, is

a highly narcissistic person who is disengaged from the world

---

[4] *The Art of Loving*, pp. 73–74.

outside. He does not really feel anything since authentic feeling is always the result of the interrelation between oneself and the world. . . . He lives in a state of narcissistic excitement since he has drowned the feeling of his isolation and emptiness in a total submission to the idol and in the simultaneous deification of his own ego, which he has made part of the idol.[5]

This is an excellent description of Richard III, Iago and Edmund in their dedication to their pseudo-Machiavellian creed of worship of a nature whose law, as Edmund proclaims it, is that of complete egoism. Each, in worshipping at this altar, is worshipping himself, his asserted superiority to mankind. In his worship of himself, he acts cold-bloodedly, without feeling toward others, but in a "state of narcissistic excitement" in which he delights in ironies which only he can apprehend. Yet Richard's sense of isolation bursts out in his words, "There is no creature loves me;/ And if I die, no soul shall pity me" (V. iii. 201–202); and Iago's inner emptiness emerges in his comment on Cassio: "He hath a daily beauty in his life/ That makes me ugly" (V. i. 19–20).

Though Shakespeare's villains have the qualities of fanatics, they also have the qualities of the calloused bureaucrat and the mechanical man of business. Goneril and Regan in their cold-blooded calculation, it has been pointed out, make frequent use of mercantile terminology and imagery. So, too, does Iago, the mercenary soldier who speaks of the "trade of war" (I. ii. 1). "Put money in thy purse; follow thou the wars," Iago tells his dupe Roderigo (I. iii. 344–345) in suggesting to him that he use money as his weapon in besieging Desdemona and gaining the prize of her love. Similarly Edmund, laying his plot against Edgar, regards his father and brother as so many counters in the

[5] *May Man Prevail?* (New York, 1961), pp. 24–25.

14

game which he is playing: "A credulous father! and a brother noble . . . I see the business" (I. iii. 195–198). The apotheosis of this attitude was reached in the sending of millions of human beings to gas chambers in an efficiently ordered assembly line, with careful accounts being kept. Fromm comments on Robert S. Bird's impression of Eichmann at his trial:

> One suddenly hears speaking the faceless "company man" of the over-sized industrial organization, the alibi-ridden, buck-passing, double-talking, reading-by-ear personality who has been drained of native emotion and principle and filled with an unreal ideology. . . . Eichmann has become more human, because we can recognize that he is as inhuman as we all are. This new kind of inhumanity . . . is the attitude of total bureaucratization that administers men as if they were things.[6]

What is dead and inhuman in us corresponds to what is in Shakespeare's villain, who indeed administers men as if they were things.

What is alive and human in us, on the other hand, corresponds to what is in his tragic hero, a man rich in humanity whose vitality reveals the possibilities of existence. John Stuart Mill in his essay "On Liberty," arguing against the Victorian conformity that would suppress as perilous strong individual desires and impulses as well as deviant opinions, enables us better to understand him:

> To say that one person's desires and feelings are stronger and more various than those of another is merely to say that he has more of the raw material of human nature, and is therefore capable, perhaps, of more evil, but certainly of more good. . . . Energy may be turned to bad uses; but more good may always be made of an energetic nature than of an

[6] Ibid., p. 198.

15

indolent and impassive one. . . . Strong susceptibilities . . .
are . . . the source from which are generated the most passionate love of virtue and the strongest self-control. It is
through the cultivation of these that society both does its
duty and protects its interests: not by rejecting the stuff of
which heroes are made, because it knows not how to
make them.[7]

It is because Shakespeare's heroes have "more of the raw material
of human nature" than ordinary men and show the potentialities
of humanity that they arouse our awe and admiration. Even a
character such as Macbeth, who, as he advances in evil, murders
women and children, never wholly loses our sympathy and always
keeps us in awe because we remember what he was and are
aware of the immense potentialities for good within him which
he has destroyed. This is true even at the conclusion when, alienated from mankind, he finds life to be terribly meaningless, a
"tale told by an idiot."

Mill regarded "the wearing down into uniformity all that is
individual" in human nature as a growing danger. Today there
is an even higher degree of unthinking and unconscious conformity. The "lonely crowd" is made up of "outer-directed"
"organization men." As Fromm puts it,

Modern capitalism . . . needs men who feel free and in-
dependent, not subject to any authority or principle or
conscience—yet willing to be commanded, to do what is
expected of them, to fit into the social machine without
friction; who can be guided without force, led without
leaders, prompted without aim. . . .[8]

Or, as Huxley's World-Controller has it, "Civilization has abso-

---

[7] *The Philosophy of John Stuart Mill*, ed. Marshall Cohen (Oxford
University Press, 1964), p. 254.
[8] *The Art of Loving*, p. 72.

lutely no need of nobility or heroism."[9] In a society which rejects "the stuff of which heroes are made," Shakespearean tragedy keeps alive the idea of the hero.

Although the Shakespearean tragic hero towers above ordinary men, he is also, in his humanity, representative of mankind. Hamlet is not merely Hamlet; he is also Everyman. We are all faced with the problem of action in an imperfect world. The suffering of the tragic hero lifts us above our own petty troubles and makes us conscious of our common humanity, of the ties that exist between all men as well as of the greatness of individual spirits. It enables each of us, in the words of Thomas Gray, "to feel what others are, and know myself a man."

Our generation has been acquainted with so much horror that it is hard to remain undulled. Can we retain the significance of Belsen and Hiroshima, of Guernica, Lidice, and the incinerated peasant villages of Vietnam? When we constantly hear calculations about how many millions would be destroyed in a nuclear war, when balance sheets of destruction are constantly being drawn up, must not human life be cheapened? William Hazlitt, living a century and a half before the horrors of our time but in the midst of the mass brutalities of the industrial revolution, found in tragedy a means by which the value of human life in general is maintained through the dramatization of the suffering of the individual:

> We have been so used to count by millions of late, that we think the units that compose them nothing. . . . If we are imbued with a deep sense of individual weal or woe, we shall be awe-struck at the idea of humanity in general. . . . I defy any great tragic writer to despise that nature which he

[9] *Brave New World* (New York, 1950), pp. 284–285.

17

understands, or that heart which he has probed, with all its rich, bleeding materials of joy and sorrow.[10]

If we accompany Lear on his purgatorial progress, we must, like him, awake to a new feeling of sympathy for our fellow man. If we witness the storm on the heath, whose winds seem like furies released from hell by the ferocity of Goneril and Regan, the possibilities of chaos are shatteringly brought home to us. "Is this the promised end?" (V. III. 264) exclaims Kent at the final, unexpected horror of Cordelia's death, recalling the promise of the Day of Judgment. In the death of Cordelia, brought about by the evil passions of man, he envisages the end of the world, causing us to do so also; but as we contemplate the self-sacrificing devotion and fortitude of Cordelia, we are piercingly aware of what the extinction of humanity, after all its travails and despite the light of love with which it has sustained itself within the darkness of life, would mean. In the age of the hydrogen bomb, Shakespearean tragedy has an ever deeper meaning.

Shakespearean tragedy heightens our feeling of the value of life through its presentation of greatness in a defeat which is in a sense a triumph. Shakespearean comedy heightens our feeling of the value of life through its presentation of human vitality winning out over the mechanical codes which would imprison it and the automatized persons who would destroy it. The hero of Shakespearean comedy is an embodiment of that ideal of the age, the gentleman, a balanced personality, poised and urbane, possessed of the social graces without being a fop, learned without being a pedant, knightly without being a military swaggerer. Opposed to him is a "humors" character, one who is ridden by a single ruling passion, whose behavior is set in advance so that he can respond to the surprises of the world only in a single

---

[10] *Complete Works*, ed. P. P. Howe (London, 1931), XII, 53–55.

mechanical way: a Shylock, obsessed by his hatred and driven by his money-madness, governed by his business code so that if compassion is not written into the contract he does not regard himself as obligated to feel it; a Don John, melancholy and malevolent, plotting compulsively; a Duke Frederick smoldering with stifled wrath or storming tyranically at each appearance; a Malvolio so "sick of self-love" that he stalks about like a supercilious marionette. Each of these "humors" characters is hostile to gaiety, to resilience, to life.

The fool, who is a kind of personified *élan vital*, buoyantly irrepressible despite his being continually squelched or "put down," as the Elizabethan idiom has it, is therefore inimical to him and associated with the hero or heroine. Shylock's house is hell, says Jessica, and Launcelot is a merry devil who makes life in it less dismal. Launcelot runs away from Shylock and goes to serve Bassanio, who will not starve him and will grant him a new livery, the fresh clothes which in Shakespeare so frequently indicate a new spirit. Touchstone's satiric wit, which had been appreciated by Rosalind's father, is regarded suspiciously by Duke Frederick, and Celia gives him a friendly warning that he will be whipped if he is not careful. He runs away with Rosalind and Celia to breathe the invigorating air of the Forest of Arden, where the rightful duke once more laughs at his sallies. Feste is contemptuously treated by Malvolio, but he is defended by Olivia, who at the end smiles at the story of his mirthful revenge and does not punish him. Under the gracious protection of the aristocracy, the fool, no longer "put down," pops up at the conclusion of the play more full of life than ever. For the victory of the gentleman, signalized by his marriage to his lady, is the triumph of life over the wasteland of the spirit and the symbol of its renewal of itself.

Significantly, Shakespearean comedy ordinarily contains what

Northrop Frye calls a "green world," a world of enchanted forest derived from the drama of folk ritual, which acts as a means for regeneration. The action of Shakespearean comedy, Frye points out,

> begins in a world represented as a normal world, moves into the green world, goes into a metamorphosis there in which the comic resolution is achieved, and returns to the normal world. The forest in this play [the early comedy, *The Two Gentlemen of Verona*] is the embryonic form of the fairy world of *A Midsummer Night's Dream*, the Forest of Arden in *As You Like It*, Windsor Forest in *The Merry Wives of Windsor*, and the pastoral world of the mythical sea-coasted Bohemia in *The Winter's Tale*. In all these comedies, there is the same rhythmic movement from normal world to green world and back again. . . . In *The Tempest* the entire action takes place in the second world, and the same may be said of *Twelfth Night*, which, as its title implies, presents a carnival society, not so much a green world as an ever-green one.[11]

It may be pointed out, however, that even in *The Tempest* Prospero abjures his magic at the conclusion and returns to his proper kingdom, and that in *Twelfth Night*, with the presiding duke freed of the love-sickness of pastoral romance, Illyria becomes a "normal" world. Through the magic of the "green world" in conjunction with the power of love, there is achieved in the "normal" world a new social order in which Antonio is no longer the king of Milan and Malvolio no longer the steward exceeding his proper function in Olivia's household. In the same fashion, in *As You Like It* and *Much Ado About Nothing*, there is achieved a new social order in which the usurping Duke

---

[11] "The Argument of Comedy," *English Institute Essays, 1948*, ed. D. A. Robertson, Jr. (Columbia University Press, 1949), p. 67.

Frederick and the mover-behind-the-scenes Don John are no longer present.

The "green world," a world of music, poetry and romance, is life as we dream it can be, life in which man is reintegrated into the nature which modern urban civilization has excluded, in which man is in harmony with the universe and at peace with himself. It is good for men and civilizations to have such dreams, for these enable them to return to the workaday world with a vision of life that may act as a model for creative endeavor. It prevents life from becoming a meaningless, mechanical round of existence as in *Brave New World*, where there is no "green world" of the spirit, only the everlasting here-and-now which is everywhere the same, with the bedrooms of every hotel all over the world equipped with "liquid air, television, vibro-vacuum massage, radio, boiling caffeine solution, hot contraceptives and eight different kinds of scent," bedrooms not so very different from those in the luxurious motor inns that dot the United States, making the traveller feel that, no matter where he is, he is in the same place.

The enchanted realm of Shakespearean comedy, therefore, like the world of poetic imagination of Shakespearean tragedy, can refresh us in our wasteland. Our salvation, to be sure, cannot be achieved by doggedly reading and rereading Shakespeare, but Shakespeare can help to renew our spirits so that we can seek that salvation out, and he can give us some idea of what it consists of.

II

The Chief Controversy in Shakespearean Criticism Today

I.

The question of questions, the main point of difference in Shakespearean criticism today, is whether or not Shakespearean tragedy is the expression of a Christian outlook on life. Many critics today have come to feel that Shakespearean tragedy is Christian in a way that previous generations had not realized; however, since many other critics have remained unconvinced that this is true, a most fundamental issue has evolved.

A number of those viewing Shakespearean tragedy as Christian have written as men who themselves are of Christian belief, and consequently there has been a tendency on the part of some to regard everyone holding this general view as a Christian apologist intent on imposing his own convictions on Shakespeare. Since the temptation to find that Shakespeare's genius has penetrated to the truth in one's own possession is undoubtedly a subtle one, and not confined to Christians, each interpretation must be examined on its own merits. Moreover, many of those who have been referred to as "Christianizers" of Shakespeare, including myself, are manifestly historical scholars who, as J. C. Maxwell said in placing himself in their company, do not have "a confessional axe to grind."[1] To dismiss the view that Shakespearean tragedy is Christian as being Christian apology has as little validity as to dismiss the criticism pointing out the importance of the doctrine of courtly love in much of medieval literature as propaganda for extramarital affairs.

For the most part the members of each of the conflicting groups have not sought to come to close combat with the opposition; rather they seem content in developing their own positions and taking an occasional shot at the other side, to say nothing of taking shots at those on their own side—neither group being of course a disciplined army. However, a number of engagements have taken place, and recently Roland M. Frye in his *Shakespeare and Christian Doctrine* trained the formidable battery of his theological learning on the "theologizers" of Shakespeare, attacking their writing as both poor theology and poor criticism. Frye's book has acted as a call to arms for me to re-affirm the position I took in *Shakespearean Tragedy and the Elizabethan Compromise* in which I sought to show how Shakespearean tragedy expresses the Christian humanism that dominated the thought of the time. There I did not engage in extended polemics; rather I presented my analysis of the nature of Shakespearean tragedy and referred the reader to those who had opposing opinions so that he might make his own comparison.

---

[1] "The Presuppositions of Tragedy," *Essays in Criticism*, V (1955), 175.

A. C. Bradley's masterly analysis of Shakespearean tragedy, I pointed out, is a necessary point of departure, but it needs to be modified and supplemented:

> Bradley found that Shakespeare's tragic universe conveys the impression of being a moral order that casts out evil by the laws of its own nature but that it mysteriously continues to engender it and expels it only through a fearsome struggle in which good as well as evil is destroyed. There are four major alterations that have to be made in his picture of Shakespearean tragedy: (1) Shakespearean tragedy conveys a sense of divine providence; (2) this divine providence visits a poetically appropriate retribution upon the guilty; (3) characters and action suggest analogies with the Bible story; (4) there are intimations of the heaven and hell of Christian religion.[2]

Because each of these four assertions has been challenged, I shall deal with the objections raised against each of them. I hope that the critics with whom I polemicize will accept the occasional fierceness of my assault as part of the game of Shakespearean criticism and that the critics who occupy the same general position as my own—they include among others Roy W. Battenhouse, Joseph H. Bryant, Jr. and Irving Ribner—will excuse me for not taking up our differences, but my hands are sufficiently full in combatting the anti-"Christianizers."

---

[2] Paul N. Siegel, *Shakespearean Tragedy and the Elizabethan Compromise* (New York University Press, 1957), p. 82. Like Bradley's analysis, much of what I have to say, although mainly concerned with *Hamlet*, *Othello*, *Macbeth* and *King Lear*, is applicable in varying degrees to the other tragedies. What most distinguishes these four tragedies from the others is their suggestions of a heaven and a hell awaiting the outcome of the struggles we witness. Such suggestions are present also in *Richard III* and *Richard II*, but they do not work upon the imagination with the force that they do in the four great tragedies.

II.

Since assertion two is a corollary of assertion one, I will discuss the two of them together. Clifford Leech finds that not only is there no divine providence represented in Shakespearean tragedy but that there cannot be: "The tragic picture is incompatible with the Christian faith. It is equally incompatible with any form of religion that assumes the existence of a personal and kindly God."[3] For the essence of tragedy is unmerited suffering which an omnipotent and benevolent God would not permit. It is the contemplation of such suffering which causes tragic terror, for we perceive that the tragic situation is recurrent in human life. At the conclusion of a Shakespearean tragedy, the evil situation is no more, but "there is nothing reassuring in the new situation, no promise that a new chain of evil will not quickly ensue, no lesson that men or the gods have learned. No message of hope for the future has been brought."[4] "Remnants of old faiths jut out now and then like rocks in a troubled sea, but there is no firm footing on them, and the sea is limitless, the laws of its tides unknown, its winds incalculable."[5]

Bradley too emphasizes the presence of unmerited suffering and death in Shakespearean tragedy, but he says that both it and the recurrence of evil create an impression which is only one of two aspects of the tragic vision, two aspects "which we can neither separate nor reconcile."[6] With the terror of Shakespearean tragedy, he points out, there comes "something like a feeling of acquiescence in the catastrophe" (p. 36). For a sense of a moral order is conveyed to us through our perception that

[3] *Shakespeare's Tragedies and Other Studies in Seventeenth Century Drama* (London, 1950), p. 18.

[4] Idem, p. 172.

[5] Idem, p. 86.

[6] A. C. Bradley, *Shakespearean Tragedy* (London, 1905), p. 37.

the catastrophe is a result of the work of evil, which is self-destructive, and that the hero, even if this evil does not have its lodging in him, nevertheless contributes in some measure to his disaster because of his own defects. What Leech and the other critics opposed to the view of Shakespearean tragedy as Christian have done is to separate the two aspects of Shakespeare's tragic vision which Bradley says cannot be separated and to ignore or deny the aspect of it that conveys a sense of moral order.

If, however, Shakespearean tragedy is, as Leech says, a revelation of a universe indifferent to man, the terror thus afforded to us being balanced only by the pride we feel as we identify ourselves with the hero in nobly withstanding destiny, why is this hero never shown as withstanding only external misfortunes that do not have any human agency? Why is the chief cause of disaster always an evil person, and why is this person always overcome at the end? Bradley's answer is that there is represented in Shakespeare's tragic universe an order that is no mere blind chance or a mechanically working destiny, for always the cosmic order is inimical to the evil which has convulsed its being and which it finally expels. To alter somewhat Leech's metaphor, the storm of devastation we witness in Shakespearean tragedy is terrifying, making life's journey hazardous and uncertain, yet the winds and the tides are governed by a law by which men, despite the treachery of the rocks and of the waters ever ready to engulf them, must seek to guide themselves.

What Bradley calls the laws of the moral order Elizabethans would have regarded as the workings of divine providence whose operations were described in numerous works of popular philosophy and religion and were presented in works of literature. One of the most important ways in which divine providence was thought to manifest itself was through the visitation of a poetically appropriate retribution upon an ill-doer.[7] When I pointed out the presence of such justice in *Othello*, Edward Hubler replied (without showing where I had wrenched the text in my demonstration of this justice): "The view of tragedy as the dispensation of justice strikes me as childish. In any case, that is the view of tragedy my freshmen are most likely to have."[8] Leaving aside the question of whether Samuel Johnson, who asked for precisely such justice, would have belonged among Hubler's freshmen, what Hubler did not perceive, although I stated that Desdemona suffers through no fault of her own, was that the poetic justice of which I was speaking was not the poetic justice of neo-classical criticism, which demanded that there be a "just distribution of good or evil."[9] In Shakespearean tragedy, contrary to Johnson's demand, the good are not rewarded at the conclusion, but the evil suffer a fate peculiarly appropriate to their offences so that more than coincidence seems to be at work. This is the kind of stroke which Aristotle commended (*Poetics*, ch. 9) for its·dramatic power: "Of the things which happen by chance, those seem to excite more wonder which appear to have happened in accordance with some design, such as when the statue of Mitys in Argos fell on the murderer of Mitys and killed him as he was witnessing a festival. Such things seem to happen according to some design."

The fact that such poetically appropriate retribution takes place is not heavily underscored, as it is in the cruder literature of Shakespeare's time, but it is there. In *Hamlet* it is more explicitly presented than in the other tragedies, given in that same

[7] Cf. Siegel, pp. 85–86, 213–214.

[8] "The Damnation of Othello: Some Limitations on the Christian View of the Play," *SQ*, IX (1958), 298.

[9] *Samuel Johnson on Shakespeare*, ed. W. K. Wimsatt, Jr. (London, 1960), p. 33.

"choral comment" in which Sylvan Barnet finds nothing but a "picture of destruction" and "irreparable ruin"[10] that is Horatio's summary of the story he has to tell:

> So shall you hear
> Of carnal, bloody, and unnatural acts,
> Of accidental judgments, casual slaughters;
> Of deaths put on by cunning and forc'd cause,
> And, in this upshot, purposes mistook
> Fall'n on the inventors' heads.
>
> (V. ii. 391–396)

The "carnal, bloody, and unnatural acts" are, of course, the adultery, murder and incest of Claudius, the acts which were revealed by a supernatural visitation and which brought about the struggle culminating in Claudius' death. "Accidental judgments," says George Lyman Kittredge, no "Christianizer" but a critic with a masterly knowledge of the Elizabethan language, are "judgments of God brought about by means apparently accidental," and "casual slaughters" "merely repeats the idea."[11] This refers to the deaths of Polonius and the Queen. "Deaths put on by cunning and forc'd cause," deaths brought about by a cunning forced to meet cunning by the necessities of self-defense, refers to the deaths of Rosencrantz and Guildenstern. "Purposes mistook/ Fall'n on the inventors' heads," miscarried intentions of murder boomeranging to return upon the plotters, refers to the deaths of Claudius and Laertes. The holocaust is not indiscriminate but the workings of an order which operates by the laws of the power that created it, an order of which seeming chance is a part.

Leech lists Polonius, Rosencrantz and Guildenstern among

---

[10] "Some Limitations of a Christian Approach to Shakespeare," *ELH*, XXII (1955), 86.

[11] *Hamlet*, ed. George Lyman Kittredge (Boston, 1939), p. 298.

the Shakespearean minor characters "whose sudden and cruel deaths do not arise out of any fault of their own" (p. 9). But is it not significant that Polonius is killed while spying, that spying so delighted in by this worldly-wise old counselor, for what else is the purpose of the Reynaldo scene if not to establish Polonius' love of devious "indirections" (II. i. 66)? Foolishly proud of his "policy," (II. ii. 47) a word which for Elizabethans had the pejorative meaning of underhandedness, Polonius eavesdrops on Hamlet, "loosing" his daughter to him to draw him out and supplying her with a religious book that she may assume "devotion's visage" (III. i. 47). The second time he eavesdrops on Hamlet he meets his death: in the game which he thinks he knows so well but whose deadliness he does not realize, twice is too much. "Take thy fortune," says Hamlet (III. iv. 32–33), on finding him dead, "Thou find'st to be too busy is some danger." This busybody ignorantly intruding himself between Claudius and Hamlet is fittingly killed while engaged in his characteristic activity. In slaying Polonius, Hamlet is indeed, as he says (III. iv. 175), acting as heaven's "scourge and minister" (how else can we take his words than that he is fulfilling the will of providence?), even though his own soul is in a perilous state as he takes on the aspect of a criminal avenger.[12]

Rosencrantz and Guildenstern have sometimes been regarded as innocent dupes of Claudius, unaware of his evil intentions, concerned for Hamlet's own sake to find out what is plaguing him and then sincerely concerned about protecting the king of Denmark from Hamlet's alleged lunacy. But Hamlet himself regards them as "adders fang'd," (III. iv. 203) sycophantic courtiers who will do anything to gain the favor of the king. This is the meaning of his jibe that they are like sponges that soak up

---

[12] Cf. Siegel, pp. 101–116.

"the king's countenance, his rewards, his authorities" (IV. ii. 16–17). We must believe him, for throughout the play he exposes the corruption underlying the fair appearance, and his view of them is accepted by Horatio whose eyes are clear if they do not pierce as deep as Hamlet's. Further Hamlet tells Gertrude that Rosencrantz and Guildenstern "must sweep my way,/ And marshal me to knavery" (III. iv. 204–205). "Tempt him with speed abroad," Claudius instructs them (IV. iii. 56). In clearing his path to destruction, hurrying him aboard ship, they are unknowingly hurrying to their own destruction. The instant death, without even waiting for the grinding of the ax, which Claudius had commanded be visited upon Hamlet, is instead visited upon them. "The engineer," as Hamlet had anticipated (III. iv. 206–207), has been "hoist with his own petar," an irony which was a favorite theme in works of moral philosophy, emblem books and literature.[13] Hamlet states "They did make love to this employment," (V. ii.58) and simply asked to be dealt with in this way, their destruction coming as a result of "their own insinuation," the eagerness with which they sought to wriggle into Claudius' favor by treacherously deceiving their erstwhile friend. Horatio's choral reference to the "forc'd cause" of their deaths confirms its place in the design of providence.

Similarly the purposes of Claudius return upon his own head. Laertes, his tool, turns against him, exposes him before the court, thrusts the unbuttoned foil Claudius has instructed him to use through his body,[14] and forces the poisoned wine between Clau-

---

[13] Cf. Russell A. Fraser, *Shakespeare's Poetics* (New York, 1962), p. 33: "The engineer, infallibly, is hoist with his own petar, an irony the emblem books adumbrate over and over."

[14] "Thus doth he [God] force the swords of wicked men," says Buckingham, being led to execution, "To turn their own points on their masters' bosoms." —*Richard III*, V. i. 23–24.

dius' lips. The ironic appropriateness is pointed up by Laertes: "He is justly served;/ It is a poison temper'd by himself" (V. ii. 338–339). Drinking of the cup prepared for others seems to have been a conventional image for a poetically appropriate divine retribution. "For the which cruell act," says Holinshed of the murder of Prince Edward, "the more part of the dooers in their latter daies dranke of the like cup, by the righteous iustice and due punishment of God."[15] Macbeth too, we may remember, had said in words that came figuratively true for himself, as they literally came true for Claudius:

> This even-handed justice
> Commends the ingredients of our poisoned chalice
> To our own lips. (I. vii. 10–12)

So too Albany says at the conclusion of *King Lear* that "all foes" will have to drink "the cup of their deservings" (V. iii. 303–304). In the dramatic representation of the image in *Hamlet*, the members of the court are grouped formally about the main characters and stand frozen in horror. The effect is suggested by the words of a student of Elizabethan stage pageantry: "utilizing . . . the older technique of the pageants, the Elizabethan dramatists stopped the flow of action at certain points, and created stage pictures to stress memorable and symbolical scenes."[16]

Laertes also points up the ironic appropriateness of his own death in this emblematic scene of divine justice. "I am justly kill'd with mine own treachery," he says (V. ii. 316–317), "as a woodcock in mine own springe," caught in his own trap like a foolish bird. This is similar to a statement in Philippe Desprez'

---

[15] Quoted by A. P. Rossiter, *Angel with Horns* (London, 1961), p. 3.
[16] Alice Venezky, *Pageantry on the Shakespearean Stage* (New York, 1951), p. 122.

emblem book *Theatre des Animaux* which Russell Fraser quotes: "the cozener is his own prime gull. . . . the hunter . . . preys on no one more than himself" (p. 33).

From this examination of retribution in *Hamlet*, then, we can say that, as opposed to Leech and Barnet, Bradley is correct and that what Bradley himself says has to be extended: not only does the fact that evil destroys itself indicate the existence of a moral order but the poetically appropriate manner of this destruction indicates, in keeping with the ideas of the period, the workings of divine providence. Bradley's other point in connection with his concept of a moral order manifesting itself, namely that the Shakespearean tragic hero has a moral imperfection that contributes to his catastrophe, has been challenged by A. P. Rossiter, another of the critics opposed to a Christian interpretation of Shakespeare.

> The theory (extracted from Aristotle) says that the hero's nature is "flawed" and his fate follows this excess or deficiency. Its effect is to shift all blame from the universe (or to give that consoling impression), and it is popular enough: both because of the ease with which "tragic weaknesses" can be diagnosed (or devised)—when we know how the story ends; and, again, because it re-establishes the comforting belief that the universe is moral, and the fates of tragic heroes somehow just.[17]

The argument here is complicated by the reference to Aristotle, an ancient stumbling-block as well as a guide. We are not concerned now with what Aristotle really meant (some classical scholars hold that he was referring to an error of judgment, not necessarily a moral flaw) or with the nature of all tragedy (I for one cannot see how Oedipus' catastrophe can be attributed

---

[17] Rossiter, pp. 261–262.

to a moral flaw), only with the nature of Shakespearean tragedy. Not only is Bradley right in speaking of a moral imperfection on the part of the Shakespearean tragic hero, but Shakespeare's audience, as Willard Farnham has shown in his painstaking analysis of how Renaissance tragedy developed a concept of tragic justice which links character and event,[18] would have associated this imperfection with the Christian notion of sin.

Rossiter is not very specific in seeking to controvert Bradley. In his sole contradiction of any of Bradley's discussions of Shakespeare's heroes, he says of Bradley's reference to Othello's "credulousness, excessive simplicity" as being a defect: "He has turned a nobility (generosity of mind) into an 'evil,' to evade the issue . . ." (p. 189). Now certainly the fact that Iago speaks contemptuously of Othello's "free and open nature," (I. iii. 405) upon which he is going to practice, heightens the impression of his villainy and the goodness of his victim, just as Claudius' similar words about Hamlet and Edmund's about Edgar do. But is not an ignorance of evil that, although allied with a noble openness of nature, permits itself to be worked upon by evil, a moral imperfection? The Elizabethans would have thought so. They would have remembered that through such ignorance "our credulous mother" Eve (*Paradise Lost*, ix. 644) sinned. Milton was not alone in thinking that a cloistered virtue that is ignorant of evil is a virtue that is unexercised and lacking its full strength: that the Red-cross Knight is deceived by Archimago into believing Una to be adulterous, as Othello is deceived by Iago, is due to the fact that the knight, on his first adventure, is new and untried. To be sure, Desdemona too is lacking in a knowledge of evil, as evidenced by her asking Emilia in wonderment if it

[18] *The Medieval Heritage of Elizabethan Tragedy* (Berkeley, Calif. 1936).

is indeed possible that there are women who deceive their husbands, but hers is an unworldly purity that is immune to evil: she does not contemplate even for a moment avenging herself by cuckolding her husband, as Emilia has jestingly suggested, figuratively turning the other cheek after he has struck her, in contrast to Othello, who accepts Iago's counsel of revenge.

Rossiter, moreover, disregards the fact that Bradley finds (p. 186) that Othello has other defects which contribute to his disaster: "His tragedy lies in this—that his whole nature was indisposed to jealousy, and yet was such that he was unusually open to deception, and, if once wrought to passion, likely to act with little reflection, with no delay, and in the most decisive manner conceivable." Beneath Othello's superb self-command is an explosiveness of passion that, when ignited by Iago, destroys him. To say that Othello bears no responsibility for committing murder and thereby destroying himself is to do violence to the play.

Bradley is, therefore, right on the second count as well as on the first in speaking of the impression we gain of the existence in Shakespearean tragedy of a moral order. This moral order, in addition to its execution of a poetically appropriate retribution, has other characteristics that would have made Elizabethans recognize it as divine providence. Ghosts, prophecies, premonitory dreams and portents are not, as Bradley says, "faint and scattered intimations" that "avail nothing to interpret the mystery" (p. 39); they are the means by which Elizabethans understood divine providence to operate and, although often doubted or disregarded by the dramatic characters, are always vindicated in the action.[19]

[19] Cf. Siegel, pp. 82–83, 113–115, 138–140, 156–159, 166–186, 223–224, 227.

In concluding his discussion of *Hamlet*, Bradley himself comes close to this perception when he states that the pirate ship incident "is meant to impress the imagination as the very reverse of accidental" and that ". . . while we do not imagine the supreme power as a divine being who avenges crime, or as a providence which supernaturally interferes, our sense of it is influenced by the fact that Shakespeare uses current religious ideas . . ." (pp. 172–174). This further strengthens the feeling we get from Hamlet's conviction that he is in the hands of providence.

What Bradley was not aware of is that divine providence was thought of by Elizabethans as manifesting itself first through natural law, the necessary consequences of a person's acts when he violates God's order, and secondly through strange events that can be explained away as chance by those disposed to do so. Here Roland M. Frye, glossing Hamlet's words as a demonstration of how Shakespeare uses theological ideas in dialogue for the purpose of characterization, supplies a valuable commentary:

Calvin's words [describe] the perils from which Hamlet has emerged, and though the parallel is not exact it is surely instructive: "If a man light among thieves or wild beasts, if by wind suddenly rising he suffer shipwreck on the sea . . . , if having been tossed with the waves, he attain to the haven, if miraculously he escape but a finger breadth from death, all these chances as well of prosperity as of adversity the reason of the flesh doth ascribe to fortune. But whosoever is taught by the mouth of Christ, that all the hairs of his head are numbered, will seek for a cause further off, and will firmly believe that all chances are governed by the secret counsel of God" [Calvin, *Inst.* I. 16, 2–Norton tr.]. Having passed through experiences like those which Calvin hypothesizes, Hamlet has come to sense in what might seem quite inconsequential details that "even in that was heaven ordinant" and to declare . . . "There's a divinity that shapes our ends. . . ."[20]

Here we may take up the challenge of another critic of the so-called Shakespearean Christianizers, Laurence Michel, who finds at the conclusion of *Hamlet* an "enforced piety" for a "baleful divinity" which demonstrates that "the Tragic Vision and Christianity are incompatible." Hamlet's "And praised be rashness for it, let us know/ Our indiscretion sometimes serves us well/ When our deep plots do pall. And that should learn us/ There's a divinity that shapes our ends,/ Rough-hew them how we will" (V. ii. 7–11) Michel regards as "disenchanted, sardonic, bitter, ironic." The divinity Hamlet has discovered is

> . . . an anti-intellectual force allied with the things Hamlet has constantly despised and feared. . . . The gratuitous doom of Rosencrantz and Guildenstern, to be murdered "not shriving time allowed," has received the seal of approval from this supposedly merciful and loving Providence too; Hamlet goes on wonderingly, incredulously: "Why, even in *that* was Heaven ordinant." . . . [When Hamlet says "There's special providence in the fall of a sparrow" (V. ii. 230–231)] he doesn't say: there's a special Providence in the well-being of a sparrow, or in its salvation; he says: this divinity we've come upon even takes a special interest in making sure of a sparrow's fall. . . .[21]

But in speaking of his "deep plots" failing, Hamlet is not, as Michel says, stating that "all his rational thinking has failed."

---

[20] Roland M. Frye, *Shakespeare and Christian Doctrine* (Princeton University Press, 1963), pp. 231–232. Frye does not concern himself with the question of whether or not the sense of a divine providence at work in human affairs is conveyed in Shakespearean tragedy although this question is central to his subject.

[21] "Hamlet: Superman, SubChristian," *The Centennial Review of Arts and Science*, VI (1962), 240–242.

"Deep plots" has a sinister connotation; it refers to his delight in intrigue when he had spoken in the vein of a malcontent avenger: "O, 'tis most sweet,/ When in one line two crafts directly meet" (III. iv. 209–210). Hamlet's "rashness" is not counterposed to "rational thinking"; it is the placing of oneself in the hands of the Lord when bold, decisive action is the only course. So Henry V before Agincourt calls upon God to take from his men "the sense of reckoning, if the opposed numbers/ Pluck their hearts from them" (IV. i. 308–309). The divinity of which Hamlet speaks is not "an anti-intellectual force" to which he gives himself up with "distaste"; it is a force which works through the actions of men, sculpting smooth the rough-hewn results of their own ineffectual efforts. So Lancaster in *Henry IV, Part II* says (IV. ii. 21–22) that our "dull workings," our inadequate mental efforts, are in need of "the grace, the sanctities of heaven," the divine force for whose reason beyond our reach the Archbishop acts as the "intelligencer" or interpreter. Divine providence assigns fit retribution to Rosencrantz and Guildenstern, not a gratuitous doom. It has no animus toward sparrows but, as implied in Matthew, controls all happenings, small things such as the fall of sparrows, as well as large, and everything serves a purpose in the scheme of things, which is ultimately beneficent. Hamlet's "we defy augury" (V. ii. 230) is not a repudiation of "his faith in the noble mind's ability to anticipate and therefore to forestall disaster" (243); it is an echo of the Old Testament's injunction against the augurs of pagan Rome: "There shall not be found with thee any one . . . that practiseth augury" (Deut. 18:10). Hamlet is rejecting the idea of an indifferent fate and relying upon the merciful justice of a divine providence, the "secret counsel of God" which governs all events. His "readiness is all" is not "stultifying nihilism" (233); it expresses the need for man, whose hairs are numbered, to be at all times ready for death. He is not to be so attached to the world, whose goods he may not take with him in death, that he is not ready to meet his Maker, "since no man has aught of what he leaves, what is't to leave betimes?"—an echo of the Anglican burial service's "We brought nothing into this world, neither may we cary anything out of this worlde."[22]

Hamlet, therefore, is expressing, as S. F. Johnson says, "good Christian doctrine, if somewhat colored later by neo-stoicism," a doctrine that is substantiated by the events of the play.[23] It is the failure to perceive the design of the play which leads Michel to twist Hamlet's words so. But if the critics of the alleged Shakespeare Christianizers have gone astray in failing to perceive the workings of divine providence in the action, what are we to say about their point that unmerited suffering is incompatible with Christian doctrine? "Rymer," says Leech, "realized far more clearly than most critics that *Othello* and Shakespeare's other great tragedies represent a view of the world that cannot be reconciled with Christianity" (p. 103). But the neo-classical view was not that the good are rewarded in life but that they should be rewarded in fiction, which in that respect is superior to life. Johnson, a devout Christian, was certainly aware that misery is not confined to the wicked. Christianity, in fact, had long insisted that we live in a vale of tears. As George Gascoigne phrased it in his translation of Innocent III's *De Contemptu Mundi*, in words similar to Lear's "Thou must be patient; we came crying hither:/ Thou know'st the first time that we smell

<hr>

[22] Richmond Noble, *Shakespeare's Biblical Knowledge* (London, 1935), p. 208. Noble also notes that this passage is based on 1 Tim. 6:7.

[23] S. F. Johnson, "The Regeneration of Hamlet," *SQ*, III (1952), 204. For fuller discussions of Hamlet's speeches as Christian doctrine, see Johnson, 203–206, and James V. Cunningham, *Woe or Wonder: The Emotional Effect of Shakespearean Tragedy* (Denver, 1951), pp. 9–14.

the air/ We waul and cry" (IV. vi. 181–183), "We are all borne crying, that we may thereby expresse our misery. . . ."[24]

The inherited medieval tradition of Shakespeare's day emphasized the wretchedness of man's lot here on earth in order to teach the need of looking to the next world. If seeming chance is a part of God's order, man is nevertheless subject here on earth to the mutability of fortune, which does not permit prosperity to stay long. Adversity, added the Renaissance works of moral philosophy, serves the function of teaching men to live better by showing them the ephemerality of material possessions and worldly power, causing them to give up their selfish striving and to grow in love for their fellow human beings and for God.[25]

In Shakespearean tragedy Desdemona and Cordelia, who suffer through no fault of their own, exemplify both this love which persists despite all wrongs and the fortitude which endures whatever God has willed; love and patience, however, have to be learned by Lear. Desdemona states the uses of adversity when, in response to Emilia's warning to husbands to use their wives well, "else let them know,/ The ills we do, their ills instruct us so," she replies: "Good night, good night: heaven me such uses send,/ Not to pick bad from bad, but by bad mend!" (IV. iii. 105–108). To Emilia's ethic of returning evil for evil, she responds with the ethic of returning good for evil and calls upon heaven to enable her to learn how to improve herself through suffering.

That Desdemona and Cordelia in a sense rise superior to their suffering and that Lear learns from his does not, however, wipe

[24] Quoted by Maynard Mack, " 'We Came Crying Hither': An Essay on Some Characteristics of *King Lear*," *Yale Review*, LIV (1965), 183. Cf. Kenneth Myrick, "Christian Pessimism in *King Lear*," *Shakespeare 1594–1964*, ed. Edward A. Bloom (Providence, 1964), pp. 56–70.

[25] Cf. Siegel, p. 215.

away the memory of that suffering. The optimistic doctrine that "Whatever is, is right," that every seeming evil is really a good since it is a necessary part of the scheme of things of a beneficent Creator, can from another point of view be regarded as horribly pessimistic, as Voltaire showed in *Candide*, for it means that all which we suffering beings must regard as evil cannot be remedied. Shakespearean tragedy, where we are afforded only brief intimations of a compensating afterlife, presents us with a complex vision that accepts life with all of its misery in a manner that combines the two views and transcends both the optimism that denies evil and the pessimism that, recoiling from the laws that govern life, rejects life. We must accept the workings of divine providence, but the suffering that takes place in this world under its control is not an illusion but a tragic fact.

Shakespearean tragedy is, as Bradley perceives (pp. 25–26) and the opponents of a "Christian" interpretation of this tragedy do not perceive, a representation of life that, although it is "piteous, fearful and mysterious," does not "leave us crushed, rebellious or desperate." Leech cites Edgar's pronouncement over the dying body of his brother concerning the misery of their father, "The gods are just, and of our pleasant vices/ Make instruments to plague us:/ The dark and vicious place where thee he got/ Cost him his eyes" (V. iii. 170–173), and comments: "This terrible sentence seems as outrageous to our moral sense as the hanging of Cordelia or the torture of Webster's Duchess. What kind of justice, we wonder, is this, which will seize on so small a fault and inflict so terrible a punishment?" (p. 14). This is to leave the imaginative experience of the play in order to ask an abstract question: where a couple have had a son without having had the prescribed words spoken over them by a clergyman, does the father merit having his eyes stamped out? The most zealous defenders of the sanctity of the marriage sacrament would scarcely assent to the enactment of such a law. But the abstract question does not rise to mind as we listen to Edgar's words, having surrendered ourselves to Shakespeare's tragedy. Bradley, who has so often been accused of judging Shakespearean characters by the moral canons of real life, knew better:

> When we are immersed in a tragedy, we feel towards dispositions, actions, and persons such emotions as attraction and repulsion, pity, wonder, fear, horror, perhaps hatred; but we do not *judge*. . . . While we are in its world we watch what is, seeing that so it happened and must have happened, feeling that it is piteous, dreadful, awful, mysterious, but neither passing sentence on the agents, nor asking whether the behaviour of the ultimate power towards them is just. (pp. 32–33)

Preceding Edgar's words is our perception that Gloucester's joking about his mistress is related to his complaisant acceptance of the ways of the world, including the abuse of power, that in losing his eyesight he had become able to see right and wrong clearly, that the ironically appropriate retribution that comes to him[26] is part of a general pattern of retribution that is visited upon the wicked as well as upon those who are more sinned against than sinning, that he has died in an ecstacy of joy, having been reunited with the son of whom he had said, "Might I but live to see thee in my touch,/I'ld say I had eyes again!" (IV. i. 22–23). Under these circumstances we do not rebel against Edgar's words. Yet we also cannot forget the words he uttered when he heard the eyeless Gloucester, the sensual man deprived of one of his senses, called "blind Cupid" (IV. vi. 141) by the mad Lear: "I would not take this from report; it is,/ And my heart breaks at it" (IV. vi. 144–145). Life is so

[26] Cf. Siegel, p. 169.

much more terrible than we had imagined; yet it also has its precious good, and it and the laws which govern it must be accepted.

Nor can we say with Rossiter that "the 'moral order' has a *double* heart: i.e. that the universe is quasi-Manichean, and that human greatness (which is one God's 'good') is the evil of the *other* God (i.e. the God of order and degree)" (p. 266). It is true that Shakespearean tragic heroes, even the comparatively innocent heroes such as Hamlet and Lear, malcontents who question the established verities or rage against them, challenge the order of things. But this challenge, which shakes up the audience and helps to induce what Prosser Frye called the "tragic qualm,"[27] does so only in order that the tragic qualm may be allayed, as the audience is reconciled to what it has been forced to witness and its "moral dizziness and nausea" is quelled. Hamlet and Lear are themselves at the end reconciled to the order of things without losing their greatness.

Although the tragic hero challenges the order of things, his greatness is not in itself opposed to this order, as Rossiter, attempting to turn Bradley's analysis against him, argues: "The Shakespearian tragic universe is such that mediocrity is pretty safe. . . . The universe produces human greatness, which is therefore *natural* to it; and yet it is antagonistic to distinction. . . . By its destruction and the calm that ensues—if Bradley is right —greatness seems *unnatural* to this world" (pp. 264–265). But mediocrity, if it is allied to evil, is not safe in this world—witness Rosencrantz and Guildenstern, Roderigo, Oswald and all the other tools of villainy. It is evil, not greatness, which is paradoxically a part of this world but hostile to its order. The tragic hero comes into conflict with the order of the universe because of the

---

[27] *Romance & Tragedy* (Boston, 1922), p. 146.

defect which is the cause of his fall, not because of his admirable traits. The greatness of Othello, for instance, that which makes him a tragic hero and distinguishes him from the jealous husbands of comedy, is his nobility and dignity, the fact that he is not meanly suspicious by nature and that he regards Desdemona not as a possession but as an ideal to which he dedicates his entire being. It is not these traits, however, which bring about his disaster, but his lack of knowledge of evil and the violence of his passion. Since Othello is not merely a collection of character traits, his credulousness in the face of evil is, to be sure, intertwined with his generosity of mind, and his intense passion is intertwined with the depth of his feeling for Desdemona, but they are not the same. He has a life-like complexity but is greater than life size, with a capacity greater than that of ordinary men for both happiness and misery, for Edenic bliss with Desdemona as well as for his subsequent agony.

Feeling intensely, the tragic hero runs the risk of being carried away by his passions, but his strength of feeling springs from a force of character which has potentialities for good as well as for evil. Because he is a magnification of ordinary humanity, the audience can both identify itself with him and regard him with awe. Othello's human weaknesses help to bring about his downfall, as do those of the ignoble Roderigo in the comic subplot of the tragedy, but, unlike Roderigo, he makes us more sharply aware of what is admirable in human nature. "O thou Othello," exclaims Lodovico (V. ii. 291–293), "that wert once so good,/ Fall'n in the practice of a damned slave,/ What shall be said to thee?" It is the realization of the existence in the tragic hero of superior spiritual qualities which gives us, on witnessing his downfall, the feeling that Bradley correctly describes (p. 37) in the sentence to which Rossiter takes objection: "It [the moral order] has lost a part of its own substance,—a part more dangerous and unquiet, but far more valuable and nearer to its heart than that which remains,—a Fortinbras, a Malcolm, an Octavius." Bradley found (p. 38) that the idea of a moral order which engenders evil within itself and then expels it at the price of losing inestimable good brings before us a "painful mystery" (p. 38). It is this quality of "painful mystery" which Laurence Michel finds to be essential to tragedy and to cause Christianity, offering, as it does, an answer to the problem of evil, to be incompatible with it. By the doctrine of redemption, "the hegemony of the devil was destroyed once and for all. . . . Sin remains, although the *devastating* effect of Original Sin has been removed, and each man must work out his salvation with diligence, if not in fear and trembling; but his life is no longer in the proper sense a predicament or a dilemma" (233).

The fact, however, that Shakespeare's tragic vision is an expression of this doctrine does not deprive his drama of a sense of life's mystery. To be saved, according to the accepted doctrine, man in his weakness has need of the grace of God. But, although "There, but for the grace of God, go I" may be said in a tone of complacent self-congratulation, it may also be said in a tone of fear and trembling: if only the grace of God has prevented me from having become like that man, why was that grace not vouchsafed him—and may it not in the future be denied me? Something like this question at times suggests itself as we witness the extraordinary temptation or other unusual circumstance with which the Shakespearean tragic hero is faced. As Bradley phrases it, "Men act, no doubt, in accordance with their characters; but what is it that brings them just the one problem which is fatal to them and would be easy to another, and sometimes brings it to them just when they are least fitted to face it?" (p. 29). Or, as Fraser states it in Elizabethan terms,

A man cannot enlist the aid of grace, as he can compel to

his support the aid of reason. Grace is not within his giving; and yet it is indispensable. . . . Innocence, then, as it turns on the accession of grace, is kindred to good fortune. It is as fragile as fortune and as dependent for its life on caprice. . . . It [the dispensation of grace] is always crucial, though Shakespeare rarely adverts to it, and for the very good reason that its felt presence is inimical to real drama. (pp. 134–135)

The theologians, like Milton's fallen angels, might seek to explain "Providence, Foreknowledge, Will, and Fate, / Fixt Fate, free will, foreknowledge absolute," to reconcile the idea of the fall of man and his subsequent proneness to sin with the concept of an omnipotent and benevolent God, but a poet, even a devout one, might give utterance to the pain of laboring under the burden of the mystery in which one is "created sick, commanded to be sound":

> Oh, wearisome condition of humanity,
> Born under one law, to another bound;
> Vainly begot, and yet forbidden vanity,
> Created sick, commanded to be sound.[28]

In the course of Shakespearean tragedy, says Bradley (p. 29), "even character itself" contributes to the "feelings of fatality" which are among the impressions we receive: "How could men escape, we cry, such vehement propensities as drive Romeo, Antony, Coriolanus, to their doom?" The doctrine of original sin, according to which each of us is born fatally sick of soul, is the theological explanation for this passion which drives man to destruction, but a sensitive Elizabethan responding to the tragedy, while accepting the dogma, would have felt the weight of the burden.

The paradox of man's greatness and his wretchedness, of his

[28] Fulke Greville, "Chorus Sacerdotum" from *Mustapha*.

glory and his blind suicidal destructiveness, which Bradley finds in Shakespearean tragedy (p. 23)—" 'What a piece of work is man,' we cry; 'so much more beautiful and so much more terrible than we knew! Why should he be so if this beauty and greatness only tortures itself and throws itself away?' "—is a frequently voiced Elizabethan theme:

> I know the heavnly nature of my mind,
> But 'tis corrupted both in wit and will.
> I know my Soul hath power to know all things,
> Yet is she blind and ignorant in all;
> I know that I am one of Nature's little kings,
> Yet to the least and vilest things am thrall.
> I know my life's a pain and but a span,
> I know my Sense is mock'd with everything:
> And to conclude, I know myself a MAN,
> Which is a proud, and yet a wretched thing.[29]

Shakespearean tragedy made the Elizabethan spectator feel much more keenly what he already knew. In it he could see the workings of providence in the fulfillment of portents and prophecies, but, in the disregard by the dramatic characters of these portents and prophecies, he could see the ironic unawareness of human beings. Through it he was given a superior vantage point from which he could act as God's spy, but he was made more sharply conscious that in the life of which tragedy is a representation he was "blind and ignorant in all." Although man may rely on the general laws by which divine providence works and must have faith in its ultimately beneficent purpose, its mysterious ways are in the last analysis beyond his comprehension.

---

[29] Sir John Davies, "Nosce Teipsum."

III.

My third modification of Bradley's analysis, the statement that there are biblical analogies in Shakespearean tragedy which suggest that men in the conduct of their lives follow the basic patterns set by Lucifer, Adam and Christ has received the strongest criticism from Roland M. Frye. He does not refer to the analogies with Lucifer and Adam which I and others have pointed out, but he is most positive concerning the falsity of what he calls "the Christ-figure mania" (p. 39):

> So far as I know, we have no objective evidence that an audience which found types of Christ in the Old Testament would have sought them in Shakespeare. Everyone admits that Elizabethans found such typology in Scripture under the old covenant, but I know of no reason to believe that Elizabethan drama was so confused with Holy Writ as to require the same methods to be applied in both cases. Nor has anyone yet made a convincing case, in terms of historical theology, for such identification.

What Frye does not perceive is that it is not a matter of the Elizabethans' method of reading the Old Testament but of their way of looking at life, their penchant for finding analogies in all things. In English history, they found, as Lily B. Campbell has shown,[30] patterns repeating themselves, one king imaging another king. Lucifer, the first rebel against God, Adam, the first sinner to repent, and Christ, the only perfect man, set more basic patterns. Adam, in "the transgressing of God's precept in eating of one apple," so roused God's wrath that He "would not be pacified but only with the blood of his own Son," and everyone who has sinned since Adam has likewise participated in

[30] *Shakespeare's "Histories," Mirrors of Elizabethan Policy* (San Marino, Calif., 1947).

47

crucifying him: "To commit sin wilfully and desperately, without fear of God, is nothing else but to crucify Christ anew. . . ."[31] But just as in sinning we crucify Christ again, so in accepting our worldly woes without rebelling against God or hating the men who misuse us we bear our crosses in imitation of him: "Yea, let us take up our cross with Christ, and follow him. His passion is not only the ransom and whole amends for our sin, but it is also a most perfect example of all patience and sufferance. . . . For surely, as saith St. Peter, *Christ therefore suffered, to leave us an example to follow his steps.*"[32]

This idea that the good life is the life most imitative of Christ, popularized by the immensely influential medieval manual of devotion *The Imitation of Christ*, of which there are many Protestant sixteenth-century editions, is repeated again and again in the Elizabethan homilies.[33] Just as men given over to evil are by their conduct, in the words of Calvin, "rightly recognized to be the children of Satan from his image, into which they have degenerated,"[34] so true Christians, Spenser indicates, are images of Christ, "ensampled" by him to follow his behest that "we louing bee,/ As he himselfe hath lou'd vs afore hand,/ . . . Him first to loue, that vs so dearely bought,/ And next, our brethren to his image wrought,"[35] our brethren created in the self-same image of God. Of course, just as man resembles God only as much as "mortall thing immortall could" resemble (l. 114), so the conduct of the Christian can only faintly resemble the per-

[31] *Certain Sermons or Homilies Appointed to be Read in Churches in the time of Queen Elizabeth of Famous Memory* (London, 1864), pp. 453–454.

[32] *Certain Sermons*, p. 442.

[33] *Certain Sermons*, pp. 63, 66, 148.

[34] Quoted by Roland M. Frye, p. 142. Cf. *Certain Sermons*, pp. 498, 588.

[35] "An Hymne of Heavenly Love," ll. 212, 185–189.

fect love of Christ. In following the way of Christ, the Christian becomes, however, as a contemporary of Milton phrased it, a "*microchristus*," for he is "the epitome of Christ mystical," just as natural man is a "*microcosmus*, an epitome of the world."[36]

It would not, therefore, have been at all strange for Shakespeare to have suggested to his audience that some of his characters resembled Christ. The most explicit of these comparisons with Christ, an oft-cited one to which Frye does not refer, is most instructive. In *Richard II* the Bishop of Carlisle says that if Richard is deposed, England will be called "the field of Golgotha" (IV. i. 144). What does Frye think is the point of this allusion to the crucifixion? Surely it emphasizes the horror of this heinous deed by suggesting a comparison between Richard and Christ. This is the significance of Carlisle's reference to Richard as "the figure of God's majesty," (IV. i. 125) the image and symbol of God. Richard's references to those who betrayed him, as "Judas did to Christ," (IV. i. 170) and to those who "with Pilate, wash your hands" and deliver him to "my sour cross" (IV. i. 239, 241) keep up the comparison, as does York's description of the crowd's mockery of Richard and the throwing of dust upon "his sacred head," which he bore with "grief and patience" (V. ii. 30, 33).

An eyewitness account of the fall of the historical Richard, Jean Creton's *Histoire du Roy d'Angleterre Richard*, which Paul Reyher and J. Dover Wilson believe Shakespeare consulted in manuscript, draws the same analogy. Speaking of Bolingbroke, it says:

> At this hour did he remind me of Pilate, who caused our Lord Jesus Christ to be scourged at the stake, and . . .

[36] *The Ancient Bounds* (London, 1645), reprinted in A. S. P. Woodhouse, *Puritanism and Liberty* (London, 1938), p. 248.

delivered our Lord unto them ["the multitude of Jews"]. Much in like manner did Duke Henry, when he gave up his rightful lord to the rabble of London, in order that, if they should put him to death, he might say, "I am innocent of this deed."[37]

So too does the anonymous *Chronicque de la Traison et Mort de Richard Deux*, another eyewitness account believed by Reyher and Wilson to be a Shakespearean source, compare Richard with Christ, as does Holinshed.[38] Whether or not we agree with Reyher and Wilson that Shakespeare used the two French medieval manuscripts—and it is not necessary to postulate this, for, aside from the possible indebtedness on this point to Holinshed, the comparison is, as Virgil K. Whitaker says, "a logical inference from the teaching of the Homilies which Shakespeare might easily have made"[39]—it is evident that Shakespeare's Richard-Christ analogy springs from a habit of thinking inherited by his time. The "Christ-figure mania" is not confined to modern Shakespearean critics.

Shakespeare's characterization of Richard is significant for our understanding of other Christ figures. The same York, a relic of a better time with the wisdom of age, who speaks of him as a divine martyr at his deposition spoke of him earlier in the play as being deaf to the dying Gaunt's inspired words because his ear is "stopp'd" with the "flattering sounds" of the praises of his dissolute favorites (II. i. 17). Richard is a self-indulgent man and a poor king, but, betrayed and scorned, he undergoes his ordeal patiently and is made to recall the supreme example of patience in suffering. He is a life-like character with human

---

[37] Quoted in *King Richard II*, ed. Peter Ure (Harvard University Press, 1956: "Arden ed."), p. xlviii.

[38] Idem, p. xlviii.

[39] *Shakespeare's Use of Learning* (San Marino, Calif., 1953), p. 160. Quoted in the Arden edition, p. xliv.

frailties, but at one moment in the drama the associations gathered about the figure of a king, the situation and the allusions make him take on the aspect of Christ.

Frye not only does not consider all of these indications that Richard is suggestive of Christ. He rejects all Christ analogies as absurd on their very face, saying of each, without examining the critical readings advanced, that they lack evidence. One gathers that evidence for him would consist of a statement by an Elizabethan theologian, preferably Hooker, to the effect that, on attending the play, he had found the character in question to be a Christ figure. Elizabethan theologians, however, were not in the habit of writing dramatic criticism, which is perhaps just as well. In want of such statements, which in any case would represent only that theologian's opinion, the evidence must be drawn from the play itself, using whatever aid a knowledge of the contemporary climate of opinion and of the dramatic practice can give us. The opponent of a critical interpretation must in turn show how the critic has wrenched or disregarded the text. But this is what Frye does not seek to do.

One cannot very well present a rebuttal to what is merely assertion rather than an attempt at refutation. However, I may elaborate on one passing reference I made to a Christ figure, since Frye singles this out as an especially horrible example. "It is particularly puzzling," he says (p. 178), "to find Timon," who "hates all men," "referred to by the theologizers as a type of Christ." And he exclaims in amazement at the vagaries of modern critics:

> Surely no one prior to our time has seen Timon of Athens as a Christ-figure. Paul N. Siegel, however, assures us that "the perceptive theatre-goer of Shakespeare's day" would have recognized in Shakespeare's "clear and distinct" allusions a "comparison between Timon's boundless generosity and Christ's overflowing love. . . ." (p. 34)

Frye does not explain that I had stated that Timon, in becoming a misanthrope, ceases to be a Christ figure and that I had given this as an instance of the fact that a character who takes on the aspect of a Christ figure may be quite blameworthy at other times in the drama. He does not, furthermore, give his reader the allusions cited by G. Wilson Knight, to whom I referred, so that the reader might judge the validity of the evidence for himself. One of these allusions, it so happens, was pointed out prior to our time. The eighteenth-century editor Steevens called attention to the similarity of phrasing in Christ's foretelling of Judas' betrayal (Matt. 26:23), "He who has dipped his hand in the dish with me, will betray me" and the First Stranger's comment about the ingratitude of Timon's friends, "Who can call him/ His friend that dips in the same dish?" (III. ii. 72–73). So too is Apemantus' earlier "It grieves me to see so many dip their meat in one man's blood . . . I wonder men dare trust themselves with men. . . . There's much example for 't. The fellow that sits next him . . . is the readiest man to kill him" (I. ii. 40–50) reminiscent of the Biblical phrase. "The example that will occur almost to everybody," says Richmond Noble (p. 237), speaking of Apemantus' reference, "will be Judas Iscariot," and the editors of the revised Arden and New Cambridge editions of the play agree with him.[40]

But what is the significance of these allusions? If his betrayers resemble Judases, then Timon resembles Christ.[41] He is not the

[40] *Timon of Athens*, ed. H. J. Oliver (London, 1959: "Arden ed."), p. 23 and *Timon of Athens*, ed. J. C. Maxwell (Cambridge, Eng., 1957), p. 113.

[41] Other examples of Christ figures who partake of a Last Supper are Duncan, who is banqueted by Macbeth before being murdered by him, and Antonio, to whose supper Shylock goes "to feed upon the prodigal Christian" (II. v. 13–14), Shakespeare assigning the same cannibalistic images to Shylock as he does to Timon's false friends and creditors.

satirized gull that he has sometimes been made out to be but
another one of Shakespeare's openhearted noble heroes. His
steward Flavius, having, in imitation of Timon, shared his
remaining money with his fellow servants left homeless after
Timon's fall, exclaims in grief over their loved master:

> Poor honest lord, brought low by his own heart,
> Undone by goodness! Strange, unusual blood,
> When man's worst sin is he does too much good!
> Who then dares to be half so kind again?
> For bounty, that makes gods, does still mar men.
> My dearest lord, blest to be most accursed,
> Rich only to be wretched, thy great fortunes
> Are made thy chief afflictions. (IV. ii. 37–44)

It is through his great goodness, his love of mankind, that Timon
has been undone. He had the bounteousness, the spirit of giving,
that characterizes gods but that causes men to come to their
ruin in this world of greedy self-seeking, just as, it might be said,
a deity taking the form of man suffered humiliation and agony
at the hands of those who were incapable of appreciating him.[42]
"How rarely does it meet with this time's guise,/ When man was
wished to love his enemies!" (IV. iii. 472–473) exclaims Flavius
later on observing the alteration in Timon. In this time, when
man was urged to love his enemies—a reference to the Gospel,
the anachronism of which is, as usual, not Shakespeare's concern
—Timon's wretched appearance, the result of the ingratitude of
his friends, who, far from loving their enemies, did not even
return the love of their benefactor, is very much in keeping with
the fashion.

---

[42] Significantly, the last three lines quoted above are similar to France's
words about the rejected Cordelia, another Christ figure: "Fairest Cordelia,
that art most rich, being poor;/ Most choice, forsaken; and most loved,
despised!" (I. i. 253–254).

The representation of Timon as a Christ image reaches its climax in a scene whose significance has not been realized, that is, the scene in which his creditors beset Timon on all sides. "Creditors? Devils!" he exclaims (III. iv. 105). In both the medieval allegories of the debate between Justice and Mercy and in the numerous medieval versions of Satan's suit before the divine tribunal for the souls of men due him, Christ was represented as paying the debt of man to the Devil, who frequently appeared as a usurer.[43] The idea was expressed in Shakespeare's own time by Launcelot Andrewes: "As debtors we were, by vertue of . . . the *handwriting* that was against us. Which was our *Bond*, and we had forfeited it. . . . Therefore Hee became bound for us also, entred bond anew, took on Him, not only our *Nature*, but our *Debt*. . . . The debt of a Capitall Law is Death."[44] Timon, urging his creditors in his anguish to cut out his heart and tell out his blood to satisfy the debt which he has contracted because of his love of man, recalls, like Antonio, baring his breast to give "this devil" Shylock (IV. i. 287) his pound of flesh, the crucifixion of Christ.

In like manner Desdemona, a loving wife, Cordelia, a loving daughter, and Duncan, a gracious, loving sovereign, become in their deaths representative of love itself with various allusions reminding the audience of the supreme example of sacrificial love. To say, as Marvin Rosenberg does, that "the symbolism that sees Othello between the Iago-devil and Desdemona-divinity . . . can be conceived only if the special human qualities of the characters are explained away"[45] is to fail to understand that

[43] Benjamin N. Nelson, *The Idea of Usury from Tribal Brotherhood to Universal Otherhood* (Princeton, N. J., 1949), p. 144n.

[44] "Christmas 1609," *XCVI Sermons*, 3rd ed. (London, 1635), p. 28. Quoted by Barbara K. Lewalski, "Biblical Allusion and Allegory in *The Merchant of Venice*," *SQ*, XIII (1962), 339–340.

[45] *The Masks of Othello* (University of California Press, 1961), p. 232.

the dramatist may, as E. M. Forster pointed out with regard to the novelist,[46] momentarily collapse a round character into a flat character, making the individual become typical and gaining a powerful effect of universalization. The Elizabethan drama, which "ostensibly imitates natural forms," but whose "dramaturgy still retains features, its stage properties, and its playwrights habits that belong to 'the artifice of eternity,'"[47] particularly lends itself to such effects. If, having lost that "alertness to symbolism" which the Elizabethans, "induced by familiarity with allegory," had and which "a more realistic convention has partly atrophied in us,"[48] we are blind to them in Shakespearean tragedy, we miss some of its most striking moments.

IV.

My fourth modification of Bradley, the assertion that there are intimations of heaven and hell in the four great tragedies, has been most vigorously opposed by Sylvan Barnet in what Roland M. Frye calls "a brilliant essay" (p. 58). "Shakespeare,"

[46] *Aspects of the Novel* (Harmondsworth, Eng., 1962: "Penguin ed."), p. 84.

[47] Bernard Spivack, *Shakespeare and the Allegory of Evil* (Columbia University Press, 1958), p. 451. Spivack's book is, of course, only one of a number of studies which have demonstrated the significance of the medieval heritage of Elizabethan drama. Rosenberg, studying the presentations of *Othello* on the post-Elizabethan stage in order to see whether any were symbolic, and Roland M. Frye, plowing through the theologians to determine how to read Shakespeare rather than taking note of the dramatic tradition, are equally off the mark and seem equally unaware of the implications of the scholarship which has shown Elizabethan drama as 'hybrid," to use Spivack's word, transitional between medieval allegory and modern naturalism.

[48] Madeleine Doran, *Endeavors of Art: A Study of Form in Elizabethan Drama* (University of Wisconsin Press, 1954), p. 99.

Barnet points out, "does not treat suicide in a consistent Christian manner. In the Roman plays it is clearly not a sin, and these dramas are not outside the pattern of Shakespearean tragedy' (89). Since they are not outside of this pattern, suicide in the other tragedies cannot have been presented as sinful and hence to regard Othello as damned is wrong. So too Frye sternly demands that the "Christianizers" be consistent in their "theologizing" (p. 27): "Siegel escapes ['damning Romeo and Juliet'] by denying in this one instance the relevance of theological norms which elsewhere he insists upon as determinative."[49]

It is a mistake, however, to assume that if there are intimations of a Christian afterlife in some Shakespearean tragedies they must be present in all of them. This is to take seriously indeed Barnet's caricature (81) of the Shakespearean tragedy of the "Christianizers" as consisting of "*exempla* in the sermon to which, it is implied, the Elizabethan was continually exposed, even when he deserted his shop for a visit to the theaters on the Bankside."[50] Shakespearean tragedy is an expression of the dominant Christian humanist ideology of his time in its representation of human life as part of a divinely appointed cosmological, social and psychological order, but this does not mean that Shakespeare was intent on expounding repeatedly the same rigid theological scheme. He could make use of the concept of a divine providence at work in *Romeo and Juliet* while making use also of the idea of the paradise for love's martyrs who are faithful to each other unto a self-inflicted death which he inherited from the religion of love of the Christian Middle Ages. He could also show divine providence at work in his Roman trage-

---

[49] For the discussion of *Romeo and Juliet* referred to by Frye, see pp. 100–107 below.

[50] It is true that some of the extreme "Christianizers" come close to this caricature.

dies[51] while presenting sympathetically the suicide of his heroes dying bravely in accordance with their Stoic philosophy.[52] In those tragedies, however, in which he looked upon the drama of human life most intensely, he made use of the afterlife of Christian religion as, to use the words I have used before, "an imposing but faintly painted and unobtrusive backdrop for the action."[53]

Barnet regards the critic who speaks of an afterlife as amusingly naive: "Here is the modern scholarly version of Mary Cowden Clarke's *Girlhood of Shakespeare's Heroines*. Not the youth, however, but the second life of the characters is sketched according to the critic's fancies" (90). If, however, Mary Cowden Clarke was, without knowing it, writing fiction rather than criticism, this does not mean that drama does not indicate a life anterior to or subsequent to the events enacted on the stage. The critic who confuses literature and life creates a world for the characters outside of the dramatist's world, that is, one which has no warrant in the text. The world of the play, however, is not rigidly confined to the action we witness. It would be absurd to speculate on Lear's married life with the woman who bore him Goneril, Regan and Cordelia, for this is manifestly extraneous to the text, but we miss much if we do not see Lear as having been blinded by the pomp of kingship so that he had "but slenderly known himself" (I. i. 296–297) and his position in the

---

[51] J. Leeds Barroll, "Shakespeare and Roman History," *MLR*, LIII (1958), 341 and n. cites a number of Elizabethan works "which regard God's providence as operant in pagan history."

[52] Theodore Spencer, *Death and Elizabethan Tragedy* (Harvard University Press, 1936), p. 165 quotes Monluc's statement about suicide, "Les Romains pouvaient faire cela, les Chretiens, non," and comments that this attitude, in which suicide was "admired in the heroes of antiquity," was "fairly widespread" during the Renaissance.

[53] Siegel, p. 90.

universe even before old age had heightened his moral infirmities. So too we miss much if we do not see Hamlet as having been the first courtier of the land, "the observed of all observers," (III. i. 162) before the revelations that came to him after his father's death.

Thus also with the life indicated subsequent to the events on the stage. "Unless we are told," says Hubler (296), "where a character goes when he goes off the stage, he doesn't go anywhere at all." But of course the dramatist does not at any time literally "tell" us directly where a character goes, for he does not speak in his own person. He speaks only through the words and actions of his characters, which we must judge in accordance with the tenor of the entire play. This was what I had contended Shakespeare had done in *Othello*: through words and actions which formed a dramatic pattern—and neither Barnet nor Hubler nor Frye tried to show that the pattern I traced is a distortion of the play—he had "told" the audience that his hero is damned. The picture of himself eternally and agonizedly separated from Desdemona and subject to the tortures of hell which Othello paints in his final speech is the culmination of this pattern and is as much a part of the imaginative effect of the play as the picture which Lavinia paints of herself living through the years in the darkened house haunted by the ghosts of the Mannons is part of the imaginative effect of Eugene O'Neill' *Mourning Becomes Electra*. In each case the dramatist "tells" us what happens to his protagonist in the only way he can.

Far from rectifying a confusion between literature and life Barnet and Hubler indulge in such confusion themselves. "The scholars who wish to apply Christian thinking to Shakespeare' plays," says Barnet, "insist that the dramas do not end with the heroes' death, but should be acted out to Judgment Day and for eternity" (88). It is doubtful that we can speak of Othello' "eternal destiny," Hubler suggests (298), for "Othello is not a man; he is a character in a play."[54] One might argue similarly that Lavinia cannot be said to live on after the curtain goes down. She lives, however, in the same way that the Lavinia on the stage does—in our imagination. To give dramatic credence to the stage-Lavinia is to give dramatic credence to the Lavinia continuing on into the indefinite future in the darkness of the shuttered Mannon house.[55] It is no different with *Othello*. The idea of hell is not a departure from the dramatic universe of the play, as Barnet and Hubler claim; it is suggested by Othello himself when he says that the "demi-devil" Iago has "ensnared" his "soul and body" and that at Judgment Day Desdemona's look "will hurl" his "soul from heaven" (V. ii. 301–302, 274). Rather than being the spokesmen for a common sense which points to the text in reply to those who would go beyond it, Barnet and Hubler disregard these explicit statements of the hero at the conclusion of his tragedy.

They are overlooked also by Bernard Harris, who in his review of my book stated: "As a Christian I find the theological discussion lacks, literally, grace, and some might say humility."[56] The idea would seem to be that I was uncharitable in regarding Othello as damned and that such judgments should be left to

[54] So too Robert H. West concludes ("The Christianness of *Othello*," *SQ*, XV [1964], 341) that, unless "the action shows some such event as devils seizing Dr. Faustus or angels declaring Margaret's salvation," a character in drama cannot be said to be either damned or saved.

[55] Roland M. Frye states (pp. 52–53), "I do not believe . . . that Shakespeare was trying to determine what would happen to Hamlet after the play ended (he knew, after all, that he would doff his costume and go home as that respectable citizen, Richard Burbage)"—as if what made it possible for the first audience to wonder what was going to happen to Hamlet in the course of the action was that Burbage had ceased to be Burbage while in costume on the stage!

[56] *MLR*, LII (1958), 564.

God. So too Hubler tells us (296) that an interpretation which "sets limits on the mercy of God" is "blasphemy." This may be sound theological advice for the conduct in life of Christian believers, but it represents another confusion between life and literature: in tragedy, we have the knowledge of God. As W. H. Auden has put it,

> In real life, when a sane person commits suicide, it is always possible for a Christian to hope that, in the last split second, he or she made an act of contrition, but a character in a play is transparent; there is no more to him than the dramatist tells us. If a dramatist makes a suicide utter words of repentance before death, then he repents; if the dramatist does not, then he dies unrepentant and goes to hell.[57]

Not only have the opponents of the "Christian" interpretation of Shakespearean tragedy confused the drama and life; they have failed to recognize the difference between the symbolic stage of the Elizabethans and the naturalistic stage of modern times. Barnet believes (92) that we should "accept the immediate impressions yielded by the plays" and not see them as "portrayed on a canvas stretching from hellmouth to heaven." As general editor of the Signet Classic Shakespeare editions, he tells the reader that the Elizabethan stage was protected by a " 'heavens' or roof" and that "certainly characters can descend from the stage through a trap or traps into the cellar or 'hell,' "[58] but these

---

[57] *Romeo and Juliet*, ed. W. H. Auden (New York, 1958: "Laurel ed."), p. 38. Auden, however, would apply this statement to all Elizabethan tragedy. In actuality it is valid only for the tragedies in which the Christian afterlife is consistently and unambiguously adumbrated. For *Romeo and Juliet*, for instance, it disregards Shakespeare's use of the tradition of the religion of love and its doctrine of the lovers' paradise.

[58] *Much Ado. About Nothing*, ed. David L. Stevenson (New York, 1964: "Signet ed."), p. xv.

stage terms have no suggestive significance for him. George R. Kernodle, however, sums up his study of the background structure of the Renaissance stage as follows:

> Shakespeare's background . . . was a complex symbol, combined out of several age-old symbols. For centuries kings had been presented to the public, whether real kings in public ceremonies or actor-kings in plays and pageants, in a throne backed by a symbol of the realm. That symbol combined elements from the pageant-castles, from the city gates, from triumphal arches, from the choir screen of the church. The throne was framed by columns supporting a canopy, a "heavens"—exactly the same kind of pavilion-canopy used to frame an altar or a tomb. Heavenly singers proclaimed the divine praises of the king, and often a figure of God sat on a heavenly throne to endorse the earthly king below. The Elizabethan stage had absorbed all these medieval symbols. Its background structure resembled a castle, a throne, a city gate, a tomb, and an altar. It was a symbol of social order and of divine order—of the real ties between man and king, between heaven and earth.[59]

The backdrop of the Christian afterlife is not an imposition of modern "Christianizers." It was suggested to the Elizabethan audience by the symbolic facade of their stage. It was suggested also by the frequently expressed idea that life is a drama arranged by God, indicated in the titles of two popular Elizabethan works, Thomas Beard's *The Theatre of God's Judgements* and Boiąstuau's *The Theetor or Rule of the World*. "What is our life?" says Sir Walter Raleigh in the opening lines of one of his poems, "a play of passion, . . . Heaven the Judicious sharpe spectator is,/ That sits and markes still who doth act amisse,/ Our graves that hide us from the searching Sun,/ Are like

---

[59] "The Open Stage: Elizabethan or Existentialist?" *SS*, XII (1959), pp. 2–3.

drawne curtaynes when the play is done." In *The History of the World*, Raleigh's expression of the idea sounds the themes of *King Lear* and furnishes an interesting commentary on it. Forgetting that "St. Paul hath promised blessedness" to those who accept the will of God and "death" to those who do not accept it, men, he states, complain about their misfortunes. But

> if an heathen wise man call the adversities of the world, but *tributa vivendi*, the tributes of living [cf. Lear's "Thou must be patient; we came crying hither" (IV. vi. 182)]; a wise Christian man ought to know them, and bear them, but as the tributes of offending. [Cf. Edgar's "The gods are just" (V. iii. 170).] . . . For, seeing God, who is the author of all our tragedies, hath written out for us, and appointed us all the parts we are to play; and hath not, in their distribution, been partial to the most mighty princes of the world . . . why should other men, who are but as the least worms, complain of wrongs? [Cf. Gloucester's "Which made me think a man a worm" (IV. i. 32) and the Gentleman's "A sight most pitiful in the meanest wretch,/ Past speaking of in a king!" (IV. vi. 208–209).] Certainly there is no other account to be made of this ridiculous world [Cf. Lear's "this great stage of fools" (IV. vi. 187)] than to resolve, that the change of fortune on the great theatre, is but as the change of garments on the less. [Cf. the mean costumes assumed by Lear, Gloucester, Kent and Edgar in their adversity.] For when, on the one and the other, every man wears but his own skin, the players are all alike. [Cf. Lear's "Robes and furr'd gowns hide all," (IV. vi. 169) and his statement that naked Poor Tom is "the thing itself" (III. iv. 111).][60]

For Barnet a backdrop of eternity must make tragedy impossible since a damned hero cannot elicit pity and a saved hero gives us the happy ending of comedy. I have, he says with regard

---

[60] Sir Walter Raleigh, *The History of the World* (Edinburgh, 1820), pp. xxxix-xl.

to the first point (90), "apparently forgotten that, under the tutelage of Vergil, Dante learned that human pity for the damned is presumptuous and incompatible with Divine Justice." But Dante did feel pity in Hell, and so must we. That a work of art is expressive of a Christian outlook does not mean it should be confused with a theological tract. Quiller-Couch, writing before the "Christianizers," stated that for the Elizabethans the fact that Macbeth embraced witchcraft meant that he "sold his soul to the devil, to become his servitor; that, for a price, he committed himself to direct reversal of the moral order; that he consented to say, 'Evil, be thou my good.' 'Satan, be thou my God.' "[61] Yet, he pointed out (p. 56), Shakespeare nevertheless "forced" his audience "into terrified sympathy" with his hero and made it feel the pity and terror of tragedy. So too the feeling evoked by *Othello*, as I have previously said, is not "he is damned—it serves him right!" but "he is damned—the pity of it!" In the tragedy of damnation, in the words of Helen Gardner, "the acceptance of the justice makes possible the pity, and the pity calls for the justice without which it would turn to loathing."[62]

[61] Arthur Quiller-Couch, *Shakespeare's Workmanship* (London, 1918), pp. 44, 56.

[62] "Milton's 'Satan' and the Theme of Damnation in Elizabethan Tragedy," *Essays and Studies*, I (1948), 63. Miss Gardner's essay, which she seems to have forgotten in attacking "a theological interpretation" of *Othello* in her lecture "The Noble Moor," answers her own assertion there that "whether or not allegorical and symbolical interpretations hold in other plays, they are defeated in *Othello* by the striking human individuality of the characters." In "Milton's 'Satan' " she had written: "Middleton is usually praised and praised rightly for the intense realism of his characterization, . . . but there is more than realism here. What Mephistophilis is to Faustus, . . . DeFlores is to Beatrice-Joanna." Shakespeare, it would seem, is as capable as Middleton of combining realism and symbolism.

In the tragedy in which we get a brief glimpse of a heaven beyond this world, the suffering of the tragic hero is not forgotten in a happy ending, for we are left not amid the glories of this heaven but with the survivors in this harsh world. Although the existence of the backdrop of eternity affects our response, contributing to a feeling of reconciliation, our attention remains fixed on the foreground, the stage upon which human beings play out their lives. That foreground is a world full of pain but governed by law, and the knowledge we have gained of it has been bought by the price of our experience of the hero's suffering and death.

Roland M. Frye, who throughout follows Barnet in rejecting the picture of an afterlife in the background as part of the universe of the play, at one point reverses himself and in so doing rephrases (p. 181) my statement (pp. 90–91) that in certain of Shakespeare's tragedies "although there is suggested to the audience's imagination a heaven and a hell awaiting the outcome of the struggles of the characters, its attention is focussed on this world, in which these struggles take place": "Richard II is one of the rare characters whom Shakespeare treats in such a way as to indicate the relevance of the kind of theological doctrines of the afterlife which we have cited here. Even so, however, it remains true that Shakespeare's focus is upon characterization and action in the theater, rather than in heaven and hell." Two pages before his comment on Richard II, Frye had said that "Shakespeare uses references to the life everlasting for the purpose of characterization within the limits of the 'two hours' traffic' of his stage." In the later passage, however, he is saying that Richard's words about an afterlife are not merely in keeping with his character but indicate that he is indeed going to the heaven of which he speaks, for Richard has prepared himself for it "by the disciplines of humility and affliction" in the manner prescribed by Calvin and Luther, whom Frye cites. "Suffering and time provide the opportunity for Richard to win a new world's crown," he comments, referring to Richard's statement "Our holy lives must win a new world's crown" (V. i. 24). In making this comment, he has worked around to the position that, although attention is focussed on this world, Richard's words adumbrate a heaven beyond it.

Thus, although Frye charges the "theologizers" with inconsistency, he is himself inconsistent. At one time he indicates that the very notion of an afterlife is incompatible with Shakespearean or other tragedy and at another time he indicates that in some rare cases a Christian afterlife is adumbrated. Attacking the "theologizers" who find Othello to be saved, he asserts (pp. 28 and 29n.) that a consistent "theological analysis" must lead one to the conclusion that he is damned—but then he rejects this conclusion even though, on the basis of such a theological analysis, he sees Richard as having won a heavenly crown. Having rejected my interpretation of Othello's tragedy although he has admitted that the theological evidence justifies it, he challenges me to produce the evidence for an afterlife in a number of other specific instances!

In finding my interpretations in these instances to be lacking in evidence, he confuses dramatic suggestion that makes more or less explicit use of current religious ideas with theological disputation. Thus he calls on me (pp. 23–24) to give "a point-by-point analysis" that would convince an imaginary "theological panel consisting of Richard Hooker, Martin Luther, and John Calvin" that Cassio attains "a state of grace leading explicitly to a state of glory," not realizing that I am writing for informed critics cognizant of the dramatic practice of Elizabethan playwrights and of the ideas and expectations of the Elizabethan audience rather than for theologians, imaginary or real. A dramatic pattern is not the same as a theological proof.

Let us conclude this section by taking up the instance of Cassio's salvation as illustration. Frye doubts that "Cassio's comic remarks made while drunk are to be taken seriously in connection with the state of his soul." What, however, it may be asked, is the function of these remarks? Why does Shakespeare instead of merely making Cassio hot in his cups make him drunkenly ludicrous? Why humor at this point, and what sort of humor is it? Why does the humor take the form of talk about salvation? These are questions which Frye does not even think to ask.

We may remember, however, that, while Coleridge rejected as an un-Shakespearean intrusion the low comedy of the *Macbeth* porter not recovered from his drunken carousing, the Porter's words are generally regarded today as masterly grim irony, his bleary fancy of being the porter of hell-gate being more true than he realizes. Is there not also a dramatic irony in the words Cassio utters in his drunken piety? "Well, God's above all, and there be souls that must be saved, and there be souls must not be saved" (II. iii. 106–108). Every one, including himself, is unaware that Iago is putting on an act, playing the hearty boon companion and manipulating him, Roderigo and Montano to deceive Othello as part of the plot in which Othello is to be destroyed. Every one is blind to what is going on—but God is above all, sees what is happening and will eventually perform justice. "For mine own part, no offence to the general, nor any man of quality, I hope to be saved" (II. iii. 109–111). Why is Cassio made, in his drunken religiousness, to apologize to his absent general for his forwardness in thrusting himself in among the saved if not to suggest that Cassio will indeed be saved while Othello will not be saved? "The lieutenant is to be saved before the ancient." In this case the one in the lower rank will be left behind, indeed left out. But, although Cassio speaks truth, he knows not what he says. He is not drunk, he protests: "This is my ancient, this is my right hand, and this is my left hand." But his ancient is not his at all; rather it is Iago who is in command. Yet, in his awareness of his wrongdoing in getting drunk on watch—"Let's to our affairs: God forgive us all!"—Cassio, although befuddled by the devilish Iago as well as by "the devil drunkenness," (II. iii. 297) possesses the possibility of that salvation which the theatre audience, acquainted with Iago's diabolism, knows is at stake even though his audience on the stage regards his words as nonsense. It is noteworthy that drunkenness has just been said to be the national vice of Englishmen, universalizing the significance of the scene, as the Porter's reference to the Gunpowder Plot does: the devil makes use of the weakness of men in Jacobean England as he does in Venice. But if the scene has a significance other than what its actors realize, it must also be significant that Cassio, juxtaposed to Othello in continuing to worship Desdemona, as Othello does not, rises in position as Othello falls into disgrace and gains the place which Othello has lost. In the light of the drunken scene the dramatic curve suggests that Cassio is saved, as Othello is damned.

V.

The objections of the anti-"Christianizers" are, therefore, without validity. It is not the critics who have Christianized Shakespearean tragedy; it is Shakespearean tragedy which is an expression of Renaissance Christian humanism. This does not, of course, mean that we have to be Renaissance Christians—or any other kind of Christians—to respond to it. As with any great art, our recognition of the system of belief lying behind it—a recognition that deepens our understanding of it—does not obligate us to accept more than provisionally that system of belief in order to respond to the emotional experience Shakespearean tragedy gives us. The feeling that life may be grimly, horribly uncertain but that we can infer laws by which we may govern our existence, that life is precious but that for it to have significance we must accept values for which we are ready, if necessary, to give up our lives, that life has immense potentialities but that few of us have the strength of character and the courage to attempt to realize them—such feelings are what Shakespearean tragedy quickens in us, as we enter into its experience. That quickening is as vital for us today, subject as we are to the dehumanizing forces of contemporary society, as ever.

III

Christianity and the Religion of Love in Romeo and Juliet[*]

I.

The long established traditional interpretation of *Romeo and Juliet* is that it is a drama of fate or of sheer misfortune in which the lovers are not at all responsible for the catastrophe they suffer.[1] Recently, however, a number of scholars have argued that

[*] Reprinted by permission from *Shakespeare Quarterly*, vol. xii, no. 4, Autumn 1961.

[1] Cf. F. S. Boas, *Shakspere and his Predecessors* (New York, 1896), p. 214; R. G. Moulton, *The Moral System of Shakespeare* (New York, 1903), p. 61; George P. Baker, *The Development of Shakespeare as a Dramatist* (New York, 1907), p. 255; C. H. Herford, *Shakespeare's Treatment of Love and Marriage* (London, 1921), p. 25; Raymond M. Alden, *Shakespeare* (New York, 1922), p. 245; Allardyce Nicoll, *British Drama* (New York, 1925), pp. 170–171; E. K. Chambers, *Shakespeare: A Survey*

the Elizabethans, with their Christian background of thought, would have regarded the lovers as guilty sinners rather than as innocent victims.[2] What has not been appreciated by either of these two groups of critics is that *Romeo and Juliet*, one of many Elizabethan adaptations of stories of disastrous love derived from Italian novelle, was affected by the manner in which these other adaptations used the ideas of the religion of love that persisted from the Middle Ages.

What had been an aristocratic cult became in the hands of the Elizabethan adapters of the Italian novelle a means of middle-class entertainment. To the straightforwardly realistic accounts of Boccaccio and Bandello, they added a further dash of spice and then a generous portion of moralization to give the mixture

(London, 1929), pp. 70–71; Elmer Edgar Stoll, *Shakespeare's Young Lovers* (London, 1937), pp. 4–5; Thomas Marc Parrott, ed., *Shakespeare: Twenty-three Plays and the Sonnets* (New York, 1938), pp. 166–167; Hazelton Spencer, *The Art and Life of William Shakespeare* (New York, 1940), p. 220; William Allan Neilson and Charles Jarvis Hill, eds., *The Complete Plays and Poems of William Shakespeare* (New York, 1942), p. 975; George Lyman Kittredge, ed., *Sixteen Plays of Shakespeare* (New York, 1948), p. 674; H. B. Charlton, *Shakespearian Tragedy* (Cambridge, Eng., 1952), p. 51; J. Dover Wilson and Ian Duthie, eds., *Romeo and Juliet* (Cambridge, Eng., 1955), pp. xxiii-xxiv.

[2] Cf. H. Edward Cain, "*Romeo and Juliet*: A Reinterpretation," SAB, XXII (1947), 163–191; Roy W. Battenhouse, "Shakespearean Tragedy: A Christian Interpretation," *The Tragic Vision and the Christian Faith*, ed. Nathan A. Scott, Jr. (New York, 1957), pp. 89–94; Franklin M. Dickey, *Not Wisely But Too Well* (San Marino, Calif., 1957); *Romeo and Juliet*, ed. Charles Jasper Sisson with a commentary by W. H. Auden (New York, 1958: "the Laurel ed."), pp. 21–39. A few recent critics (Harley Granville-Barker, *Prefaces to Shakespeare* [Princeton, N. J., 1941], II, 340–342; Donald Stauffer, *Shakespeare's World of Images* [New York, 1949], pp. 55–57; Oscar James Campbell, ed., *The Living Shakespeare* [New York, 1949], p. 313) have assigned responsibility to Romeo and Juliet with a better sense of proportion. Cf. also Bradley, p. 29. My study in part supports and extends what these critics have to say.

a properly medicinal flavor for an audience that thought of literature as a sugar-coated pill, increasing the amount of these ingredients already increased in intervening French translations.[3] Their books, which Roger Ascham lamented could be found in "every shop in London,"[4] anticipated *Pamela, Charlotte Temple* and the modern Hollywood Biblical "epics," in which the audience is invited to sin vicariously with the pagans while being edified by the pious sentiments of the Christians. In their stories dealing with love the reader could find sensational incidents providing gratifying thrills presented to him as moral instruction. Each of them proclaimed that passionate love brought destruction and death, but at the same time glorified this love and, in keeping with the doctrine of the religion of love, presented faithfulness in it as the highest virtue.

What is in the other Elizabethan works drawn from the Italian novelle a crudely mechanical mixture of a glorification of passionate love and a Christian moralistic condemnation of it is in Shakespeare's *Romeo and Juliet* a subtle blend of these two ingredients. In the other adaptations the author oscillates between frivolously inconsistent attitudes toward the lovers; in *Romeo and Juliet* these mutually contradictory attitudes are transformed into a complexly unified attitude. As in Shakespearian tragedy generally, perception of the hero's fatal lack of balance does not preclude admiration and sympathy. Moreover, the ideas of the religion of love and those of Christianity, instead of merely being

[3] Cf. René Pruvost, *Matteo Bandello and Elizabethan Fiction* (Paris, 1937), pp. 106–108. For a discussion of the moral surface for poetry demanded by the middle-class audience, see J. W. Saunders, "The Facade of Morality," *That Soueraine Light: Essays in Honor of Edmund Spenser,* ed. William R. Mueller and Don Cameron Allen (Baltimore, 1952), pp. 1–34.

[4] Roger Ascham, *The Scholemaster,* ed. Edward Arber (Boston, 1898), p. 80.

placed in incongruous juxtaposition as in the other novella adaptations, are in *Romeo and Juliet* interwoven into a unified artistic pattern. Thus in the other adaptations the idea that Love is a god in supreme control over human beings and the idea that divine providence rules the affairs of men are juggled without rime or reason. In *Romeo and Juliet* the medieval and Renaissance concept that sexual love is a manifestation of the cosmic love of God, which holds together the universe in a chain of love and imposes order on it, acts as a nexus between the two doctrines. It may be said of Shakespeare's drama, as Harold S. Wilson said of Chaucer's "Knight's Tale," "Divine love providentially works through imperfect human love to a higher end."[5]

This is not to say that Shakespeare expressed a logically consistent outlook encompassing the ideas of both Christianity and the religion of love. He was concerned with artistic unity, not with logical unity. The ideas of the religion of love and those of Christianity not only work together; they also pull in opposite directions, creating a dramatic tension which is relieved only with the transcendence of love at the very end. According to a tenet of the medieval religion of love that continued to be expressed in the Elizabethan adaptations of novelle, joining the loved one in death qualifies the lover as one of Cupid's saints and ensures that the two meet in the "Paradise in which dwelt the god of love, and in which were reserved places for his disciples."[6] According to Christianity, suicide, unless repentance occurs between the act and death, ensures damnation. In *Romeo and Juliet*, unlike *Hamlet*, *Othello*, *Macbeth* and *King Lear*, it is the lovers' paradise of the religion of love, not the afterlife of

---

[5] "*The Knight's Tale* and the *Teseida* Again," *University of Toronto Quarterly*, XVIII (1949), 145.

[6] William G. Dodd, *Courtly Love in Chaucer and Gower* (Boston, 1913), p. 18.

Christian religion, which is adumbrated at the close of the tragedy. W. H. Auden's statement that the Elizabethans must have believed that any stage character who committed suicide without expressing repentance before his death was going to hell[7] is valid only for a play such as *Othello*, where the Christian afterlife is consistently and unambiguously though faintly adumbrated. It is not valid for *Romeo and Juliet* since it does not take into account Shakespeare's use of the tradition of the religion of love and its doctrine of the lovers' paradise. If it seems strange that dramatic use of this tradition was accepted by the Christian Elizabethans, it should be remembered that it originated in the Christian Middle Ages. In this tradition, C. S. Lewis points out, love, at times "an escape from religion" and at other times "a rival religion," can also be "an extension of religion" and even a "combination" of all of these things.[8]

II.

We had best begin by reviewing the group of Elizabethan adaptations of novelle that tell the "tragical histories" of unfortunate lovers who meet family hostility and finally die for love. In this review we shall not be concerned with the deviations of these adaptations from their originals, for what is of sole interest to us is the attitudes toward passionate love which the Elizabethan popular audience found in them. We shall see how the tenets of the religion of love—that Love is an all-powerful god, that he exercises his dominion particularly over the young, that his rule is a law of nature—are used to justify and exalt passionate love, and how at the same time orthodox Christian ethics

[7] *Romeo and Juliet* ("the Laurel ed."), p. 38. For a discussion of the intimations of Othello's damnation, see Siegel, pp. 121–140.

[8] *The Allegory of Love* (Oxford Univ. Press, 1936), pp. 21–22.

are used to condemn it. By examining first the mechanical mixture of glorification and condemnation in these adaptations, we shall be better able to analyze the blend of these two ingredients in *Romeo and Juliet*. In addition, the reader will note the references to an afterlife, both those to the paradise of the religion of love for those faithful to love in death and those to the hell of Christianity. Our observation of these will alert us to such references in *Romeo and Juliet* and will enable us to understand more fully their significance.

The first published work in this group of adaptations is William Walter's *Guystarde and Sygysmonde* (1532), a versified adaptation of Boccaccio's tale of Guiscardo and Ghismonda in the *Decameron*. This tale, with whose retellings we shall begin, was, with the tale of Romeo and Juliet, with which it was more than once linked, the most popular of the novella stories. Thomas Peend spoke of the two stories as among the great love stories of all time in *The Pleasant Fable of Hermaphroditus and Salamacis* (1565), and Barnaby Rich spoke of their fame in *A Right Exelent and Pleasaunt Dialogue betwene Mercury and an English Souldier* (1574).[9] William Painter included both in his *Palace of Pleasure* (1566).

The tale told by Boccaccio is of Ghismonda, a widow who, knowing that her father Tancred will not permit her to remarry, looks about for the secret solace of love and finds it in the person of Guiscardo, her father's servant. Caught *in flagrante delicto* by Tancred, she is imprisoned by him and sent the heart of her murdered lover in the bottom of a cup. Calling to her lover that she is coming to him, she poisons herself. The author's sympathy is with his worldly, sophisticated heroine, and a good deal of the

---

[9] *Early English Versions of the Tales of Guiscardo and Ghismonda and Titus and Gisippus from the Decameron*, ed. Herbert G. Wright, EETS (New York, 1937), p. cviii.

story is given over to her spirited defense of herself in reply to her father's upbraiding of her, for which the story may almost be said to exist. This defense in which, speaking of her youth and natural desires, she asserts that if her father did not want her to have an illicit affair he should have got her married off instead of keeping her by him presents the case for the sovereignty of love.

Walter tells the story in a fairly straightforward way, but it is punctuated throughout by the obtrusive comments of the printer, R. Coplande, delivered with the regularity but not the lyricism of a Greek chorus. These comments have a schizophrenic character, for at some crises Coplande condemns the lovers and at others he exalts them. As Herbert G. Wright points out, there is no reason to believe that Coplande's sermonizing met with Walter's disapproval, as Walter himself inveighed against the bad effects of idleness in the prologue he wrote to *The Spectacle of Lovers* in the same way that the prologue to *Guystarde and Sygysmonde* does.[10] Coplande's comments, however, are certainly inorganic. When Guystarde and Sygysmonde give themselves up to love, Coplande exclaims:

> O folysshe Guystarde/ O vnwyse Sygysmonde
> O newe Pryamus [sic]/ O yonge wanton Thysbe. (p. 106)

He comments otherwise, however, after Sygysmonde's defense of herself to her father. Reminding him that she is young and made of flesh and blood, not iron or stone, she asserts:

> I beynge in voluptuousyte
> Bothe nyght and day my mynde I dyd apply
> My flamynge hete how quenced it myght be. (p. 117)

---

[10] *Early English Versions*, p. lxvi.

This speech makes Coplande exclaim:

> O constant lady/ O lyght of louers shene
> O turtle true. . . . (p. 120)

Walter himself excuses Sygysmonde because of her faithfulness:

> Alas swete woman/ thou loued not for mede.
> Nor yete in comune/ but stedfastly to one. (p. 121)

At the end he follows the medieval convention of praying for his hero and heroine:

> To these two louers Iesu of his grace
> Graunt mercy & in heuen to haue a place. Amen.

Coplande, however, adds to this conclusion a moralistic envoy in which he calls on the poem to "shewe example/ wylfull appetyte" to those who "chayned be in loue" (pp. 128–129).

The next version of the Guiscardo-Ghismonda story is that of Painter, who as he generally does, gives a quite direct translation; his version is the closest one to Boccaccio. In his dedicatory epistle, however, he insists on his moralistic intention. While admitting that "by the first face and view, some of these [stories] may seeme to intreat of vnlawful loue," he defends them on the ground that they teach that passion leads to "ruine, ouerthrow, inconuenience and displeasure."[11] Yet, despite Painter's announced moralistic purpose, he permits Gismonda to deliver with as much spirit as ever her speech in which she charges her father with having disregarded "the lawe of youth" (I. 171) that impels young people to gratify their sexual desire. And, although Gismonda is described at the beginning as a lady who, "yonge, lustie, and more wise peraduenture then a woman ought to be"

---

[11] William Painter, *The Palace of Pleasure*, ed. Joseph Haslewood (London, 1813), I, iii.

(I. 166), decides to find a man to be her lover, she is later presented as admirable in her fidelity. At the end her father, repentant, respects her dying wish and causes the lovers "honorablie to be buried, and intombed both in one grave, not without great sorowe of all the people of Salerne" (I. 175).

The next version of the story, a play, *The Tragedie of Tancred and Gismund* by Robert Wilmot and others, was published in 1591 after having been acted at court in 1567. *The Tragedie of Tancred and Gismund* is an austere Senecan drama, complete with choruses and furies, but it continues to mix condemnation and glorification of the lovers. The dedicatory epistle to "the Gentlemen Students of the Inner Temple" states that the play is concerned with "commending vertue, detesting vice, and liuely deciphering their ouerthrow that suppresse not their vnruely affections"; the "preface to the Queenes Maidens of Honor" states that through the play the dead Gismunda prays for them "to pittie her annoy." Gismunda is shown as pitiable in her thwarted desire to marry Guiszhard, but her succumbing to love is spoken of in terms of moral condemnation. At the same time it is presented as virtually inevitable. Thus Cupid, proclaiming his power, says:

> Gismund I haue entised to forget
> > her widdowes weedes, and burne in raging lust . . .
> Twas I allur'd her once againe to trie
> > the sower sweetes that Louers buy too deere.[12]

Gismunda herself says to her father that she is deserving of death, pleading only that Love "would not endure controlment any more:/ But violently enforst my feebled heart" (ll. 1171–1172). When she comes to commit suicide, however, she dies ex-

---

[12] *The Tragedy of Tancred and Gismund*, The Malone Society Reprints (Oxford Univ. Press, 1914), ll. 594–599.

altedly, not repentantly, exclaiming as she takes the poison, "Dreadlesse of death (mine Earle) I drink to thee" (l. 1719). It is Tancred who points a moral as he kills himself:

> Now fathers learn by me,
> Be wise, be warnde to vse more tenderly
> The jewels of your ioyes. (ll. 1855–1857)

At the conclusion Iulio, one of Tancred's gentlemen, acting as the moralizing epilogue, informs the audience of Tancred's damnation for having committed suicide in "despaire": "With violent hands he that his life doth end,/ His damned soul to endles night doth wend" (ll. 1863–1864). He says nothing about the fate of Gismunda's soul, but she herself in committing suicide had said: "Now passe I to the pleasant land of loue,/ Where heauenly loue immortall flourisheth" (ll. 1725–1726). The "pleasant land of loue" of which she speaks is evidently the lovers' paradise of the religion of love, the same paradise for which one of the heroines in George Pettie's love stories presents her credentials as a martyr of love in committing suicide: "I think myself to have satisfied my duty, and purchased thereby a passport to the place and paradise where my husband hath his habitation."[13] Yet the destination of Gismunda's soul is uncertain, for she concludes her speech by calling upon hell, not heaven, to witness that she dies for Guiszhard's "pure love," and Iulio in the epilogue condemns her by implication: "Now humbly pray we that our English dames . . . their honors may auoid the shames/ That follows such as liue in wanton lust" (ll. 1877–1880).

The last published Elizabethan version of the Guiscardo-Ghis-

---

[13] George Pettie, *A Petite Pallace of Pettie his Pleasure*, ed. I. Gollancz (London, 1908), I, 45–46.

monda story, a narrative poem "The Statly Tragedy of Guistard and Sismond," was printed in 1597 from a manuscript written during the latter half of the fifteenth century. In this poem, although Sismond's sexual passion is not blinked at ("lustie youth and corage brent her as fyre"),[14] Guistard and Sismond are presented as models of true gentility rather than as the worldly-wise creatures that Boccaccio's hero and heroine are. The conclusion, which is copied from an earlier fifteenth-century manuscript, Gilbert Banester's "The Tale of Guiscardo and Ghismonda," is very sympathetic to the lovers. The moral drawn is that love is irresistible to youth and should not be opposed by cruel parents:

> Youth will to youth, loue will to loue euermore,
> And shortly in my minde this processe to conclude,
> Each thing will draw to his similitude.   (p. 97)

Tancred's soul is said to be "in great perill" because he would not let Sismond get married. The poet prays, however, for his heroine's soul and at the same time holds her up as a model of womanhood, as, according to the religion of love, she was:

> That as I trust she is in blisse celestiall,
> As of faith and troth all louers surmounting,
> She was a mirrour vnto women all,
> Example of true and stedfast loue giuing:
> Wherefore I beseech him that is of all thing
> Lord gouernour, and comfort agen bale,
> Graunt all louers ioy. And thus endeth my tale.
>   (p. 99)

The God of Christianity and the god of love are here indeed confused.

---

[14] *Early English Versions*, p. 43.

The next two tales of unfortunate lovers thwarted by parental opposition, aside from Arthur Brooke's "Tragicall Historye of Romeus and Juliet" and Painter's version of the story, which I shall leave to the end of my survey, appear in Geoffrey Fenton's *Certaine Tragicall Discourses* (1567), translations of stories derived from Bandello. Fenton, like Painter, while admitting that "at the firste sighte, theis discourses maye importe certeyne vanytyes or fonde practises in love," affirms that they demonstrate "the inconvenience happenynge by the pursute of lycenceous desyer."[15] Fenton's moralizing is much heavier than that of Painter, but his sensationalism is also greater, and his sympathy for his lovers, guilty or not, is evident.

The title of the first of his stories that I shall examine, which deserves to be quoted in full, is indicative of its tone: "The Long and Loyall Love betwene Lyvyo and Camylla, together with their lamentable death; the one dying of a passion of joye the first night he embraced his mystres in bedde; the other passed also the same way, as overcome with present sorow for the death of him whom she loved no lesse then herselfe" (I. 85). Fenton condemns the lovers' excessive passion as causing their damnation, asserting flatly that they were "th' unnatural morderers of their owne soules" (I. 88), but the moral is laid on as with a trowel. It does not at all grow out of the story in which the lovers, forbidden to see each other by Camilla's father, are sympathetically depicted and their passion is presented as irresistible. "What angrye dome of the godds or sinyster permission of the fates is this," cries Livio, on finding that Love has "made himselfe lord" (I. 91, 89) over his mind. Their brief but intense

---

[15] *Certain Tragical Discourses of Bandello*, trans. Geoffrey Fenton (London, 1953), I, 8.

delight, moreover, is so described that many undoubtedly would have felt as Byron did in commenting that he could not pity Juan even if he had been squeezed to death between Julia and Antonia. Although Fenton condemns such secret marriages as that of Livio and Camilla as a violation of filial obedience that must be punished by God, at the conclusion he blames not the lovers but Camilla's brother, who instigated her father: his "cruelty was the cause of the death of the ii only flowers and peragons in Italy" (I. 128). The lovers themselves are enshrined in a burial vault of marble.

In Fenton's other story of parental opposition to love, Perillo, a prodigal young bankrupt, who "seamed invincible againste all good councel," falls in love with Carmosyna and is "made tractable" by Love, which "plieth the most stronge and stubborne uppon earthe," so that "one poyson driveth oute an other" (II. 218). Her father, a wealthy merchant, refuses the match, but Perillo, after much hardship and adventure, gains riches and marries her. On the marriage night, however, the hot June weather breeds a thunderstorm, "whereof (as the feare of the tempest hadd dryven the bride and bridgrom to embrace one another) so one of the sayd fatall mynisters of destenye, whyche we call properly thunderbolts, darted with suche vehemencie uppon the one and other lover . . . that it gave ende to their pleasure and life at one blowe." So Perillo was not able to avoid "the furie of the heavens and inclemencye of his fates" or "the greate wronge which the guider of amarus destinies seemed to do to the loyalte of the younge man" (II. 234). Thus the ultimate power is left indecisively poised between divine providence, fate and the god of love.

Our last two stories of the type, aside from the Romeo-Juliet story itself, are verse translations of tales from Boccaccio in

George Turberville's *Tragical Tales* (1587).[16] The first is from the well-known tale which was the source of Keats's *Isabella, or the Pot of Basil.* In Turberville's poem Elizabeth, a wealthy merchant's daughter, falls in love with the boy who keeps her brothers' shop. The lovers

> Sport as the maner is
> Of wanton Cupids crue,
> That more respect the present toyes,
> Than troubles that ensue.[17]

Elizabeth, however, is excused, as Ghismonda was, because

> she was ripe to wed.
> And yet without a married mate,
> Her lustie prime shee led. (p. 185)

Her pining away after her brothers steal from her the basil pot in which she has buried the head of the lover they have murdered is described in a manner as pathetic as the pedestrian verse allows, but Turberville draws a moral at the conclusion:

> Loe here the lotte of wicked loue,
> Behold the wretched end
> Of willful wightes, that wholy doe
> On Cupides lawes depend. (p. 199)

---

[16] I shall omit from this survey the stories of Germanicus and Agrippina and of Curatius and Horatia in *A Petite Pallace of Pettie his Pleasure,* for, although influenced by the adaptations of novelle, Pettie's book retells classical love stories rather than those in the Italian novelle. Moreover, it has a sophisticated wit which, together with the dedication to "the gentle gentlewomen readers," leads one to suspect that it was written for a more courtly audience than the volumes of Painter and Fenton. Pettie has sensational incident, glorification of passionate love and moralization, as do the adaptations of novelle, but the sensationalism and the glorification of love are undercut by the play of wit, and the moralization is clearly tongue-in-cheek.

[17] (Edinburgh, 1837), p. 186.

In his envoy, however, Turberville acknowledges the sovereignty of Cupid and condemns not the lovers but the brothers:

> By nature so the law of loue is set,
> As none hath wil or power from him to wrest . . .
>   Wherefore this wrong was great they did this maide:
> The brothers were a little not to blame,
> That would the wench from fixed fansie staid:
> And thought by force to quench her kindled flame. (p. 202)

Turberville's other verse tale can only be described as a burlesque, witting or unwitting, of the type. Girolamus, the fourteen-year-old son of a rich merchant's widow, is madly in love with his playmate from babyhood, Salvestra, a tailor's daughter, who desires him equally ardently. His mother, wishing a better match and seeing that whippings do not do any good, sends him off to Paris. While he is there, Salvestra is married to a curtainmaker. Girolamus, hotter in love than ever, comes back. He steals into her house at night and makes his way to the bed where she lies by her soundly sleeping husband. There follows an erotic scene in which he begs her to yield grace and she refuses. Finally, he entreats her, since he is frozen, to permit him "to warme himselfe within her bed," promising her he would not "her naked carkasse with / His manly members tutche" (p. 273). To this she assents. As he lies there thinking of her "shamefull scorne," he is "brought to deep despaire" and, deciding "not to live," gives up the ghost forthwith and lies lifeless "by Saluestras sauage side" (p. 274). She wakes her husband, tells him the story and has him bring the corpse to the door of Girolamus' mother. At the funeral pity comes to Salvestra too late. Throwing herself on Girolamus' body, she expires. Turberville gravely appends (p. 283) three different morals to the story. First, since Cupid is all-powerful, parents should "giue consent, / And not repine when mindes to match are bent." Second, women should "peruse the plague of her that pyty lackt" and take example their "rygor to remoue." Third, "Cupidos knyghts" should "take heede" to "courte no mans wyfe embrace no maryage bed," for married women who submit must prove faithless.

The tellings of the Romeo-Juliet story before Shakespeare contain the same mixture of the Christian moralistic condemnation and the glorification of passionate love as the other Elizabethan adaptations of the Italian novelle. Arthur Brooke in his prefatory address to the reader accuses the lovers of "thralling themselves to unhonest desire" and of "abusyng the honorable name of lawefull mariage, to cloke the shame of stolne contractes."[18] This, however, is only the moral surface conventionally expected in these adaptations. His sympathy in the poem itself is entirely with the lovers. He describes the marriage night with considerable zest, making bawdy jokes and exclaiming in transport, "I graunt that I envie the blisse they lived in. . . . Fortune such delight as theyrs dyd never graunt me yet" (p. 309). And when Juliet commits suicide, she speaks of her and Romeus' "parted sprites" as being reunited to live together eternally "in place of endlesse light and blisse" (p. 357) without a word of authorial disapproval. On the contrary, Brooke concludes his poem with a reverential description of the monument erected by their parents to commemorate "so perfect, sound, and so approved love" (p. 363).

So too, although Painter, as we have seen, insisted that his love stories were meant to show the destructive consequences of passion, his "Rhomeo and Julietta" is entirely sympathetic to the lovers. As in Brooke, the marriage night is described ecstatically, and the lovers' paradise of the religion of love is referred

---

[18] *Narrative and Dramatic Sources of Shakespeare*, ed. Geoffrey Bullough (Columbia Univ. Press, 1957), p. 284–285.

to by Julietta when she commits suicide saying that she "frankly offreth vp hir soule . . . that our soules passing from this light, may eternally liue together in the place of euerlasting ioy" (II. 387).

III.

The love of Romeo and Juliet is the passionate love described in these Elizabethan adaptations of Italian novelle. We need not turn aside with Victorian prudishness from Juliet's anticipation of the marriage night in her "Gallop apace, you fiery-footed steeds" soliloquy (III. ii. 1–33) to affirm that no other Shakespearian heroine could have uttered it. Desdemona elopes with Othello, but her love for him is spiritual ("I saw Othello's visage in his mind"—I. iii. 253) rather than physical, and the consummation of their marriage is postponed, as is clear from the herald's announcement of the nuptial festivities and the marriage morning serenade of Cassio's musicians, until they are at Cyprus. Ophelia, far from being swept away by her love, permits herself to be lessoned by her father and her brother to return Hamlet's gifts. As for the romantic comedy heroines, they are, as Rosalind says, apter to love than to confess they do, engaging their lovers in skirmishes of wit before laying down their arms. One cannot imagine Juliet spending her time dressed as a boy making mock-love to Romeo. Friar Laurence, on hearing the ardor of their expressions of love, hastens to perform the marriage ceremony before their passion gets out of hand: "By your leaves, you shall not stay alone/ Till holy church incorporate two in one" (II. vi. 36–37).

Intense though their passion is, however, it is exalted. The salaciousness present in many of the adaptations of novelle is refined away. Juliet is not a Ghismonda making approaches to

Guiscardo or an Elizabeth making approaches to her brothers' apprentice. Shakespeare departs from Brooke, who has Juliet, falling in love with Romeus at first sight, whisper to him at the dance "I am yours," as "all her partes did shake" (p. 294) with passion. The avowal of love of Shakespeare's Juliet comes after Romeo has already heard her divulge it in soliloquy so that, romantically ardent though she is, she retains her maidenly modesty. So too, if Juliet is an eager bride, she is also a blushing one who calls upon night to "hood my unmann'd blood, bating in my cheeks,/ With thy black mantle" (III. ii. 14–15). And, dangerous though the prudent Friar Laurence may find it to leave them alone unmarried, their "bent of love" is "honorable," their "purpose marriage."[19] In Brooke, on the other hand, Friar Laurence relates that they threatened that "except he graunt the rytes of church to geve,/ They shalbe forst by earnest love in sinnefull state to live" (p. 361).

Shakespeare, then, took care not to lose his audience's sympathy for the lovers. Romantically passionate though their love is, it is, like that of Fenton's Livio and Camilla, consummated only in marriage. Like that of Fenton's lovers, it is, however, a marriage which has the savor of a hurriedly snatched illicit delight. This love is too intense, too precipitate, to bring anything but disaster. This is the burden of Friar Laurence's warnings: "Love moderately; long love doth so;/ Too swift arrives as tardy as too slow" (II. vi. 14–15).

Since Dowden's arraignment of Gervinus, it has been customary to regard Friar Laurence as a fussy, even comical, old busy-

---

[19] II. ii. 143–144. The fact that the love of Romeo and Juliet is not adulterous is one of the things which make it a deviation from the love-death myth, in which love and death are blended in a mystic ecstacy. This myth has been traced by Denis de Rougemont in *Love in the Western World* (New York, 1940).

body, utterly incapable of performing a choric function. Thus Duthie speaks of him as "this well-meaning but dull, timid and unimaginative cleric" (p. xx). The man who agrees to marry Romeo and Juliet in secret and who devises the plan of the potion can scarcely, however, be called timid and unimaginative. And before dismissing his sententious utterances as dull it is well ·to examine them.

Friar Laurence supplies the moralizing with which the authors of the adaptations of novelle would garnish them. In Shakespeare, however, this moralizing is not extraneous to the work, although it does not contain within itself its complexity. Friar Laurence's comments concerning the conduct of Romeo are just and foreshadow the conclusion. His warnings about immoderateness and reckless abandon, in fact, only repeat the misgivings of Juliet at the time of their avowals of love:

> I have no joy of this contract to-night:
> It is too rash, too unadvised, too sudden;
> Too like the lightning, which doth cease to be
> Ere one can say "It lightens." (II. ii. 117–120)

It is not merely the failure of Friar John to get to Mantua, the last accident in a fatal chain of mishaps, that brings about the death of the lovers; it is the speed with which Romeo acts, a speed which distinguishes the lovers' action throughout. Romeo's drive to death in the last act is only the culmination of a drive which reaches its goal at the conclusion. The words "I long to die" (IV. i. 66), with which Juliet, threatening, knife in hand, to kill herself, impels Friar Laurence to his desperate stratagem, express well the drive to death of the two lovers. Ready like half-cocked pistols to go off or, as Friar Laurence says of Romeo, "like powder in a skilless soldier's flask" (III. iii. 132), they are prone to suicide. The hasty jumping to conclusions and the

thoughts of death with which each responds to the initial disaster of Tybalt's death foreshadow the suicides as the result of
misunderstanding at the end as surely as the frequently pointed
out dreams, premonitions, references to death as a lover and
mentions of fate. Juliet, mistaking the Nurse's lamentations over
Tybalt for an announcement of Romeo's death, exclaims: "Vile
earth, to earth resign; end motion here;/ And thou and Romeo
press one heavy bier!" (III. ii. 59–60). When Romeo will in fact
be dead, having killed himself in the mistaken belief that she is
dead, she will indeed join him to lie in one grave with him.

So too Romeo, overwhelmed at the thought of his banishment
and mistaking the Nurse's description of Juliet's grief for an indication that she is sorrowing over Tybalt and has rejected him, is
about to kill himself when Friar Laurence restrains him, reclaim-
ing him from despair with a lengthy speech that contains some
prophetic passages:

> Hold thy desperate hand:
> Art thou a man? . . .
> Thy wild acts denote
> The unreasonable fury of a beast. . . .
> Wilt thou slay thyself?
> And slay thy lady too that lives in thee,
> By doing damnèd hate upon thyself? . . .
> Take heed, take heed, for such die miserable. (III. iii. 108–145)

"Desperate" is a word that Romeo uses about himself at the
end, as he immediately thinks of the means by which he may kill
himself: "O mischief, thou art swift/ To enter in the thoughts
of desperate men!" (V. i. 35–36). He also uses the same image of
the wild beast—it is, as G. Wilson Knight has pointed out, one
of the "disorder" images that run through Shakespeare's work[20]

[20] *The Shakespearian Tempest* (Oxford Univ. Press, 1932), *passim*.

—to describe his mood in warning Balthasar not to spy on him in the graveyard:

> The time and my intents are savage-wild,
> More fierce and more inexorable far
> Than empty tigers or the roaring sea. (V. iii. 37–39)

And in slaying himself he does indeed slay Juliet.

If, however, Friar Laurence's warning is prophetic, the intensity of the love of Romeo and Juliet is presented as its own justification. Their love is reckless, tending to destruction, but it is glorious. Each utterance of Friar Laurence is balanced by one of Romeo. We should not, with Dowden, disregard those of Friar Laurence or, with Dickey, disregard those of Romeo: both sets of utterances have validity. What in the other novella adaptations are two opposing views of love voiced by the author without regard for self-contradiction are here two views appropriately voiced by two dramatic characters, for each of whom the audience has sympathetic understanding.

Of the philosophical discussion of his situation in which Friar Laurence wishes to engage him Romeo says:

> Thou canst not speak of that thou doest not feel:
> Wert thou as young as I, Juliet thy love,
> An hour but married, Tybalt murdered,
> Doting like me and like me banished,
> Then mightst thou speak. . . . (III. iii. 64–68)

The advice of the philosopher is no doubt wise, but would he himself be able to follow it if he had the youthful heart of Romeo? If not, "hang up philosophy!" (l. 57). Philosophy is for the old, not for the young, who must follow the law of love taught to them by their hearts. The sensitive members of the Elizabethan audience would have looked upon the participants of this dialogue with a double vision. They would have been able to see Romeo through the eyes of Friar Laurence as a "fond mad man" "with his own tears made drunk" (ll. 52, 83), one who violated all the familiar preachings of the moral philosophers and the divines by permitting his passion to overcome his reason. At the same time, responding sympathetically to Romeo's statement of the familiar idea that love has an irresistible power over youth, they would also have been able to see Friar Laurence through his eyes as an old man incapable of genuinely entering into the feelings of the young.

Moreover, Romeo expresses not merely the power of the love glorified in the novelle but also its rewards. Side by side with Friar Laurence's adjuration that immoderate love must come to speedy destruction is Romeo's assertion, a kind of dedication to love made immediately before the sacrament of marriage is performed:

> Come what sorrow can,
> It cannot countervail the exchange of joy
> That one short minute gives me in her sight:
> Do thou but close our hands with holy words,
> Then love-devouring death do what he dare;
> It is enough I may but call her mine. (II. vi. 3–8)

If such love brings sorrow and death, it is nevertheless worth it.

Friar Laurence's own image captures the ambivalent feeling toward Romeo and Juliet's love projected by the play:

> These violent delights have violent ends
> And in their triumph die, like fire and powder,
> Which as they kiss consume. (II. vi. 9–11)

If this love is destructive, it is also ecstatic. Taken in conjunction with "kiss," "die" suggests the consummation of the sexual act which is one of the Elizabethan meanings of the word. Such violent delight may be short-lived, but its completion is a "triumph," a word that means not only "rapturous delight" but "splendor" and "victory" (*NED*, 2, 3, 5). Burning one's candle at both ends, Edna St. Vincent Millay found, makes a lovely light; by the same token, bringing fire and gunpowder together makes a splendid explosion. The image of the explosion or flash of lightning, an important running image throughout the play, is Shakespeare's artistic means of expressing that view of passionate love which was expressed with crude sensationalism in Fenton's description of bride and bridegroom struck down together by lightning in their nuptial embrace.

IV.

Destructive as their love for each other is to the lovers, through it providence is shown as working out its own ends. But before we can discuss this aspect of *Romeo and Juliet*, we must first look at the history of the concept that sexual love is a manifestation of the all-pervading love of God, through which the universe is governed.

This concept, as Alan M. F. Gunn has pointed out, is an extension of the classical-Christian doctrine of the Middle Ages and the Renaissance that God, overflowing with love, created a universe, hierarchically ordered, in which everything conceivable is present.

> The philosophy of plenitude and the idea of the Scale of Being demanded, not only that all possibilities—from the highest to the lowest—be realized, but that when once realized in the various elements and species of the created universe, they be maintained by the creatures' constant exercise of the reproductive, the generative power with which they had been endowed by Nature acting as the deputy of the Eternal Being. . . . By fulfilling the reproductive function, the creatures would be participating or cooper-

ating in the creative or generative activity of the Eternal Being, that activity in which . . . his "goodness" and his "love" were believed to lie.[21]

Gunn finds that this concept, although it had been foreshadowed before, received its first full exposition in Jean de Meun's portion of the *Roman de la Rose*. Rosemond Tuve, tracing it from the Middle Ages to Spenser, finds it expressed in diverse places, in "courtly romances set in the garden of the God of Love," in "praises sung to the power of Love, of Venus, or of Dame Nature," in "half-scientific, half-philosophical treatises with a Neo-Platonic cast of thought" and in "didactic poetry intent (like the treatises) upon preaching certain tenets of Christian theology."[22]

In poems written in the courtly love tradition the praise of sexual love as a manifestation of God's creative energy is unqualified; in other works the praise of sexual love among human beings is restricted to love within marriage. Common to both, however, is the idea that a cosmic love, permeating the universe and finding expression in sexual love, works against the chaos which would otherwise prevail. Opposed to "the power of Mutability" is "the power of Love (Peace, Natura, Harmony, the Providence or Wisdom of God)."[23] The power of love holds together the universe, which is constantly threatening to get out of order. It brings about universal and social harmony, reconciling the elements, which would otherwise be at war with each other, and doing the same for men.

It is with the operation of the cosmic love in society, in other

---

[21] *The Mirror of Love: A Reinterpretation of "The Romance of the Rose"* (Texas Tech Press, 1952), p. 212.

[22] "A Medieval Commonplace in Spenser's Cosmology," *SP*, **XXX** (1933), 147.

[23] Tuve, 143n.

human relations as well as in sexual love, that we are here concerned. Since God loves, says Chaucer in his invocation to Venus in the proem to Book three of *Troilus and Criseyde*, He will not refuse love to others. Love, the source of all happiness, animates all living things in their seasons and among human beings holds together in unity realm and household. This concept of love as the bond holding together human society as well as the universe itself was also expressed during the Renaissance.

Thus in Barnaby Googe's *Zodiac of Life*, a translation of Marcellus Palengenius' *Zodiacus Vitae* often used as a textbook in Shakespeare's time, there is a passage[24] beginning with the statement of the traditional themes of the universality of love among all creatures, which feel "Cupids flame"; of "loues assured knot," but for which "the worlde should straight be at an end, and the elements decay"; of the "principle of replenishment"[25] by which "the loue of God, that all doth guide," maintains everlasting order by continuing the species despite the death of individuals. It then exalts peace as ministering to the universal fecundity: "In time of peace do all things growe, and all things liuely be." Next it laments the loss of the golden age and the triumph of Discord:

All things does Discorde vile disturbe, with raged motion sad,
Nowe fierce we forced are to be, and lawes with sword to
   stake:
The furies all of hell they swarme, a thousand brondes they
   .shake,
A thousand snakes withall, and moue the proud hie minded
   Kings
And common people mad to be. . . .

[24] *The Zodiake of Life* (London, 1588), pp. 50–51. John Erskine Hankins has strongly argued for the influence of Googe on Shakespeare in *Shakespeare's Derived Imagery* (University of Kansas Press, 1953).

[25] Gunn, p. 213.

The contradiction between the picture of a universe governed by the love of God and the picture of society ruled by Discord is resolved in a later passage on mutability by the Boethian[26] philosophy of a law underlying seeming aimless turmoil and of a divine providence by which God uses seeming accident and evil for an ultimately good purpose:

> But whether Fortune gouerne all, or howsoeuer it be,
> Or Diuels guide the state of men: yet without Destinie
> Doth nothing passe. But all things rulde by mind of God on hie,
> Without whose power nothing is done. (p. 139)

Spenser's description of Concord is an allegorical representation of the operation in human society of the cosmic love which is also manifested in the love between the sexes. Concord, the mother of "blessed Peace" and "Friendship," sits at the doorway of the Temple of Venus, who is "there worshipped of euery liuing wight" (*F. Q.*, IV. x. 34, 29). Close by is a garden of marvelous fecundity and seemly order, where lovers "frankely there their loues desire possesse" (st. 28). This is appropriate, for Venus, by whom "all the world . . . was made," does daily "the same repayre" by causing all living things to seek "in generation . . . to quench their inward fire" (st. 47, 46). On either side of Concord are two young men, Hate and Love, who are half-brothers and "both strongly arm'd, as fearing one another," whom Concord "forced hand to ioyne in hand,/ Albe that *Hat-*

. [26] Although Gunn does not cite Boethius as one of those who anticipated the concept of sexual love as an expression of God's pervasive universal love, Boethius had stated that the "loue of God" governs the universe and human relations: it "kepyth the world in due order and good accorde" and "knitteth together the sacramēt of wedlocke with chaste loue between man and wyfe"—*Boethius' Consolation of Philosophy*, trans. George Colville, 1556, ed. Ernest Belfort Bax (London, 1897), pp. 51–52. Boethius, translated by both Jean de Meun and Chaucer, continued to be translated and read during the Elizabethan period.

red was thereto full loth" (st. 32, 33). Concord subdues "strife, and warre, and anger" and indeed contains the conflict of the elements themselves, holding them as "their Almightie maker first ordained,/ And bound them with inuiolable bands" (st. 34, 35). Opposed to Concord is "*Ate*, mother of debate,/ And all dissention, which doth dayly grow/ Amongst fraile men, that many a publike state/ And many a priuate oft doth ouerthrow" (IV. i. 19). Ate's malice is such that she maligns "euen th' Almightie self," because His overflowing love makes Him merciful to man and "vnto all his creatures so benigne." "For all this worlds faire workmanship she tride,/ Vnto his last confusion to bring,/ And that great golden chaine quite to diuide,/ With which it blessed Concord hath together tide" (IV. i. 30). Concord thus has the same function as Google's Cupid, who retains "all things created" in "loues assured knot," and Ate has the same function as Google's Discord, whose power seems to be daily increasing but who really cannot undo the order established by God. So too Concord is similar to Nature, and Ate is similar to Mutability in Spenser's *Cantos of Mutability*, where the conflict between the two is resolved in a Boethian manner.[27]

Romeo and Juliet dramatizes this concept of a cosmic love manifesting itself through sexual love and working against strife and disorder in society. The love of Romeo and Juliet is opposed to the hate of their parents. Although the lightning power of their love helps to bring about their destruction, it is, after all, only the hatred existing between the two houses that makes fatal the magnetic attraction toward each other of the two young lovers. As in Shakespearian tragedy generally, although the hero contributes to his own disaster, the main cause of it lies outside

---

[27] Cf. Brents Stirling, "The Concluding Stanzas of *Mutabilitie*," *SP*, XXX (1933), 193–204. Stirling finds that Boethius influenced Spenser directly.

of him. The lovers may be imprudent, but the parents are guilty. The swift and violent passion of Romeo and Juliet is the answering force to their parents' furious and violent hate. Hate kills the lovers, but love, the love of heaven, redressing order and restoring concord through the love of Romeo and Juliet, triumphs over the hate which has endangered the peace of Verona.

At one crucial point, however, the time that he kills Tybalt, Romeo gives up love for hate. For, in killing Tybalt, he acts in the vengeful manner of Tybalt.

Tybalt, a follower of the latest foreign-imported, new-fangled affectations and an accomplished duelist who fights by the book, both in his manner of fencing and in his observation of a highly formalized code of honor, resembles those members of the Elizabethan feudalistic nobility who adopted Italian manners. Animated by the enduring enmity of the Italianate, he causes the strife between the two houses, burning less strongly because of the age of the chief participants and its suppression by the Prince, to flare up again. In the first sentence he utters, "I hate the word ['peace']" (I. i. 77), he proclaims his identity, as it were, as the incarnation of the spirit of hatred governing the feud. A two-dimensional "humors" character, he no doubt would have been reminiscent to Elizabethans of such personified abstractions as Discord and Ate.[28] In fact, his opening words resemble those of Envy, who in the Tudor morality play *Impatient Poverty* announces it as his function to unravel the ties of love between man and wife and between human beings generally:

[28] Cain cites (p. 176) Choler's description of himself as an Italianate duelist in Thomas Nabbes' *Microcosmus: A Moral Mask*, produced almost a half century after *Romeo and Juliet*, and comments with but little exaggeration: "He seems to differ from Tybalt only in name."

> I hate Conscience, Peace, Love and Rest;
> Debate and strife, that love I best,
> According to my property.
> When a man loveth well his wife,
> I bring them at debate and strife . . .
> There shall no neighbour love another
> Where I dwell by.[29]

When Tybalt confronts Romeo, therefore, it is ireful Hate confronting Love. Tybalt's sharp insult, "Romeo, the hate I bear thee can afford/ No better term than this,—thou art a villain," is met by Romeo's gentle rejoinder,

> Tybalt, the reason that I have to love thee
> Doth much excuse the appertaining rage
> To such a greeting. (III. i. 63–67)

In making this reply, Romeo, fresh from his marriage and over-flowing with tenderness, is following the Christian ethic of loving his neighbor as himself, returning love for hate. When he goes on to say that he loves the name of Capulet as his own, we see at work that cosmic love which makes use of sexual love to knit together the fragmented portions of what should be a unified social organism.

But the forces of disorder are too strong for such a knitting together to take place without pain and sacrifice. Romeo and Tybalt cannot be reconciled as yet. When Mercutio is killed by Tybalt, Romeo exclaims:

> O sweet Juliet,
> Thy beauty hath made me effeminate
> And in my temper soften'd valour's steel! (ll. 118–120)

---

[29] *Early English Dramatists*, ed. John S. Farmer (London, 1907), p. 329.

His love, he feels, has deprived him of the spirit of a true man, one who will brook no injury. When the "furious Tybalt" comes back, fury is this time met by an "appertaining rage," not by love as before. "Away to heaven, respective lenity," Romeo cries out, "And fire-eyed fury be my conduct now!" (ll. 128–129). Considerate gentleness, Christian forgiveness, he consigns to heaven; fury looking through eyes of fire that are blind to mercy, the fury of Tybalt, is now to be his guide. His words are like those of Othello when Othello deposes love, the Christian love and forgiveness of Desdemona, as his ruler and sets up hate, the Satanic hate and vengefulness of Iago, in its stead:

> All my fond love thus do I blow to heaven. . . .
> Yield up, O love, thy crown and hearted throne
> To tyrannous hate! (III. iii. 445–449)

And hate and vengeful fury lead Romeo to disaster.

But this aberration from love is only momentary, as is Juliet's violent denunciation of Romeo when she is told in the next scene that he has killed Tybalt. It is, moreover, one that would have elicited the highest sympathy from an Elizabethan audience. Dueling was interdicted by Elizabeth, but the prohibition was widely disregarded. In the popular drama the Italianate's sensitivity to anything resembling a slight, his concern with the punctilios of the duello, his readiness to use any underhanded method to avenge his honor, are frequently attacked; however, the poltroonery of a Sir Andrew Aguecheek, who will take any insult without fighting, is as frequently mocked. The general feeling seems to have been that the Biblical text often cited by the Elizabethan moralists and preachers, "Recompense to no man evil for evil. . . . Dearly beloved, avenge not yourselves, but rather give place to wrath," while the highest standard of morality, could in life be carried only so far. To be a professional duelist or a Machiavellian avenger was one thing; to refuse to fight under any circumstances was another. The deeply religious Sir Philip Sidney, the hero of the London masses, although denouncing extreme touchiness of spirit and perseverence in enmity in *Arcadia*,[30] sought permission from Elizabeth to fight a duel with the Earl of Oxford. The Elizabethan audience would, therefore, have regarded Romeo not so much as a sinner as one forced by the irony of fate to depart immediately after his marriage from his course of love, the course to which God's love, acting upon the universe and constantly re-establishing order, directs him.

In returning to their course of love Romeo and Juliet fulfil their adverse destiny, but it is a destiny which serves the purpose of divine providence. "A greater power than we can contradict," Friar Laurence tells Juliet, "Hath thwarted our intents" (V. iii. 153–154), and in recounting to the Prince what had happened he reiterates his faith in God's mysterious ways: "I entreated her come forth,/ And bear this work of heaven with patience" (ll. 260–261). His faith is justified by the conclusion. Romeo and Juliet are, as Capulet says, the "poor sacrifices" of their parents' enmity, the tragic scapegoats through whom their parents expiate the sin of their vengefulness. As was stated in the prologue, which the Prince's concluding formal speech recalls, "their parents' rage, . . . but their children's end, naught could remove." The death of the lovers, says the Prince, acting as a moralizing epilogue, is the awful retribution of heaven upon their feuding families:

> Capulet, Montague,
> See what a scourge is laid upon your hate,
> That heaven finds means to kill your joys with love!
> (ll. 291–293)

[30] *The Countess of Pembroke's Arcadia*, ed. Albert Feuillerat (Cambridge Univ. Press, 1922), p. 439.

His words are rich in significance, bearing a number of meanings dependent on different meanings of the word "love": (1) see how heaven finds means to kill your happiness, punishing you through the love of your children; (2) see how heaven finds means to kill your happiness, punishing you while loving you; (3) see how heaven finds means to kill your happiness, punishing you while destroying your hate through the force of cosmic love.

V.

If, however, *Romeo and Juliet* makes use of the reconciliation between Cupid and God that had been effected by having Cupid act as a minister of God in maintaining social harmony, it also makes use of the ancient conflict between Cupid and God. Most critics have observed that the love of Romeo and Juliet is transcendent in death. They have not observed, however, how the ideas of the religion of love are used to gain this effect, and they have not seen the tension that was resolved by this transcendence of love.

We have seen the prophetic force of Friar Laurence's warning in the lines quoted earlier; this warning, however, is concerned not only with what will happen to Romeo here on earth. It is concerned also with what will happen to him after death. Like the moralizing Fenton, who, as we have seen, asserted that his hero and heroine are damned, the moralizing Friar Laurence speaks of damnation. "Desperate" connoted to Elizabethans despair, a heinous sin. To die in despair—and this is what is implied by the phrase "die miserable"—is to ensure perdition. In committing suicide Romeo would do "damnèd hate" upon himself because suicide is an act of self-hatred that is damnable.

The idea is made even more explicit in the lines that follow:

> Why rail'st thou on thy birth, the heaven, and earth?
> Since birth, and heaven, and earth, all three do meet
> In thee at once; which thou at once wouldst lose.
>
> (III. iii. 119–121)

As Kittredge comments, "heaven" refers to "heaven's mercy," on which Romeo has railed and which he would "lose"—that is, "abandon—i.e., by the sin of suicide."[31] Is this warning of damnation prophetic? This is the question that hangs heavy over the last act. It is answered only with Romeo's final speech.

The act begins with Romeo's telling of the happy dream he has had, in which Juliet, finding him dead, "breathed such life with kisses in my lips" that he "revived, and was an emperor" (V. i. 8–9). This dream is ironically false in accordance with the folk belief that dreams go by contraries. In another sense, however, it is profoundly true, for, as we shall see, it signifies the coming triumph of the lovers over death.

Immediately after Romeo tells of his dream of death and reawakening, he receives the fatal misinformation of Juliet's death. The exclamation that he utters is a contrast to his exclamation over the corpse of Tybalt. No longer does he passively accept himself as "fortune's fool" (III. i. 141): "Is it even so? then I defy you, stars!" (1. 24). With the quiet strength of this line Romeo attains tragic heroism. He is no longer the helpless plaything of Fortune since he can by a single act deprive her of her power over him. Totally committed to love, he chooses death. But is he a tragic hero eternally doomed? His defiance of the stars could be taken as a rejection of the destiny which God has fixed and which operates through the celestial constellations. In

---

[31] Kittredge, p. 746.

this view, the traditional Christian view, by not accepting Juliet's death as the will of God and by determining to commit self-slaughter, he is damned. It could also be taken, however, as the expression of superiority over earthly mutability of one who, like the Christian saints, is renouncing the world. In this view, the view of the religion of love, by going to join Juliet, he is achieving martyrdom and gaining the paradise of true lovers.

The first way of regarding Romeo is suggested by Balthasar's entreaty "Have patience" (l. 27), which echoes Friar Laurence's adjuration "Be patient" (III. iii. 16). "Patience" connotes the Christian fortitude in accepting the evil of this world as serving God's purposes that is best exemplified by the conduct of Christ and the saints. But Romeo's calmness, as Balthasar realizes, is in reality a controlled frenzy of despair that is revealed in his wild looks and that impels him to commit violence upon himself. Just as in Skelton's morality play *Magnificence*, Mischief, coming after Despair, proclaims to the titular hero, "And I, Myschefe, am comyn at nede/Out of thy lyfe the for to lede,"[32] so "mischief" is "swift/ To enter in the thoughts" of the desperate Romeo.

The second way of regarding Romeo is suggested by his words to the apothecary:

> There is thy gold, worse poison to men's souls,
> Doing more murders in this loathsome world,
> Than these poor compounds that thou mayst not sell.
> I sell thee poison; thou hast sold me none.
> Farewell: buy food, and get thyself in flesh. (ll. 80–84)

The "loathsome world" is here contemned in orthodox *de contemptu mundi* terms. The haggard apothecary represents that wretched poverty driven to sinful envy and repining against its

[32] John Skelton, *Magnificence*, EETS (London, 1908), ll. 2309–2310.

lot attacked by Chaucer's Man of Law in the prologue to his tale and personified in *Impatient Poverty.* "The world is not thy friend nor the world's law" (1. 72), Romeo tells him. But the desperate apothecary, unlike the desperate Romeo, comes to terms with the world. He accepts gold, which is so frequently associated in the morality plays with the things of this world and opposed to the things of the spirit. "Get thyself in flesh," Romeo tells him with contemptuous pity, as he himself rejects the world and the flesh. The apothecary has taken what proved to the three revelers of "The Pardoner's Tale" to be just what Romeo calls gold: poison. Romeo acquires from him "not poison" but "cordial" (1. 85), a restorative that will give him not death but everlasting life.

We have here something of the same paradox that underlies Donne's "The Canonization," in which Donne, following his custom of giving old ideas new twists, presents himself and his mistress as "unworldly lovers, love's saints," who, "like the holy anchorite," "have given up the world" and "win a better world by giving up this one."[33] This paradox was prepared for in the first act. In their playful exchange at their first meeting, Romeo had addressed Juliet as "saint" and Juliet had addressed Romeo as "pilgrim,"[34] and Romeo had continued to call Juliet "saint" throughout the balcony scene. Looking up at her from below the window, he had imagined her a bright angel. She was, indeed, marked to be one of Cupid's saints, a martyr of love, and Romeo, a pilgrim of love, in finding her had been initiated into love's mystery.

[33] Cleanth Brooks, *The Well Wrought Urn* (New York, 1947), p. 12.
[34] Cf. Kittredge, p. 1085: "That lovers are pilgrims and their lady-loves are saints was a common metaphor." Probably, as Halliwell (Furness Variorum edition of *Romeo and Juliet,* pp. 80–81) and Campbell (p. 326) believe, Romeo is dressed in the masquerade costume of a pilgrim.

When Romeo, however, warns Paris not to prevent him from doing what he has to do, his language once more suggests the view that he is a Christian sinner rather than Cupid's saint:

> Good gentle youth, tempt not a desperate man. . . .
> I beseech thee, youth,
> Put not another sin upon my head,
> By urging me to fury: O, be gone!
> By heaven, I love thee better than myself;
> For I come hither armed against myself.
> Stay not, be gone; live, and hereafter say,
> A madman's mercy bade thee run away. (V. iii. 59–67)

Romeo indeed speaks in the manner of a madman proceeding upon his purposes in the grip of a fixed idea but able at the same time to look upon himself from the outside and to observe his irrational behavior. He realizes that he is about to commit a sin and begs not to be compelled to add the sin of murder to that of suicide. He has come armed against himself, ready to do "damnèd hate" against himself, but in the midst of his "madness" he has the compassion for Paris to warn him not to interfere. Again, as in the Tybalt scene, he speaks to his antagonist of his love for him—and again, on being provoked by him, gives way to fury.

But on hearing Paris' dying words, "If thou be merciful,/ Open the tomb, lay me with Juliet" (ll. 72–73), Romeo wakes as from a feverish dream:

> What said my man, when my betossèd soul
> Did not attend him as we rode? I think
> He told me Paris should have married Juliet:
> Said he not so? or did I dream so? (ll. 76–79)

Although Romeo remains steadfast in his purpose, he no longer proceeds in a frenzy but with meditative deliberation. He clasps

Paris' hand in friendship and compassionately grants him his request. Lover, beloved and rejected rival are to be united in the grave in a general reconciliation. Tybalt, whom Romeo perceives in the tomb, shares in the reconciliation: "Forgive me, cousin!" (l. 101). Love finally conquers in this scene in more than one sense.

For Romeo's suicide is a triumph over death and fate as well as a defeat. Throughout the play there had been intimations of the conclusion in the images of death as a bridegroom taking Juliet. But now Romeo, thinking Juliet dead, says:

> Ah, dear Juliet,
> Why are thou yet so fair? shall I believe
> That unsubstantial death is amorous,
> And that the lean abhorrèd monster keeps
> Thee here in dark to be his paramour?
> For fear of that, I still will stay with thee;
> And never from this palace of dim night,
> Depart again. (ll. 101–108)

Death the conqueror has "not conquered" Juliet (l. 94), for her beauty remains intact. Now, united with his wife in the "bed of death" (l. 28), Romeo will deprive the grim skeleton who would be her lover of his prize. He and Juliet are, as it were, wedded again in their mutual renunciation of life, with the "bed of death" their marital bed. Just so does Sidney's Erona speak of her desire "to send her soule . . . to be maried in the eternall church with him" (p. 233), when she contemplates killing herself to join her supposedly dead lover.

Romeo's words concerning his and Juliet's reunion and everlasting triumph over death must have suggested to the Elizabethan audience the paradise of lovers of the religion of love, the "place of endlesse light and blisse" to which Brooke, Shakespeare's source, and other adapters of novelle referred. Othello, having betrayed love in dedicating himself to vengeance, says that he is parted from Desdemona forever (V. ii. 273–275): "When we shall meet at compt,/ This look of thine will hurl my soul from heaven,/ And fiends will snatch at it." Romeo, faithful in love, says, "I still will stay with thee." Othello makes use of the traditional imagery of hell in his final speech. Romeo makes use of the image of the princely court which recurs in descriptions of the paradise of love[35]: the vault is "a feasting presence full of light" (1. 86), the brilliantly lit presence chamber used by kings for state occasions. In the "palace of dim night" of the Capulet vault, it is intimated, Romeo is to be an emperor, as he had dreamed, with Juliet his ever-radiant bride. There is a similar effect in *Antony and Cleopatra*, in which Shakespeare makes use of the tradition of the two as martyrs of love (cf. Pettie, I, 179) as well as of the tradition of the infatuated Antony ruined by the seductive Cleopatra (cf. Dickey, pp. 156–160). As Romeo said, "I dreamt . . . that I revived, and was an emperor," so Cleopatra says (V. ii. 76–78), "I dream'd there was an Emperor Antony./ O, such another sleep, that I might see/ But such another man." At the conclusion she does indeed go to meet Antony in a death in which she "looks like sleep" (V. ii. 394). So too Juliet, awakened from a sleep

[35] Cf. Andreas Capellanus, *The Art of Courtly Love*, ed. John Parry (Columbia Univ. Press, 1941), pp. 78–80; *The English Works of John Gower*, ed. G. C. Macaulay, EETS (London, 1901), II, 451–453; *The Works of Geoffrey Chaucer*, ed. F. N. Robinson (Boston, 1957), p. 489. Spenser's "thousand payres of louers" in the garden of the Temple of Venus, said to be a "second paradise" (*FQ*, IV. x. 23), do not assemble as a court attending upon the King and Queen of Love, for Spenser is primarily concerned with the aspect of Venus as a goddess rather than with her aspect as a queen. Cupid is, however, later spoken of as commanding "the wide kingdome of loue with Lordly sway" and Venus is spoken of as "Queene of beautie and of grace" (st. 42, 44).

that seems to be death, goes to a death that she regards as life: she kisses Romeo's lips, saying that the poison on them may make her "die with a restorative" (1. 166). In the suicide speech of Antony, he and Cleopatra, in a description reminiscent of those of the King and Queen of Love in the paradise of true lovers,[36] are pictured as emperor and empress in an afterlife. The intimation that Romeo and Juliet are an emperor and his bride in death would seem, then, to have been likewise suggested by the descriptions of the King and Queen of Love.

Thus Shakespeare exploited imaginatively the concept of the lovers' paradise to further a feeling of reconciliation. This feeling of reconciliation, as we have seen, is also ministered to by a sense of the richness of the lives of Romeo and Juliet, brief as they were, by a sense of the inevitability of the catastrophe, given the reckless abandon of the lovers in their situation, and by the larger perception that their disastrous fate serves the end of providence. The feeling of reconciliation and indeed of exaltation at the close of the play does not, however, cause us to forget the tragic fact of the death of the two young people who have so deeply engaged our sympathies. For the glorification of the love of Romeo and Juliet involves a basic acceptance of this world, that acceptance which is necessary if suffering and death are to be tragically meaningful.

[36] Cupid and Venus are ordinarily the King and Queen of Love. In Chaucer's "The Legend of Good Women," however, Cupid's queen is Alcest, one of the famous lovers of history. The members of her court are other famous lovers, and they sing that she surpasses all in beauty and trueness.

IV

Shakespeare's Kneeling-Resurrection Pattern and the Meaning of King Lear

I.

"The overriding critical problem in *King Lear*," says J. Stampfer rightly, "is that of its ending. The deaths of Lear and Cordelia confront us like a raw, fresh wound where our every instinct calls for healing and reconciliation."[1] Samuel Johnson found the conclusion so harrowing that he could not endure to read it. Nahum Tate, in an adaptation which held the stage for a century and a half, gave the play a happy ending in which Lear and Cordelia continued to live. Bradley, while following the romantic critics in heaping contumely on the taste which

---

[1] "The Catharsis of *King Lear*," SS, XIII (1960), 1. Cf. also Nicholas Brooke, "The Ending of *King Lear*," *Shakespeare 1564–1964*, pp. 71–87.

permitted this adaptation to be popular, admitted that, although one does not ask for a happy ending in tragedy, in the case of *King Lear* we desire for Lear something more than he receives. In an interpretation which he feared would be regarded as fantastic, he found that Lear's last words indicate that he dies in the belief that Cordelia is alive and stated: "To us, perhaps, the knowledge that he is deceived may bring a culmination of pain: but, if it brings *only* that, I believe we are false to Shakespeare. . . ."[2]

Bradley's interpretation, while it has been accepted by such critics as Granville-Barker, Empson and Kenneth Muir, has, as J. K. Walton has pointed out, been rather widely disregarded.[3] R. W. Chambers, however, in a notable lecture went further than Bradley and stated that in view of the Christian tenor of the play Lear's dying belief that Cordelia is alive must be construed as suggesting a "symbolic truth."[4] His comment has received little notice.[5] However, I believe that it is the completion of a remarkable discovery of Shakespeare's meaning. I have previously sought to substantiate this opinion by showing that

---

[2] Bradley, p. 291.

[3] J. K. Walton, "Lear's Last Speech," SS, XIII (1960), 18.

[4] *King Lear* (Glasgow, 1940), p. 47. Walton, denying Bradley's interpretation, argues that for Lear to die deceived would go counter to the movement of the play in which he grows in knowledge. He does not take up Chambers' point that Lear's belief contains a "symbolic truth" and that the elaborate parallelism of the drama demands that Lear's heart, like Gloucester's, should "burst smilingly" (V. iii. 199).

[5] It was agreed with by Oscar James Campbell, "The Salvation of Lear," ELH, XV (1948), 93–109, who seems to have arrived at his interpretation independently through a study of the morality plays, and accepted by Geoffrey Bush, *Shakespeare and the Natural Condition* (Cambridge, Mass., 1956), p. 128 and by Harold S. Wilson, *On the Design of Shakespearean Tragedy* (Toronto, 1957), p. 204. It is contested by Stampfer.

the ending of *King Lear* can be properly understood only if we note the repeated kneelings throughout the play which are followed by events that seem miraculous, blessings of heaven in reply to prayer, humility and forgiveness.[6] In presenting the conclusion of *King Lear* in relation to this pattern of repeated kneelings in the play, I failed, however, to observe its relation to the conclusions of other Shakespearean plays where such kneelings are significant.

In the conclusion of play after play kneeling is followed by the appearance of a supposedly dead person. All of these plays are comedies, for the actualization of what is merely suggested in *King Lear* is appropriate to comedy rather than tragedy. In the repeated kneeling and "resurrections" of the tragi-comedies, the kneeling-resurrection pattern achieves its most elaborate form. The repetitiveness is similar to that of *King Lear*, which was written shortly before the tragi-comedies and which bears other significant resemblances to them. These similarities confirm the genuineness of the pattern in *Lear* and enable us to find further significance in it.

II.

Before we discuss the kneeling-resurrection pattern in the comedies and its culmination in the tragi-comedies, it will be necessary to summarize what I said about it in *Lear*.

I noted that after Gloucester prays on his knees to the gods "If Edgar lives, O, bless him" (IV. vi. 40), he is saved from despairing suicide by the son whom he had cast out and who tells him, "Thy life's a miracle" (IV. vi. 55). He is saved again by his unrecognized son, this time from being killed by Oswald,

[6] Siegel, pp. 174–186.

immediately after he has asked for him "the bounty and the benison of heaven" (IV. vi. 229), a blessing which would seem also to have been made on his knees, for he has just directed to the gods a fervent plea that he not be tempted again to suicide which elicits from Edgar the words "Well pray you, father" (IV. vi. 223). Finally, Gloucester dies of the joy which triumphs in his conflict of emotions as Edgar, asking for his blessing, presumably on his knees, tells him how he had guided and sustained him.

So too Lear, on waking and seeing Cordelia as an angel of mercy, kneels to her, as she is kneeling to him in asking for his blessing.[7] He is repeating without realizing it the attitude he had taken in kneeling in bitter mockery to Regan to demonstrate how ridiculous it would be to beg forgiveness of Goneril. With heart-felt contrition he does now beg for forgiveness from Cordelia. His kneeling to her, in a sense unnatural, is a miracle accompanying the restoration of order, indicated by Cordelia speaking to him with the affectionate deference of a daughter. In his welcoming of prison with her as a heaven, Lear recalls this moment and finds the greatest blessedness in the kneeling for forgiveness that calls down divine benediction: "When thou dost ask me blessing, I'll kneel down,/ And ask of thee forgiveness" (V. iii. 10–11).

In the concluding scene, I argued, Lear must lay the dead Cordelia down, as it would be too strained and awkward, indeed well-nigh impossible, for the actor to stand holding her throughout the scene while impersonating an eighty-year-old man. His exclamation "This feather stirs; she lives!" (V. iii. 265) indicates that, applying desperately the tests of life which he mentions,

---

[7] Perhaps Cordelia, kissing Lear as he sits asleep slumped over in his chair, should kneel rather than stoop over him.

he is convinced for the moment that she is alive. But in order for him to place first the looking-glass and then the feather to her lips, he must kneel by her, a position which helps to rivet the audience's attention on Cordelia's inert body.[8] The position would have suggested to sensitive members of the Elizabethan audience that Lear's conviction in death that Cordelia is alive is the last blessing bestowed upon him as he is kneeling, that it is the mysterious insight which they believed a dying man to possess.[9] The heaven with Cordelia which he had envisaged, while ironically false as a picture of what awaited them in prison, was an intimation of an afterlife, also suggested by his awakening to the sight of Cordelia, as if from purgatory.

III.

In analyzing them, we find that the conclusions of almost all—perhaps all—of the large number of Shakespeare's plays in which a supposedly dead person is revealed to be alive are scenes in which kneeling plays a significant part in the action. Of course, kneeling also takes place in Shakespeare in scenes that are not "resurrection" scenes,[10] but in view of the fact that kneeling in *King Lear* consistently accompanies happenings that bear the aspect of miracle, this conjunction of kneeling and

[8] Kean, Phelps and Salvini played the scene kneeling beside Cordelia. Cf. Arthur Colby Sprague, *Shakespeare and the Actors* (Cambridge, Mass., 1945), pp. 296–297. It is not clear from the records which Sprague cites whether or not other nineteenth-century actors knelt.

[9] Cf. *Richard II*, II. i. 31–32.

[10] Iago kneels side by side with Othello, as he vows revenge, exchanging oaths with him in a kind of black mass. The moment contrasts with Desdemona's later kneeling in the presence of Iago to vow that she will continue to love Othello no matter what he does to her. Mother, wife and son kneel before Coriolanus, effecting a kind of miracle, the turning from his purpose of destruction, even though it means the sacrifice of his life, of one who had seemed a god of war incapable of mercy.

resurrection—a resurrection which is also presented as a rebirth—
is surely significant.

In so early and unlikely a play as the farcical *Comedy of
Errors* we find the kneeling-resurrection pattern, even though
here the characters were lost at sea rather than regarded as dead.
Adriana tells her sister, before the identities of the various persons thought to be lost are revealed, that she will beg the Duke
to release her husband from the priory: "Come, go, I will fall
prostrate at his feet,/ And never rise until my tears and prayers/
Have won his grace to come in person hither" (V. i. 114–116).
She evidently does kneel at his feet when she shrilly calls for
justice against the prioress; moreover, when her husband, echo-
ing her, calls for justice against her, he evidently does likewise.
In the midst of the confusion the prioress reappears, and as
R. A. Foakes says, "It is as if, through her intervention, the
harsh justice embodied in the Duke is tempered by a Christian
grace and mercy."[11] The prioress, revealed to be the long-lost
wife of Egeon and the mother of their two lost sons, says that
since the shipwreck she has "gone in travail/ Of you, my sons,
and till this present hour/ My heavy burden ne'er delivered" and
invites every one to "a gossip's feast" (V. i. 400–405), a feast
of sponsors at a christening.[12] Thus the theme of rebirth, which

---

[11] R. A. Foakes, "Introduction," *The Comedy of Errors* (Harvard University Press, 1962: "Arden ed."), p. xlix.

[12] Shylock is told by Portia, when she informs him that his life lies at
the mercy of the Duke, "Down, therefore, and beg mercy of the Duke"
(IV. i. 363). Presumably, crushed by the fact that the law, on which he
had insisted, has turned against him, he does fall to his knees, but before
he can utter a word, the Duke grants him his life. He gains his life on
the condition that he be baptized, and Gratiano comments, "In christening thou shalt have two godfathers," (IV. i. 398) the Duke and Antonio
acting as his figurative sponsors in the ritual which, as Elizabethans would
have believed, gives him the opportunity for new life in more than one
sense.

is to dominate the romances, is sounded early.

In *All's Well That Ends Well* Helena, preparing for the moment when she is to appear, as though a ghost from the grave, instructs Diana (IV. iv. 3–4) that "'tis needful" for her "to kneel" before the King "ere I can perfect mine intents," and Diana evidently does so when she presents her petition. Probably Bertram too kneels to the King when he says "My high-repented blames/ Dear sovereign, pardon to me" (V. iii. 36–37) and to Helena when, thoroughly humbled and enraptured by her saving of his honor, symbolized by his ancestral ring, he exclaims "O pardon!" (V. iii. 302). He has already been "chang'd almost into another man" (IV. iii. 4) by his mother's letter telling of Helena's pilgrimage and death. His rebirth is complete when he begs for pardon from the wife whom he has despised, who had said she would "his name with zealous fervor sanctify" (III. iv. 11), that is, redeem his name by repeating it in her prayers. Life emerges out of death. As Diana says in her gnomic rime: "Dead though she be she feels her young one kick./ So there's my riddle: one that's dead is quick" (V. iii. 297–298).

In *Measure for Measure* Isabella, at the entreaty of the kneeling Mariana, herself wronged, as Isabella was, by Angelo, finds it in herself to kneel before the Duke to beg for Angelo's life. Probably Angelo had also knelt to the Duke when, overwhelmed by his realization that the Duke, "like power divine," had observed his trespasses throughout, he asked that his trial consist only of his "confession": "Immediate sentence then and sequent death/ Is all the grace I beg" (V. i. 370–377). The Duke, in response to Mariana's entreaty to Isabella, says, "Should she kneel down in mercy of this fact,/ Her brother's ghost his paved bed would break,/ And take her hence in horror" (V. i 437–439). Claudio does appear, as if from the grave, although

114

not as a ghost of horror, resurrected by Angelo's repentance and Isabella's forgiveness.

In *Pericles*, the first of the tragi-comedies, the king, overwhelmed by grief at the loss of Marina, awakes to her singing, as Lear had awaked to the sound of music and found Cordelia. He proclaims her to be his daughter, miraculously restored to him from supposed death, as she kneels before him for his blessing: "Now, blessing on thee! rise; thou art my child" (V. i. 212). He fears (V. i. 191–193) that he will die of an ecstacy of joy, as Lear does, and bids Helicanus to thank the gods on his knees. Thaisa, also believed to have been dead, faints when she finds Pericles to be alive, but awakes from her faint as if revived from another death. Marina kneels to her (V. iii. 46), possibly as Thaisa is still lying on the ground. Possibly also Pericles kneels to embrace Thaisa as he says (V. iii. 43–44), "O come, be buried/ A second time within these arms," a burial that will be a new life.

In *Cymbeline*, Guiderius and Arviragus kneel to be dubbed knights by the King. They are shortly after revealed to be his sons, thought to be dead. The ghosts of Posthumus' father, mother and two brothers in his vision fall on their knees before Jupiter, begging that he be freed of his miseries, and Imogen, supposedly dead, is restored to him. She is, as it were, recovered a second time by Posthumus when, after he has struck the "scornful page," (V. v. 228) Imogen in her disguise as Fidele, she faints—"You ne'er kill'd Imogen till now" exclaims Pisanio (V. v. 231)—only to revive, probably as Posthumus is anxiously kneeling by her. She kneels to Cymbeline to ask his blessing, and immediately after Guiderius and Arviragus are revealed not only as the sons of Cymbeline but also as the brothers of the Fidele they had thought dead. Cymbeline, like Pericles, says that "the gods do mean to strike me/ To death with mortal joy" (V. v. 234–235) as Lear was killed by a happiness he could not bear. Finally Iachimo kneels to Posthumus, saying that he had been downed in battle by Posthumus and had had his life spared but that he is now again on his knees to beg him to take that life which he owes him on so many counts. Instead Posthumus forgives him, setting the example for Cymbeline, who proclaims "Pardon's the word to all" (V. v. 422).

At the beginning of the final act of *The Winter's Tale*, Cleomenes tells Leontes that his "penitence," his "saint-like sorrow" (V. i. 2. 4), has atoned for his misdeeds. This penitence was, Leontes tells us later (V. iii. 139–141), expressed in prayers at the alleged grave of the supposedly dead Hermione, and this atonement on his knees effects her return.[13] She comes alive after Perdita kneels to the seeming statue of her mother to implore her blessing, a blessing which is conferred upon her after she kneels again when it is realized that it is indeed the queen before them. Before this Leontes had said that if he were to marry again, Hermione's "sainted spirit" would "again possess her corpse" and incense him "to murder her I married," (V. i. 57–58, 61–62) and in a sense he is married once more—to Hermione—and Hermione is revived from the dead. He does not, however, kill again the wife he remarries, just as Posthumus only seems to kill Imogen again in striking her. Not only is Hermione restored to Leontes, but the "couple," the son and daughter he "lost," (V. i. 131) are restored to him in the persons of Florizel and Perdita. The latter, on hearing that Polixenes had impris-

---

[13] Cf. the ideas of saintliness, kneeling in prayer and repeated death and revival in the words of Macduff to Macbeth (IV. iii. 108–111): "Thy royal father/ Was a most sainted King: the Queen, that bore thee,/ Oftener upon her knees than on her feet,/ Died every day she liv'd." With the last line Malone compared 1 Cor. 15: 31: "I die dayly."

oned her supposed father and brother and that he had requested Leontes to imprison Florizel because of the elopement, had apparently knelt with her head bowed, for Florizel said "Dear, look up" (V. i. 214). The Old Shepherd and the Clown too had knelt, said the lord who bears the message from Polixenes (V. i. 198), kissing the earth and swearing that Perdita was not their kin; however, the heedless Polixenes only threatened them with "divers deaths in death" (V. i. 201)—another linkage of kneeling and repeated death and revival. Now, on the discovery of the parentage of Perdita, they are made gentlemen by the king and are in a sense reborn, having each become, as the Clown puts it, "a gentleman born" (V. ii. 139–140).

At the conclusion of *The Tempest*, when Prospero shows Alonso the supposedly dead Ferdinand in a loving chess-game with Miranda, Alonso exclaims: "If this prove/ A vision of the island, one dear son/ Shall I twice lose" (V. i. 175–177). He had lost Ferdinand once, seemingly in death, and now he has lost him again, to Miranda—but in losing him again, he has gained him. Ferdinand evidently kneels to his father to be blessed by him, for Alonso says, "Now all the blessings/ Of a glad father compass thee about!/ Arise . . ." (V. i. 179–181). In telling of the gift "immortal Providence" has given him, the wondrous Miranda, Ferdinand says that he has "receiv'd a second life" (V. i. 189, 195) from Prospero, that is, his new life with Miranda as well as his rescue from the sea. Thus in more than one sense has Alonso received "a second life" from Prospero. For one thing, through Ariel and his fellows, the "ministers of Fate" (III. iii. 61), Prospero has caused the "never-surfeited sea" to belch him up. For another thing, Alonso says that he wishes himself "mudded in that oozy bed/ Where my son lies" (V. i. 150–151) if this would enable his lost son and Prospero's lost daughter to return to life as king and queen of

117

Naples. He thus rises as it were, a second time from the sea, for he gains his wish without having to make the sacrifice of his life. He has received "a second life" too in becoming a "second father" (V. i. 195) to Miranda. In a reminiscence of *Lear* he exclaims: "O, how oddly will it sound that I / Must ask my child forgiveness" (V. i. 198–199). Prayers for forgiveness and blessing, kneeling, resurrection—the ideas are constantly related to each other.[14]

---

[14] In the three other plays with "resurrection" conclusions, *Much Ado About Nothing*, *Twelfth Night* and *Henry IV, Part I*, there are certain indications of kneeling only in *Henry IV, Part I*. However, it seems highly probable that Claudio, paying his "penance" for his "sin" at the tomb of the supposedly dead Hero, should kneel at the conclusion of the "solemn hymn" which begins "Pardon, goddess of the night, / Those that slew thy virgin knight" and ends "Graves, yawn and yield your dead" (V. iii 12–21). With the atonement of Claudio the "greater birth" which the Friar had looked for to result from "this travail" (IV. i. 215) is effected Possibly the Viola of Shakespeare's company threw herself at the feet of the infuriated Orsino when she exclaimed, in the presence of the priest who had said that he had married her to Olivia, "My Lord, I do protest' (V. i. 173). There is some hint of resurrection and rebirth: Sebastian thought to be a ghost returned from his "watery tomb," in affirming that he is alive affirms the existence of an immortal soul only temporarily inhabiting an earthly body ("A spirit I am indeed, / But am in that dimension grossly clad, / Which from the womb I did participate" (V. i. 241, 243–245), and Viola, ready to die "a thousand deaths" as a sacrificial "lamb" (V. i. 136,134) for the love of Orsino, who threatens to kill her, may be said to be reborn as a maiden. *Henry IV, Part I*, however, although Hal must kneel to place his plume on the face of the dead Hotspur, cannot be said to exhibit the kneeling-resurrection pattern. Hal' act of chivalric generosity to his foe is unrelated to the rising of the seemingly dead Falstaff. Moreover, the unregenerate Falstaff can scarcely be said to have experienced a rebirth. Representative of the life-force of the natural man, not of the immortality of the soul, he sees a dead man as dead: a corpse is "but the counterfeit of a man, who hath not the life of a man" (V. v. 117–119). He denies that he is a "double man (V. v. 141–142), a wraith, and is indeed far too solid and substantial for that.

IV.

King Lear, like each of the romances, may be said to be a story of lost children recovered, of the discarded Edgar and Cordelia restored to their fathers, each of whom has said that the restoration of his child would recompense him for all his suffering. The final scene grows in significance as we remember the repeated deaths and revivals in the romances. "The medieval basis" for the "artistic principle of parallelism" underlying *King Lear*, as George R. Kernodle has well said, "was the doctrine of prefiguration. . . . each event is the prefiguration of some other. . . ."[15] When Lear wakes to see Cordelia, he says "You are a spirit, I know; where did you die?" (IV. vii. 49). But as he comes to his senses and his vision of Cordelia as "a soul in bliss" fades, he becomes uncertain as to where he is and what he sees. Is his vision illusion or reality? "I am mightily abus'd," deluded by magic, he says, although he has just stated that he knows Cordelia is a spirit. "I should e'en die with pity/ To see another thus," (IV. vii. 53–54) he continues, even though he has just said that he is already dead. What is real, what is false? He cannot even swear that his hands are his own.

So Edgar exclaims over the prostrate body of his father, by which he no doubt kneels in order to examine it anxiously, "Alive or dead?" (IV. vi. 86). Alive or dead—that is the question raised in these two scenes and in the final scene where Lear kneels by the body of Cordelia: "I know when one is dead, and when one lives;/ She's dead as earth" (V. iii. 260–261). But does he really know? Next he asks for a looking-glass to test whether she is alive, just as he had previously pricked his hand with a pin to determine whether or not he was dead. A little later,

---

[15] "The Symphonic Form of *King Lear*," *Elizabethan Studies and Other Essays in Honor of George F. Reynolds* (Boulder, Colorado, 1945), p. 186.

immediately after he has exclaimed "She's gone for ever!" he calls on Cordelia to remain alive a while longer: "Cordelia, Cordelia! stay a little" (V. iii. 270–271). What is real, what is false? He had thought that he was dead and taken out of his grave, only to find that he was alive, but in a sense did not the old Lear indeed die and was not a new Lear, who knew love and humility, born, just as Gloucester had risen from the depths of despair into which he had fallen? He had thought Cordelia dead and found her to be alive, but in a sense does he not make the same discovery with his dying perception?

And may not this discovery have a wider meaning? "Is this the promis'd end?" exclaims Kent, thunderstruck, as Lear enters with Cordelia dead in his arms, referring to the end of the world which is promised in the Bible. "Or image of that horror?" adds Edgar. When Polixenes and Leontes learn of the marvelous restoration of Perdita, their wonderment and strength of emotion is so great that it cannot be told from their appearance whether they are transported by joy or sorrow, and they look "as they heard of a world ransom'd, or one destroyed" (V. ii. 16–17). Does the horror of Cordelia's death signalize the imminent end of the world or prefigure it? Or does the sacrifice she has made for the father who had rejected her symbolize the redemption of the world? Does it perhaps symbolize both, the "new heaven" and "new earth" of the Apocalypse (John, 21: 1–5) that Christ was to bring with his second coming at the time of the Last Judgment?

That there is a suggestion of a resurrection at the conclusion of *King Lear*, as there are resurrections in the romances and a number of the comedies, will not be surprising to those who remember Northrop Frye's observation that "the ritual of the struggle, death, and rebirth of a God-Man" out of which tragedy developed is also the origin of comedy.

> Comedy grows out of the same ritual, for in the ritual the tragic story has a comic sequel. . . . The ritual pattern behind the catharsis of comedy is the resurrection that follows the death, the epiphany or manifestation of the risen hero. . . . Tragedy is really implicit or uncompleted comedy. . . . From the point of view of Christianity, too, tragedy is an episode in that larger scheme of redemption and resurrection to which Dante gave the name of *commedia*.[16]

The fact that there is a suggestion of life emerging from death, as in the romances, does not make *Lear* a romance or a tragicomedy. Tragedy may be "implicit or uncompleted comedy," but it remains tragedy. In *Lear*, the darkest of the tragedies in its view of life in this world, the suggestion of life emerging from death is only a suggestion, a hint, a fleeting vision; it contributes to a sense of reconciliation but does not nullify the suffering we have witnessed. It helps to heal the wound, but it does not wipe out the memory of the pain. I do not believe, however, that the fact that this suggestion is Shakespeare's, not a product of critics' fancies, can now properly be doubted.

[16] "The Argument of Comedy," pp. 63–64.

V

Shakespeare and the Neo-Chivalric Cult of Honor*

I.

Many critics of *Henry IV, Part I* and *Troilus and Cressida* and some few of *All's Well That Ends Well, Coriolanus* and *Timon of Athens* have realized the importance of the theme of honor in these plays. However, they have not been studied together as presenting a certain current concept of honor as a false cult. Consequently, their contemporaneousness for Elizabethans, despite the fact that their settings are in turn medieval England, a medievalized Troy, Renaissance France, the Roman

* Reprinted with some additions and by permission from *The Centennial Review*, vol. VIII   no. 1, Winter 1964.

republic and ancient Greece, has been in good part missed and much of significance has been misunderstood.

To be sure, the subject of Shakespeare's use of the ideas on honor of his time has received book-length treatment in Curtis Brown Watson's *Shakespeare and the Renaissance Concept of Honor*. Although, however, Watson has presented much new and interesting material and put us in a position to understand better an important aspect of Renaissance thought, he has confused the subject as much as he has clarified it. Watson finds that there were during the Renaissance two major ethical systems, Christianity and a revived Greco-Roman humanism. The values of these two systems interpenetrated to form a new fusion, Christian humanism, but in large areas the tenets of the two systems came into conflict. Thus some elements of the ideal of honor, a pagan concept foreign to medieval Christianity, were assimilated into Christian humanism, but other elements, the duel and the taking of private revenge, could not be reconciled with it. Shakespeare, according to Watson, reflects "with an inconsistency which has to be admitted and accepted, both the Christian and the pagan humanist values of his time," but "he favors those definitions of good and evil which his age had inherited from the pagan humanists."[1] Watson goes on to summarize:

> When Shakespeare's protagonists seek revenge, their aim is usually in strict accord with Cicero's dictum that no one should do "harm to another, unless provoked by wrong." Thus, Hamlet, Laertes, and Macduff seek revenge for the death of a kinsman, Romeo for the death of a friend, Coriolanus and Alcibiades for the ingratitude shown them by their country, and Othello and Posthumus for the presumed adultery of their wives which will rob them of hon-

[1] *Shakespeare and the Renaissance Concept of Honor* (Princeton University Press, 1960), p. 6.

our. . . . The tragedies . . . reflect, primarily, the quick
sensitivity to affront which the Renaissance had acquired
from Aristotle through his numerous Renaissance disciples.
Indignation, anger, and the desire for revenge are not,
therefore, disparaged.[2]

The weakness of Watson's method of discussing Shakespeare
is that, using the plays to illustrate the various ideas on honor,
he does not explore any play thoroughly. He slights such elementary critical questions as the character of the individual
behaving in accordance with a given concept of honor and the
consequence of his action. Hamlet, Laertes, Macduff, Romeo,
Coriolanus, Alcibiades, Othello and Posthumus are put into one
pigeon-hole as seekers of revenge. The significance of the differences between the hesitant Hamlet pondering about what awaits
him after death, the blindly passionate Laertes proclaiming his
readiness to kill his father's slayer in church and defying damnation, and the grimly determined Macduff calling upon God to
bring Macbeth before him on the field of battle is not examined
by him.

But it is not merely in the critical analysis of how Shakespeare used the ideas on honor of his time for dramatic purposes
that Watson is deficient. He has confused two opposing Renaissance concepts of honor, what we might call the Christian
humanist ideal of honor and the neo-chivalric cult of honor.
We must understand the difference between them before we
can understand more fully the five plays of Shakespeare in which
the neo-chivalric cult of honor is so important.

The Christian humanist ideal of honor is expounded in the
courtesy books and the works of moral philosophy. This ideal is,
as I have shown in *Shakespearean Tragedy And The Elizabethan*

---

[2] Watson, pp. 354–362.

Compromise, an integral part of the new ideal of the courtier, in which the virtues of the humanistic scholar, learned in the classics and indebted to them, are united with those of the medieval knight, an ideal which governed the new Tudor aristocracy. The neo-chivalric cult of honor is expounded in the dueling treatises. It stems primarily from the chivalric notion of personal military glory. Contrary to Watson, it is this feudal chivalric tradition rather than revived classicism which is in conflict with the Christian humanist ideal of honor. To be sure, the writers of the dueling treatises made frequent reference to a few quotations from Aristotle, and the writers of the courtesy books incorporated elements of the chivalric ideal in formulating the ideal of the Christian gentleman who was to gain honor in the service of his prince, but the primacy of the chivalric tradition for the neo-chivalric cult of honor and of classical philosophy for the Christian humanist ideal of honor is clear enough.[3]

Central to the Christian humanist ideal of honor is moral virtue as understood in the Christian humanist system of ethics. As Watson puts it: "The Renaissance moralists cite endlessly this cardinal tenet of classical humanism: virtue is as inextricably connected with honor as the body is with the shadow" (p. 3n.). The neo-chivalric cult of honor, however, consisted of the artificial rules of a decadent chivalry which set the devotee

---

[3] For the relation between medieval chivalry and the Renaissance cult of honor, cf. F. Warre Cornish, *Chivalry* (New York, 1911), p. 340. See also Fredson Thayer Bowers, *Elizabethan Revenge Tragedy, 1587–1642* (Princeton, N. J., 1940), pp. 15–16 for a tracing of the idea of redress by private action in the cult of honor to the traditions of the feudal nobility of the Middle Ages. For the indebtedness of the courtesy-book concepts of honor to classical literature, see Ruth Kelso, *The Doctrine of the English Gentleman in the Sixteenth Century, University of Illinois Studies in Language and Literature,* XIV, 1–2 (Urbana, Illinois, 1929), p. 12.

apart from ordinary mortals, even to the extent of violating conventional morality. Bryson notes that the sixteenth-century Italian code of honor, imported into England, was the basis for the cult: "The code of honor is concerned less with virtue than with reputation. . . . The demands of so-called 'knightly honor' were considered inexorable. . . . It is to be preferred to one's father, one's ruler, one's country, and life itself."[4]

The Italianates at the Elizabethan court headed by the Earl of Oxford, members of the old aristocracy with strong feudal traditions and their hangers-on and apes in the city[5] were the most dedicated devotees of the neo-chivalric cult of honor. Spenser in *Mother Hubberds Tale* contrasts the Italianate courtier ape, who entices (11. 821–829) the "noble wits he led" from "desire of honor" and "loue of letters," with the true courtier, who seeks honor in the service of his prince out of desire for the esteem of his peers and as a sign of the grace of God. The "desire of honor" and the "loue of letters" are interlinked in the Christian humanist ideal because learning enables the

---

[4] Frederick Robertson Bryson, *The Point of Honor in Sixteenth-century Italy* (Chicago, 1935), pp. 12–13. Hiram Haydn (*The Counter-Renaissance* [New York, 1950], p. 572), in opposing to each other the Christian humanist and the "Counter-Renaissance" positions on honor, makes a distinction similar to the one which I am making. However, although he suggests in a footnote that the "counter-Renaissance" concept of honor had "roots" in the "medieval chivalric tradition," he does not develop the point. In his analyses of *Henry IV, Part I* and *Troilus and Cressida*, he discusses these plays as intellectual documents illustrative of the opposing Christian humanist and "Counter-Renaissance" concepts of honor, but he does not discuss the significance of the plays' medieval settings. I am indebted to these analyses, but I am in disagreement with his statement that Shakespeare varies his attitude toward honor from play to play and that in *Coriolanus* he "confines his consideration of honor to the traditional humanist interpretation" (p. 598).

[5] For a discussion of Italianism at court and in the city, see Siegel, pp. 59–60.

courtier to aid his prince in peace, as his soldierly ability enables him to do so in war, each contributing to gain him the honor which is the reward for public service; in the neo-chivalric cult, though, honor is not concerned with public service. As Charles Barber has shown in *The Idea of Honour in the English Drama* (1591–1700), it is concerned with maintaining the reputation for the personal courage and the spirit sensitive to anything remotely resembling a slight deemed to be proper for a man of birth. Learning tends to be held in contempt as suitable for scholars rather than aristocrats. Thus Spenser in "The Tears of the Muses" describes (11. 571–588) how "mightie Peeres" reject learning, "that is the girlond of Nobilitie," as a "base thing" and "onely boast of Armes and Auncestrie."[6]

In the courtesy books, while birth is emphasized as giving a pre-disposition to virtue and affording the cultural milieu which makes it possible, it is also emphasized that ancestry by itself is not enough and that falling away from the virtue of one's noble progenitors is most shameful. Room is also afforded for "nobility dative," the acquiring of nobility from the king by extraordinary public service.[7] The herald Sir William Segar and the Italian fencing master Vincentio Saviolo echo this idea in their dueling treatises, but in their description of the elaborate punctilio of the duel, rank is of high importance. The man of noble birth might refuse to fight a mere gentleman, appointing instead one of a position corresponding to that of his challenger to fight in his place.[8] When Sir Philip Sidney asked Elizabeth for permis-

[6] For further discussion of the hostility to learning among the old families with feudal traditions, see Siegel, pp. 199–200.

[7] Ibid., pp. 51–52 and Watson, pp. 76–82.

[8] Sir William Segar, *The Booke of Honor and Armes* (London, 1590), p. 35 and Vincentio Saviolo, *His Practice* (London, 1595), Bk. 2, Sig. Cg2. As the entry on Saviolo in *DNB* points out, Shakespeare probably knew his work, for Touchstone's satiric description of how courtiers quarrel "by the book" (*As You Like It*, V. iv. 48–100) is very close to

sion to duel with Oxford, the queen reminded him of the difference in rank between an earl and a gentleman. Sidney replied that ancient nobility should not be permitted to maintain its arrogance, citing the example of Henry VIII, who encouraged the gentry to appeal to him against the oppression of the powerful noblemen.[9] In his aphorisms Sidney wrote: "I am no herald to inquire of men's pedigrees; it sufficeth me, if I know their virtues."[10]

English Christian humanists were very much aware of the opposition between their ideal of honor and what they regarded as a false cult. Lodowick Bryskett in his dialogue *A Discourse of Civil Life*, in which he makes his friend Edmund Spenser one of the participants, denounces this cult as contrary to morality, reason and patriotism:

> Such as come to the combat [the dueling field] vpon points of honour, as men do now a dayes for the most part, make not any shew of their fortitude, but onely of their strength and abilitie of body, and of their courage: whereas true fortitude, is to vse these gifts well and honestly according to reason. And what honestie or reason can there be in this so

his serious description of the rules and the incident of Orlando's wrestling match resembles an anecdote in Saviolo.

[9] Sir Fulke Greville, *Life of Sir Philip Sidney* (New York, 1907), pp. 67–69.

[10] Sir Philip Sidney, *Aphorisms* (London, 1807), I, 3. Quoted by Watson, p. 77. It is true, however, that Sidney, in answering the detractors of his uncle Leicester, indignantly rejected the charges that Leicester was of base lineage. The emphasis on birth varied with the particular occasion, the new aristocracy itself delighting in claiming ancient lineage even though it inveighed against the degeneracy of the old nobility. It is doubtful, however, that Sidney would have written Oxford's lost poem expressing discontent "at the rising of a mean gentleman in the English court" (cf. B. M. Ward, *The Seventeenth Earl of Oxford* [London, 1928], p. 244n.), just as it is doubtful that Oxford would have written Sidney's aphorism.

mischieuous and wicked a fight? which neuertheles these men so farre allow and commend, as they are not ashamed to say (moued surely by some diuellish spirit) that a man for cause of honour may arme himselfe against his country, the respect whereof is and euer was so holy; yea euē against his father. . . . What iniuries can a father or a mans country do vnto him that may make him not to acknowledge his countrey, which ought to be deerer vnto him then his life, or to cast off the reuerence due to his father?[11]

He goes on to argue that reputation should be gained in war against a national enemy, not by dueling, which is contrary to ancient practice and precept, unreasonable, damnable and similar to civil war, and that controversies between gentlemen should engender emulation on the field of battle rather than be settled on the dueling field. In thus denouncing the cult of dueling as both damnable and unpatriotic, Bryskett is exhibiting the fusion of Christianity and classical humanism. As Watson says:

> The patriotic sentiment of the Renaissance drew great moral support from the humanist philosophers of antiquity. The intense patriotic fervor of the Roman writers in particular was rapidly picked up by the 16th century moralists. Cicero's definition of glory in *The Phillippics* as "praise as won by honourable deeds, and great service toward the state" reveals the close correlation between individual achievement and social obligation, the twin poles of Renaissance morality. (pp. 96–97)

The demands of honor of the neo-chivalric cult, however, superseded one's obedience to his prince as the writers of the dueling treatises, although of necessity not going so far as the unnamed proponents of the cult attacked by Bryskett, indicated.

---

[11] Lodowick Bryskett, A *Discourse of Civil Life* (London, 1606), pp. 74–75.

Sir William Segar wrote that one should ask his prince for permission to duel, but ". . . not obtaining it, shall without license go vnto the place of Combat, and with Armes answere the Enemie; for the obligation of honor is to bee preferred before all other" (p. 36). Saviolo added: "Neither according to my simple conceite, ought any prince to look for any thing at his subiects hands that may impaire their reputation, or woorke their dishonour" (Part II, Book II, Sig. Y 4).

The neo-chivalric cult of honor demanded an extreme sensitivity to any thing which might be construed as an affront. The kinds and degrees of affronts, witting or unwitting, and the etiquette by which reparation might be made within "terms of honor" or by which duels were to be conducted were codified in the treatises on the subject. James Cleland in his courtesy book *The Institution of a Young Noble Man* comments satirically on the practice of consulting a friend expert in "terms of honor" to determine whether or not one has been insulted: "Then he consulteth, if he hath sustained anie wronge, and considereth if his honour hath bin aniwais imparied, in remitting it into his friends hands, as vnable to keep it himselfe."[12]

One of the worst kinds of affronts was "to give the lie," that is, assert that some one had lied, for the man of honor's word was not to be questioned. Here too the neo-chivalric cult of honor required that ordinary considerations of morality be transcended. "Brainlesse boutefeux," states a work attacking the code of the duello, argued that "what soeuer a man hath once affirmed be it true or false; nay thoughe he knowe in his own conscience that the grounde is vniuste vppon wch he gaue the

---

[12] James Cleland, *The Institution of a Young Noble Man*, 1607, Scholars' Facsimiles & Reprints (New York, 1948), p. 232.

Lie, yet he must constantly mayntayne it, only because it came once out of his lippes."[13]

The Christian humanists did not exclude duels under all circumstances (even Bryskett goes on to permit duels which rise out of an instantaneous response to insult, not out of a cherished grudge), but they were opposed to the excessive touchiness of spirit and the perseverance in enmity in rigid adherence to a code that was demanded by the neo-chivalric cult. Thus Cleland, while not condemning dueling altogether, wrote: "There is no Valour, or great Courage to be euery day swagring and running to the field, with litle or no regard of your life, which is the Kings" (p. 234). So too Sir Philip Sidney, although he sought to fight Oxford after he had been insulted by him, condemned "proud Anaxius" in similar terms in *Arcadia*: "For, by a strange composition of minde, there was no man more tenderly sensible in any thing offred to himselfe, which in the farthest-fette construction, might be wrested to the name of wrõg; no man that in his own actions could worse distinguish between Valour and Violence . . . falsely accounting an unflexible anger, a couragious constancie."[14]

The Italian code of honor not only laid down elaborate rules concerning dueling; for some offences such as sexual relations with one's wife it sanctioned assassination as a form of revenge. Although the persistence of the feudal tradition of personal redress kept alive sympathy for those who revenged themselves in the heat of passion, vengeance was constantly inveighed against by moralists, preachers and political theorists as contrary to Christianity and as weakening the authority of the state. Especially were the enduring enmity and the underhanded methods

---

[13] Cotton MS., Titus C IV, fol. 300. Quoted by Bowers, pp. 32–33.
[14] Sidney, *The Countess of Pembroke's Arcadia*, p. 439.

of the English Italianates attacked. These were not the mere inventions of Italian-hating nationalists. Segar did not scruple to say: "And in mine opinion, whosoeuer receiueth an Iniurie in deeds dishonorablie offred, is thereby neither dishonored nor burthened: and for reuenge of such cowardlie and bestiall offences, it is allowable to use any aduantage or subtilitie, according to the Italian proverbe . . . that one aduantage requireth another, and one treason may be with another acquited." (p. 20) Oxford, it was alleged by his former associates, sought to have Sidney killed by hired bravi.

Tybalt is Shakespeare's most complete portrait of the Italianate devotee of the neo-chivalric cult of honor.[15] He is, says Mercutio in his satirical description, one of "these fashion-mongers, these perdonami's" (II. iv. 34). By the "perdonami's" Shakespeare, with his customary disregard of anachronism for the sake of topical allusion, identifies Tybalt, despite the fact that the locale is Italy and the characters Italian, as an Italianate Englishman who affectedly uses Italian phrases. He is "the courageous captain of compliments," that is, a master of the ceremony and ritual of the duel, "a duelist, a duelist, a gentleman of the very first house, of the first and second cause," one who fights by the book of the very finest schools of dueling and in accordance with the precise rules governing the issuance of challenges. He has the touchy sense of honor and of family pride demanded by the cult and, without regard for the law of hospitality observed by old Capulet, is ready to fall on Romeo without warning because

---

[15] Another such Italianate devotee is Laertes, a travelled young nobleman who has sowed his wild oats abroad and absorbed the Italian code of honor. Laertes renounces his duty as a subject and dares damnation in seeking revenge against Claudius. He uses poison in seeking to avenge his honor in the Italian fashion against Hamlet. His behavior in the duel scene contrasts with that of Hamlet, who is representative of the true gentleman.

he regards his presence at the Capulets' masquerade ball as an affront: "Now, by the stock and honour of my kin,/ To strike him dead I hold it not a sin" (I. v. 60–61). When Capulet does not permit him to attack Romeo, he leaves with sinister, threatening words that reveal the enduring enmity of the Italianate: "I will withdraw: but this intrusion shall/ Now seeming sweet convert to bitter gall" (I. v. 93–94).

II.

In the five plays which we shall now examine, Shakespeare does not draw similar portraits of the contemporary Italianate devotee of the neo-chivalric cult of honor. Instead, while presenting the destructiveness of the cult, he also, by associating it with military glory and the glamour of a bygone chivalry, makes more complex use of it.

That Hotspur is representative of feudal chivalry at its best, but with its characteristic defects, has long been realized. Boas said, in *Shakespeare And His Predecessors*, that in depicting him Shakespeare ". . . laid bare the fatal flaw of the medieval system—its glorification of individual 'honor' and prowess at the expense of national well-being. The champion of chivalry fascinates all eyes, but the moral order of society demands that he should go down before the patriot prince."[16] This interpretation, enriched by the modern knowledge of the Tudor concept of social and psychological hierarchy, is the prevalent one today and is surely correct. Hotblooded, carried away by his martial ardor, Hotspur does not have the harmony of nature which would attune him to the sweetness of music and enable him to govern himself or a kingdom. Engaging though Hotspur's boyish

---

[16] Boas, pp. 268–269.

lack of restraint may be, it enables the crafty Worcester to work upon him, as Claudius does with the similarly hotblooded, honor-spurred Laertes, and carries him, "drunk with choler," (I. iii. 129) into the rebellion.

What is not so well realized, however, is that, despite the play's medieval setting, Hotspur is a figure representative of the Elizabethan period as well as of the feudal past. For S. L. Bethell, Hotspur, in speaking of honor, voices "literary-romantic notions" which are contrasted with the views of Falstaff, "a 'modern' man," who causes the play to take on a contemporary significance: "Through Falstaff, who all along has been strictly a contemporary figure, the audience, instead of regarding Hotspur's heroics in remote complacency, were forced to realize the civil war situation as a present possibility."[17] Those who, unlike Bethell, have seen Hotspur as an Elizabethan figure have gone astray. For John F. Danby, "Hotspur, too, is a New Man. His cult of 'honour' cannot be mistaken for a knightly ideal of 'maydenhead.' For Hotspur war is a game really played for the sidestakes of 'reputation.' "[18] For J. Dover Wilson, Hotspur's views on honor ". . . were no doubt those of most Elizabethan gentlemen."[19]

Hotspur's concept of honor, however, is not that of the new Tudor aristocracy but that of the devotees of the neo-chivalric cult of honor who argued, according to Bryskett, that ". . . a man for cause of honour may arme himselfe against his country." Full of the sense of his family's "nobility and power," he feels that Henry has disgraced it and seeks to avenge the family honor, urging his father and uncle to "redeem/ Your banished honors"

---

[17] *Shakespeare and the Popular Dramatic Tradition* (Duke University Press, 1944), p. 56.

[18] *Shakespeare's Doctrine of Nature* (London, 1949), p. 88.

[19] *The Fortunes of Falstaff* (Cambridge University Press, 1944). p. 71.

and "revenge the jeering and disdained contempt/ Of this proud king" (I. iii. 167–186).

Hotspur is not like the Italianized members of the old nobility at the Elizabethan court, but he recalls one of the powerful nobles of the "North Parts" which remained half feudal up to the civil war of the next century. As Lily B. Campbell has pointed out in *Shakespeare's "Histories,"* there are a number of significant parallels between the Northern Rebellion early in Elizabeth's reign, the memory of which the "Homily Against Disobedience and Willful Rebellion" kept ever fresh, and the rebellions in the two parts of *Henry IV.*[20] Elizabethan Londoners, watching the rebels plotting to destroy the sacred national unity of England, must have remembered the saying current at the beginning of Elizabeth's reign, "Throughout the North they know no other prince but Percy," and have reflected on this great family in feudal northern England, whose way of life, whose power and whose threat to the state seemed to have remained virtually changeless throughout the years. At the time of the Northern Rebellion the members of this family had proclaimed that they only wanted to protect themselves against the newly made peers of the queen, who were plotting to suppress the ancient nobility, and to defend the old religion against the heresy which the new peers had set up. In the time of Henry IV, the dramatized history the Elizabethan spectators were witnessing showed, they stated that "for fear of swallowing" they "were enforc'd, for safety sake" to "raise this present head" (*1 Henry IV*, V. i. 64–66) and gave the name of "religion" to insurrection (*2 Henry IV*, I. i. 201). The actors of the two historic dramas seemed to be the same. We may add to Professor Campbell's evidence that the Elizabethan Percy

[20] Campbell, pp. 231–237.

appears to have been of the same feudal chivalric type as his ancestor, "this northern youth," "this gallant Hotspur, all-praisèd knight" (*1 Henry IV*, III. ii. 140–145). Spenser speaks of his Sir Blandamour, identified by Upton as the Percy of the Northern Rebellion, as "the hot-spurre youth" and describes him as

> a iollie youthfull knight,
> That bore great sway in armes and chiualrie,
> And was indeed a man of mickle might.
> (*The Faerie Queene*, IV, i, 32)[21]

Like the "mightie Peeres" attacked by Spenser, Hotspur has the old feudal contempt of the humanistic virtues of the gentleman. Although Tillyard comes close to the truth in finding Hotspur ". . . the northern provincial in contrast to that finished Renaissance gentleman, the Prince," his statement that ". . . Glendower's solemn profession of being given to the arts of poetry and music stings him into an attack on them that is not necessarily in keeping with his nature at all"[22] has no validity. Hotspur is not the man for what he calls "mincing poetry" (III. i. 34). Hunting and war are his pursuits. He had rather hear his hunting dog "howl in Irish" than hear Glendower's daughter sing in Welsh (III. i. 239). This is in the vein of those attacked by Cleland: "Ignorance is thought an essential marke of a Noble mā by many. If a yoūg chile loveth not a Hawke and a Dogge while he sitteth vpon his nurses lap, it is a token, saie they, he degenerates" (p. 134).

In war, Hotspur's is the individual prowess of the feudal lord

---

[21] Like Shakespeare's Hotspur, the Elizabethan Percy "had no political ambitions, . . . had inherited a strong sense of his own and his family's importance in the border country" and, feeling aggrieved by the orders given him by the crown, was spurred to rebellion by his kinsmen and his Northern friends and neighbors. See *DNB*.

[22] E. M. W. Tillyard, *Shakespeare's History Plays* (London, 1956), p. 284.

who can command "tenants, friends, and neighboring gentlemen" in battle (III. i. 90) but is unlearned in the new Renaissance military science; he does not have the leadership of the
military commander. Vernon urges that "well-respected honor,"
honor that has prudently considered the situation and is not
merely foolhardy, bids them defer the battle, but Hotspur's ill-
advised impatience and rashness contribute to the rebels' disaster,
"want of government" (III. i. 184) bringing its own undoing.
He resembles Sidney's Amphialus, who is reprimanded by his
counselor for being more concerned with "the glorie of a private
fighter, than of a wise Generall." His example inspires his men,
and for a time it seems as if the rebels will win the battle, but
his death is the end of their hopes.

In killing Hotspur, Hal, who has "a truant been to chivalry,"
(V. i. 94) takes over Hotspur's chivalric virtues, but he purges
them of their accompanying faults.[23] He is not concerned, as
is Hotspur, who could brook no "corrival," (I. iii. 207) with a

---

[23] In assuming the chivalric virtues in modified form, Hal gives up the
frivolous irresponsibility of the tavern knight Falstaff, for whom honor is
but an empty word. Although many literary traditions went into the
making of Shakespeare's rich comic creation, Falstaff is modelled on a
social type that existed in Shakespeare's own London, the member of the
city's demi-monde who boasts that he is of ancient lineage but that the
times have reduced him to these circumstances. Samuel Rowlands drew a
burlesque of this type in "The Melancholy Knight" (*Works*, Hunterian
Club ed., 1874, II, 23). Falstaff, like the "melancholy knight," is vain of
his knighthood (*2 Henry IV*, II. ii. 118–124), declaims against "these
costermongers' times" (*2 Henry IV*, I. ii. 191), this commercial age of successful tradesmen, in which he is expected to pay for what he buys, and
mournfully deplores his comedown and his way of life (*1 Henry IV*, III.
iii. 15–22; V. iv. 167–169). Full of vitality though he be, he likes to
speak of himself as a melancholiac (*1 Henry IV*, II. iv. 365–366). When
he is given the lie, he is no more ready to fight than "the melancholy
knight" is, but escapes doing so with his customary mental agility. He is
the degenerate descendant of the feudal gentry, as Hotspur is the best
representative of feudal chivalry.

reputation for preeminent valor, but is rather concerned with the honor that comes from doing public service, an honor that in his speech before Agincourt in *Henry V* he calls upon the commonest soldier to share with him: "For he to-day that sheds his blood with me/ Shall be my brother; be he ne'er so vile,/ This day shall gentle his condition" (IV. iii. 61–63). J. Dover Wilson comments:

> The Prince, who is to figure in the sequel to *Henry IV* as "the mirror of all Christian kings," is already at Shrewsbury the soul of true honour, caring nothing for renown, for the outward show of honour in the eyes of men, so long as he has proved himself worthy of its inner substance in his own. And this substance is only personal in so far as every patriot may share in it; for the honour he covets is to add to the honour of England. It is a conception peculiar to himself. . . . It would be interesting to enquire how far it was also new to Shakespeare.[24]

This is essentially correct, but, as we have seen, the honor with which Hal is concerned is not a new concept but the ideal of Christian humanism, in which honor follows virtue and patriotic service as the shadow follows the body.[25]

III.

As far back as A. W. Schlegel, in *Lectures on Dramatic Art and Literature*, it was realized that *Troilus and Cressida*, follow-

---

[24] Pp. 72–73.

[25] It should be added that Wilson overstates somewhat. It is not that Hal cares nothing for renown: he glories in the thought that he and his army will be remembered. He is not, however, concerned with the shadow to the exclusion of the substance, and he is not jealous of the honor of those who are fighting with him for England, expressing his sense of brotherhood in battle with John at Shrewsbury as he does with all of his army at Agincourt.

ing medieval tradition, depicts the Homeric war as a war of knights conducting themselves in accordance with the chivalric code of love and honor, but a chivalric code which is presented with ironic cynicism. It is this cynicism on the part of "gentle Shakespeare" which made the play so bafflling to the older critics before the current of feeling represented by Elizabethan satire was explored.

However, the question of the play's contemporary philosophical significance has not been settled. In *The Wheel of Fire*, G. Wilson Knight, holding that ". . . the Trojan party stands for human beauty and worth, the Greek party for the bestial and stupid elements of man," has declared: "Troy is a world breathing the air of medieval storied romance; the Greek camp exists on that of Renaissance satire and disillusion."[26] Oscar James Campbell, on the other hand, who sees the play as an expression of *fin de siècle* satire addressed to a sophisticatedly cynical Inns of Court audience, regards both sides as the object of derisive mirth: "The Trojans in *Troilus and Cressida* fare no better than the Greeks. . . . In spite of critics, like G. Wilson Knight, who believe that the Trojans were intended to represent some sort of ideal values, Shakespeare presents them as predominantly irrational and foolish."[27]

There is something of truth in each position. Although the fall of Troy comes from the disregard of reason, with Troy goes something fine and grand. It is true that the conversations of those light ladies, Cressida and Helen, with the leering old sensualist Pandarus set the social tone of a society in which chivalry is a cloak for libertinage and where love is not an inspiration but a dissipation. In this Shakespeare is representing the practices of

[26] (London, 1949), pp. 47, 62.
[27] *Comicall Satire and Shakespeare's Troilus and Cressida* (San Marino, Calif., 1938), p. 205.

chivalric love at the court of Elizabeth, where they continued as the diversion of the old feudalistic aristocracy although the spirit of chivalric love was gone. Thus the Ape as Italianate courtier in *Mother Hubberds Tale* writes "fine louing verses" with the "sugrie sweete" of which the "yong lustie gallants" whom "he did chose to follow" entice "Chaste Ladies eares to fantasies impure" (11. 797–820). In *Colin Clouts Come Home Again* (11. 775–790), Spenser attacks this group at court as "vaine votaries of laesie loue" who speak of nothing but "loue, and loue, and loue my deare," but who sin against true love with "lewd speeches and licentious deeds." So in the hothouse atmosphere of sexual dalliance of the Trojan court Pandarus sings a song whose first line (III. i. 125) is "Love, love, nothing but love, still love, still more" and which can only be described as sexual intercourse in musical form. Yet, decadent as this chivalric society is, its finest flowers stand in contrast to the besieging Greeks, who represent rude force: the courtly Aeneas to the blockish Ajax; the noble Hector to the base Achilles, who looses his Myrmidons on him while Hector is unarmed; the naively idealistic Troilus to the self-assured, brusque Diomedes, who knows how to make the woman whom Troilus has placed on so lofty a height stoop to him.

With the ardor of youth Troilus takes the knightly code of honor as well as the code of chivalric love seriously. Although the sophisticated young law students of Shakespeare's audience no doubt looked upon Troilus' idealism with amusement (had not one of their number, Jack Donne, cynically rejected in his poem "Love's Wars" the honor to be gained in war for the pleasures of unabashed sensuality?), they would also have sympathized with his disillusionment. Troilus is, as he expresses his worshipful awe of the shallow coquette whose name had become a byword of inconstancy, more directly satirized than is Hotspur, but he remains, like Hotspur, a sympathetic figure. He is the "prince of chivalry," (I. ii. 249) as Hotspur was the "king of honor" (IV. i. 10).

In his exaltation of honor, as in his love, Troilus sets reason aside, carrying the Trojan council with him in his passionate plea.

> Manhood and honour
> Should have hare hearts, would they but fat their thoughts
> With this cramm'd reason. Reason and respect
> Makes livers pale and lustihood deject. (II. ii. 47–50)

This is in the very vein of Hotspur's attack on the "frosty-spirited rogue" for the "fear and cold heart" which prevent him from partaking in "so honourable an action" as the rebellion (II. iii. 20, 33, 36–37). Like the devotees of the neo-chivalric cult of honor, Troilus is skeptical of all values other than those dictated by honor. "What is aught, but as 'tis valued?" (II. ii. 53). Helen may be a wanton, but her retention is worth the death of thousands if honor demands it. It had been agreed by the Trojans that Paris should abduct Helen to "do some vengeance on the Greeks" (II. ii. 73). They must, therefore, persist in their decision or fail to wipe out the slight that had been suffered by them. "There can be no evasion/To blench from this and to stand firm by honour" (II. ii. 67–68). Like those who argued that, though a man ". . . knowe in his own conscience that the grounde is vniuste," he must maintain his position for honor's sake once he has taken it, he is not concerned with right and wrong. The prophecies of Cassandra "cannot distaste the goodness of a quarrel/ Which hath our several honours all engag'd/ To make it gracious" (II. ii. 123–125). The goodness of the quarrel consists not in its righteousness but in the fact that their honor is involved in it.

Hector, in answering Troilus (II. ii. 163–188), speaks in

accordance with the Christian humanist tenet that honor cannot be opposed to reason and virtue. He points out that Troilus, incited by the desire for "revenge," seeks to provoke "the hot passion of distemp'red blood" rather than "to make up a free determination/ 'Twixt right and wrong." They are transgressing the "law of nature," the elementary principles of justice imprinted in men's souls to be perceived by their unaided reason, and are striking a blow at the very foundations of the social order in encouraging a violation of the marital tie. "Nature craves/ All dues be rend'red to their owners: now,/ What nearer debt in all humanity/ Than wife is to the husband?" He argues, moreover, against the idea of honor that one must at all events maintain his position even if in error: "Thus to persist/ In doing wrong extenuates not wrong,/ But makes it much more heavy."

But Hector's statement of the Christian humanist position proves only a formal obeisance to it preliminary to leaving it to join Troilus in his worship of honor. For Hector, who quixotically spares fallen Greeks on the field of battle, is himself imbued with the spirit of chivalry. His mistaken sense of honor is the direct cause of his death and of the fall of Troy. Angered by Achilles' insolence, he is, for once, "ungently temper'd" (V. iii. 1) and goes to battle in spite of his wife's ominous dreams, his father's and his mother's prophetic visions and Cassandra's warnings, exclaiming that he has vowed to do so and that, having given his word, he must be guided by his honor: "Mine honour keeps the weather of my fate" (V. iii. 26). Thus he too feels he must be true to his word, no matter how rashly he has spoken. "The gods are deaf to hot and peevish vows," Cassandra tells him (V. iii. 16), but he will not be persuaded.[28]

---

[28] So too Bertram, Coriolanus and Timon refer to vows they have taken as reasons for persisting in a wrong course of action (*All's Well That Ends Well*, III. ii. 23–24; *Coriolanus*, V. iii, 19–21; *Timon of Athens*, IV. iii.

Just as the Trojans do not heed Hector's plea that they follow an honor governed by reason rather than an honor opposed to reason, so the Greeks do not heed Ulysses' plea that they observe the principle of degree according to which the arm of the body politic does the bidding of the head. Their chief warrior Achilles, "the sinew and forehand" of the army (I. iii. 143), vain and self-willed, regards statesmanship and staff-work with contempt, and this attitude has spread among the others. With Achilles' private force of Myrmidons and his and Ajax's personal loyalties, the Greek host resembles an army of banded feudal barons who absent themselves from combat or fight in accordance with their whim. Thersites summarizes the situation in his characteristic comment on Ulysses' strategy in seeking to spur Achilles to action by crying up Ajax as the Greeks' chief warrior and in this way appealing to Achilles' emulousness since he has no sense of duty: "They set me up, in policy, that mongrel cur, Ajax, against that dog of as bad a kind, Achilles; and now is the cur Ajax prouder than the cur Achilles, and will not arm to-day; where-upon the Grecians begin to proclaim barbarism, and policy grows into an ill opinion" (V. iv. 13–18). The Greeks "begin to proclaim barbarism," to hail brute force. Achilles and Ajax return to battle as incensed bullies who have received personal injuries rather than as soldiers obeying their commander in the service of the state. Achilles arms "weeping, cursing, vowing vengeance" (V. v. 31); Ajax "foams at mouth," as he goes "roaring" about the battlefield (V. v. 36–37). Achilles' dastardly slaying of the unarmed Hector signalizes the victory of the utter

---

26–27). Shylock, although scarcely a follower of chivalry, also cites a vow he has taken as a reason for continuing in his revenge (IV. i. 35–37 and 228–229). Cf. also Othello's vow of vengeance (III. iii. 460–462) and Lear's punishment of Kent for having sought to make him break his oath to disavow Cordelia (I. i. 171–175).

barbarian without a sense of honor at all over a noble warrior, misguided in his search for honor.[29] A splendid but decadent chivalric society has left to it only the bitterness of despair with which Troilus summons it to fight in the twilight of civilization.

IV.

The importance of Elizabethan ideas on nobility and honor in our next play, *All's Well That Ends Well*, was not realized until it was recently brought to light by Muriel C. Bradbrook.[30] In doing so, Professor Bradbrook clarified much that had previously baffled commentators. She showed that the king's speech on nobility (II. iii. 129 ff.) is the structural center of the play and that it echoes the standard courtesy-book criticism of the pride of a degenerate nobility. She showed, furthermore, that Bertram is like the other young French nobles in his degeneracy, the other virtuous characters, aside from Helena, who stands for true nobility,[31] being elderly representatives of a better day.

---

[29] The strangely mysterious figure, the Greek in "sumptuous armor," whom Hector addresses as "most putrified core, so fair without," (V. viii. I) after he has wearied himself, to the cost of his life, in pursuing him to gain his armor, is perhaps symbolic of the vainglory of the purely personal honor which has been Hector's object. So Hotspur, led by his "ill-weaved ambition," becomes "dust" and food "for worms" (V. iv. 85–88).

[30] "Virtue is the True Nobility," *RES* (*New Series*), I (1950), 289–301.

[31] Miss Bradbrook finds operative in the play the medieval idea, voiced by Dante, Chaucer and many others, that virtue is the true nobility. It must be recognized, however, that this medieval concept was used differently than the similar one in Renaissance courtesy books: it was used not to defend new men making their way into the aristocracy but to suggest that one should accept one's place in the social order and practice the virtues appropriate to that place. The contrast between Helena and Chaucer's Griselda is instructive. Griselda is of peasant family, the simple, hard-working uncomplaining peasant often being idealized in medieval literature as representative of Christianity. She is industrious as her fa-

What Miss Bradbrook did not realize, however, is that Bertram is the follower of a contemporary cult, the neo-chivalric cult of honor, whose devotees also followed the traditions of chivalric love. He feels that the king, in requiring the marriage, is demanding something which would disgrace him, disregarding, in his pride of birth, the "nobility dative" which the king has conferred upon Helena. As Segar had advocated in such a circumstance, he disobeys his sovereign and, abandoning his wife, leaves the country without permission to seek honor in war. This war is a war conducted by a foreign state in which he can win personal glory but does not render patriotic service. But Bertram is not concerned with serving the state; he is governed by a concept of personal honor. "As thou lov'st her," says the king to him of Helena (II. iii. 189–190), "Thy love's to me religious; else, does err." In renouncing a marriage which he regards as dishonorable, Bertram is severing the sacred ties wrought by church and state and is in reality dishonoring himself. "His sword can never win/ The honour that he loses," says his mother (III. ii. 96–97).

The theme of honor and the theme of love are, as in *Troilus and Cressida*, interrelated. "They say the French count has done most honourable service," says Diana, and immediately after she is told (III. v. 3–4, 12–14): "The honour of a maid is her name, and no legacy is so rich as honesty." He gains honor on the field of battle, but he would have her lose her

ther's daughter and graciously charitable as a nobleman's lady, a perfect Christian in her humble submissiveness, whatever her lot in life. Her lord giveth and her lord taketh away, and she murmurs not a word. Helena, the daughter of a physician, Gerard de Narbon, is of the lowest ranks of the gentry. She is respectful of nobility, but she becomes a member of it by her own efforts, gaining the favor of the king, thanks to her learning, by curing his illness, which symbolizes the illness of his kingdom.

honor. But in besieging Diana, who, says her mother (III. v. 76–77), employing the traditional martial imagery of chivalric love poetry, "is arm'd for him, and keeps her guard / In honestest defence," Bertram loses more honor than he has gained by his valor. About his vows of love Diana wisely comments:

> 'Tis not the many oaths that makes the truth,
> But the plain single vow that is vow'd true. . . .
>   This has no holding,
> To swear by Him whom I protest to love,
> That I will work against Him. (IV. ii. 21–29)

To vow in the name of God that one will be true in adultery is to make a pledge which has no validity. That which has validity is not the fervid oaths of the chivalric lover who promises, as Bertram does (IV. ii. 17), "all rights of service," but the "plain single vow" of the marriage sacrament. In the neo-chivalric cult of honor to break one's word was the highest disgrace; yet, ironically, the devotees of this cult disregarded the violation of the marriage vow and made use of false protestations of love in pursuing the aristocratic sport of seduction. The ring which Bertram gives Diana, "an honour . . . bequeathed down from many ancestors," (IV. ii. 42–43) symbolizes, as Miss Bradbrook points out, the virtue or true honor of his ancestors. This he gives away to satisfy his lust, as the noble young knight seduced by Acrasia "fowly ra'st" his "braue shield, full of old moniments," the tokens of honor won by his ancestors, giving up "honour" for "lewd loues" (*F. Q.*, II. xii. 80). His relinquishment of his ring is the equivalent of Parolles' relinquishment of his drum despite all of his boastful protestations.

Bertram's dishonor comes about as a result of his acceptance of the guidance of Parolles, his boon companion who encourages him in his desertion of Helena with the statement, characteristic of the Italianate "contemners of marriage" whom

146

Ascham decried,[32] "A young man married is a man that's marred" (II. iii. 315). Parolles poses as a gentleman, but the wise old courtier Lafeu sees through his Italianate pretensions and furbelows without much difficulty: "I did think thee, for two ordinaries, to be a pretty wise fellow. Thou didst make tolerable vent of thy travel; it might pass: yet the scarfs and bannerets about thee did manifestly dissuade me from believing thee a vessel of too great burden. I have now found thee. . . . Go to, sir; you were beaten in Italy for picking a kernel out of a pomegranate. You are a vagabond and no true traveller" (II. iii. 211–217, 275–277).

Parolles has the fawning ways and the lack of moral principle of the Italianate, advising Bertram to use a "spacious ceremony" to those who "wear themselves in the cap of the time" and adding that "though the devil lead the measure, such are to be followed" (II. i. 51–58). He acts in Bertram's behalf in his attempted seduction of Diana, using "promises, enticements, oaths, tokens, and all these engines of lust" (III. v. 19–21). Bertram, wooing Diana, employs the same argument that virginity is contrary to nature and self-destructive that Parolles had developed in his wittily cynical jesting with Helena, as Spenser's Italianate courtier Ape sought to entice "Chaste Ladies eares to fantasies impure." Indeed Parolles becomes the symbol of Italianism corrupting the entire younger generation. "Your son," Lafeu tells the Countess (IV. v. 1–4), "was misled with a snipt-taffeta fellow there, whose villainous saffron would have made all the unbak'd and doughy youth of a nation in his colour."

Bertram, however, is not the utter blackguard that he is generally made out to be by critics. Thus W. W. Lawrence speaks

---

[32] Roger Ascham, *English Works*, ed. William Aldis Wright (Cambridge University Press, 1904), p. 235.

of him as ". . . a thoroughly disagreeable, peevish, and vicious person" and adds: "The dramatic justification for giving Bertram so bad a character is clear . . . it explains his willingness to commit adultery. . . . In Boccaccio's day, when adultery was sanctioned, and even demanded, by the code of courtly love, no such explanation of Bertram's act would have been necessary."[33] Lawrence's Bertram is a Victorian villain whose attempt at seduction can only be explained by the blackness of his character. In courting Diana, however, Bertram is engaging in a contemporary aristocratic divertisement. This divertisement is condemned as dishonorable, but Bertram himself is presented as a spirited young man of genuine quality misled by the fashion of a decadent aristocracy. With his "arched brows, his hawking eye, his curls" (I. i. 105) and his "plume" (III. v. 81), he is a dashing cavalier whose aristocratic appearance makes Helena worship him and causes even the chaste Diana to exclaim "Is't not a handsome gentleman?" (III. v. 83). Both his mother and the king state that he derives his handsomeness from his father, whose solid virtue is contrasted with the degeneracy of the present generation, and express the hope that he will also inherit his father's moral qualities. The fact that Bertram is his father's son is the earnest that he will realize his promise.

This promise is never allowed to be forgotten. Bertram's youth and inexperience are emphasized throughout as mitigating factors.[34] His behavior is to be regarded, as the Countess says (V. iii. 6), as "natural rebellion, done i' th' blaze of youth," the

---

[33] *Shakespeare's Problem Comedies* (New York, 1931), pp. 61–63.

[34] It is noteworthy that the youth of Hotspur, Troilus, Bertram, Coriolanus and Alcibiades is emphasized. For Elizabethan defenses of the youthful aristocrat impelled by anger or sexual passion on the ground of his immaturity, see Haydn, pp. 588–589 and Paul N. Siegel, "The Petrarchan Sonneters and Neo-Platonic Love," *SP*, XLII (1945), 176.

rebellion of the passions of youthful human nature against the reason. He is therefore excused as sharing in the common frailty of mankind and as needing, like all men, the grace of God to be added to his own strength. "Now God delay our rebellion!" exclaims the Second Lord when he hears of Bertram's supposed seduction of Diana (IV. iii. 23–24). "As we are ourselves, what things are we!"

Bertram undergoes, moreover, a process of regeneration that begins immediately after he has been successful, as he thinks, in his adultery. We are told by the First Lord that when he received the letter from his mother informing him of Helena's pure love and devotion, his conscience was so touched that "he chang'd almost into another man" (IV. iii. 5–6). The exposure of Parolles, who in revealing himself also reveals Bertram as a "lascivious young boy" (IV. iii. 334), furthers Bertram's education. His shame and repentance, however, are not complete until the end when, twist and turn as he will, he is utterly disgraced, only to have his honor miraculously restored to him by the appearance of Helena, like a vision from the dead, with his symbolic ancestral ring upon her finger. She is indeed, as the Countess had said (III. iv. 25–29), an "angel" whose prayers, which "heaven delights to hear/ And loves to grant," reprieve him "from the wrath/ Of greatest justice," both the earthly justice of the king and the divine justice of God.

V.

Critics of *Coriolanus*, the next play we have to consider, have commonly spoken of the hero's pride, but J. Dover Wilson in his edition of the play has recently emphasized that ". . . as Professor Alexander alone among critics seems to have realized, it is not pride," in the sense of personal vanity or of a feeling of superiority over other patricians, ". . . but his spiritual integrity, his sense of honor," which animates Coriolanus.[35] Professor Wilson points out that Coriolanus is sincerely embarrassed by any praise of his heroism. His aristocratic assumption is that one is

> . . . neither to give nor to expect any praise for conduct which merely conforms to the code that all gentlemen are supposed to observe as a matter of course. And this code which is to a large extent simply the code of medieval chivalry still in vogue among Elizabethan and Jacobean gentlemen involves of necessity a rigid adherence to one's pledged word. Thus "I do hate thee" Marcius cries on meeting his bitterest foe in the field "worse than a promise-breaker." (ibid.)

However, although Professor Wilson is right in sensing that Coriolanus is following an Elizabethan code of honor, his misunderstanding of this code causes him to say: "Shakespeare offers no explanation to account for the *volte-face* which brings Marcius [in joining the Volsces] to deny everything he has hitherto stood for, and worst of all which makes him a promise-breaker and the traitor his soul loathes."[36] But it is precisely Coriolanus' sense of honor which causes him to seek revenge against the country that has wronged him and to become a traitor, for he, like Hotspur, is moved by the principles of the neo-chivalric cult of honor in which honor may dictate war against one's own country.

The key to Coriolanus' behavior is given by the First Citizen in the opening scene, before Coriolanus' entrance. The services which Coriolanus has rendered Rome, the First Citizen says: "though soft-conscienced men can be content to say it was for

[35] *The Tragedy of Coriolanus*, ed. J. Dover Wilson (Cambridge University Press, 1960: "The New Shakespeare"), p. xvii.

[36] Wilson, p. xxxvi.

his country, he did it to please his mother and to be partly proud" (I. i. 37–40). It is aristocratic family pride, not either egotistical vanity or patriotism, which spurs Coriolanus. To be sure, Coriolanus at one point modestly tells Titus Lartius (I. ix. 15–17), in reply to Titus's praise, that he has merely done, as Titus has, as much as he can for his country, but in voicing this conventional sentiment of Roman patriotism he is self-deceived. Coriolanus, like Hotspur, is really concerned not with country but with honor. Speaking of his rivalry with Aufidius, he exclaims:

> Were half to half the world by the ears, and he
> Upon my party, I'd revolt, to make
> Only my wars with him: He is a lion
> That I am proud to hunt. (I. i. 237–240)

He fights not for patriotism and moral right but for the delight of battle and the pursuit of unrivalled glory, to gain which he would change sides. Inveighing against the Roman common soldiers, whom he despises, he threatens to "make my wars on you" (I. iv. 40). Not for him is the patriotic fellowship of Henry V with his commonest soldier. These speeches foreshadow Coriolanus' later assumption of military leadership against Rome.

Coriolanus' joining with the Volsces is, therefore, prepared for and in character. Only when he is "full quit" (IV. v. 88) of those who banished him, he feels, will his honor be restored. He, who had gained so many honors, has had them ignobly stripped from him by the "cruelty and envy of the people,/ Permitted by our dastard nobles" (IV. v. 79–80) and has been left only with the name of Coriolanus. He, who had been escorted through Rome in triumph, has been "whoop'd out of Rome" (IV. v. 83). The shame of the hooting he suffered can only be expunged by the levelling of Rome. His honor is, moreover, further engaged in wreaking revenge upon Rome, for he has sworn to the Volsces that he will not make peace with his former country upon any terms. To keep one's word of honor was, as we have seen, of paramount importance in the neo chivalric cult of honor, no matter to what impious purpose one had pledged it.

In the climactic meeting between Coriolanus and his family, this artificial cult comes into splintering conflict with the law of nature. As he sees his wife, mother and young son approach- ing, he exclaims:

> But out, affection!
> All bond and privilege of nature, break!
> Let it be virtuous to be obstinate. (V. iii. 24–26)

He feels the tug of love for his family, but he calls upon him- self to break this tie of nature in order to adhere to his oath and the claims of honor. Like Troilus, he pits the passionate vengefulness demanded by his code of honor against the reason through which the law of nature voices its commands:

> Tell me not
> Wherein I seem unnatural: desire not
> To allay my rages and revenges with
> Your colder reasons. (V. iii. 83–86)

He entreats his pathetically grieving wife, whose tender love has all along been counterposed to his fierce martial spirit:

> Best of my flesh,
> Forgive my tyranny; but do not say,
> For that "Forgive our Romans." (V. iii. 42–44)

Begging that he be forgiven, he will not offer in exchange for- giveness for the Romans who have wronged him. He rejects, that is, the ethic of "Forgive us our trepasses as we forgive those who trepass against us."

152

If Coriolanus' wife Virgilia stands for the ethic of love and forgiveness in this scene, his mother Volumnia stands for the virtue of patriotism. The Roman matron personifies the Roman motherland itself, "our dear nurse," (110) whose "bowels" (103) Coriolanus would tear out. He will no sooner "march to assault thy country," she asserts (122–123), than he will "tread . . . on thy mother's womb."

Volumnia's pride in her son had been prompted as much by the martial glory he had gained as by the public service he had rendered. Now she finds martial glory and patriotism to be opposed to each other:

> We must find
> An evident calamity, though we had
> Our wish, which side should win; for either thou
> Must, as a foreign recreant, be led
> With manacles thorough our street, or else
> Triumphantly tread on thy country's ruin. (V. iii. 111–116)

Her appeal to him, therefore, is on the basis of a concept of honor in which honor cannot be incompatible with patriotism, the concept of honor of Christian humanism. She urges that the keeping of his oath would eternally dishonor him as the destroyer of his country and that a reconciliation effected by him between the Romans and the Volsces would not make him untrue to the Volsces. To his rigid code of meeting wrongs with wrongs, she counterposes the idea that magnanimous forgiveness is the true mark of the nobleman:

> Thou has affected the fine strains of honour,
> To imitate the graces of the gods. . .
> Think'st thou it honourable for a noble man
> Still to remember wrongs? (V. iii. 149–155)

Coriolanus had previously also been compared to a god, a god

who, aloof, austere and wrathful, is terrifying in his distance
from ordinary man as well as awesomely admirable (III. i. 80–
82; IV. vi. 90–95). The climax of the descriptions of Coriolanus
as a god comes when Menenius, unaware that Coriolanus' iron
relentlessness has melted before the piteous and unnatural spectacle of mother, wife, child and chaste virgin kneeling before
him, tells of his behavior: "When he walks, he moves like an
engine, and the ground shrinks before his treading: he is able
to pierce a corslet with his eye; talks like a knell, and his hum
is a battery. He sits in his state, as a thing made for Alexander.
What he bids be done is finished with his bidding. He wants
nothing of a god but eternity and a heaven to throne in." "Yes,
mercy," replies Sicinius, "if you report him truly" (V. iv. 18–26).

To his other god-like attributes Coriolanus adds that of mercy.
He does not abide by the dictates of the neo-chivalric cult of
honor which call for revenge even against one's country and
parents. The god of war is transformed into a god of forgiveness. In saving Rome, moreover, he is, like Christ, consciously
sacrificing himself:

> But, for your son, believe it, O, believe it,
> Most dangerously you have with him prevail'd,
> If not most mortal to him. But let it come. (V. iii. 187–189)

Aufidius says of him that he is "with his charity slain" (V. vi.
12). And, like Christ, he dies as a result of treachery on the part
of one of his associates.

Although his renouncing his revenge is a splendid, truly god-
like act that gains him immortal fame and glory instead of the
ever-lasting shame he would have gained by rigid adherence to
the tenets of the neo-chivalric cult of honor, he remains true to
his character at the end, flaring up when Aufidius speaks of
him as a weakling who easily dissolves into tears when his emo-

tions are appealed to and as a traitor who breaks his oath. Blinded by his anger, he proudly recounts his feat at Carioli, thereby making it possible for the conspirators to kill him under the cover of the popular rage. His death is thus in part the result of his own defects. Yet in his very defiance of the Volsces he recalls his role as tragic scapegoat: "Cut me to pieces, Volsces; men and lads,/ Stain all your edges on me" (V. vi. 111–112). He is borne away to the dead march of a soldier's funeral, and the last words of the play are "Yet he shall have a noble memory."

VI.

Alcibiades, who figures in *Timon of Athens*, the last play we have to examine, was early recognized by F. S. Boas as ". . . the victim of the chivalrous principle of honour."[37] John W. Draper and E. C. Pettet too have seen him as representative of the chivalric code of honor of a bygone day, but they have added that it was a code that had survived and was now succumbing to the forces of capitalism of Shakespeare's time.[38] However, neither of these critics has used his sociological analysis to grapple with the long-standing problem of the character and function of Alcibiades, concerning which H. J. Oliver, summing up past criticism in the Arden edition of the play, wrote:

> The scene of his [Alcibiades'] banishment from Athens . . . was a particular puzzle; and E. H. Wright, for one, proclaimed that it "has not the slightest reference to Timon or the remotest reference to anything whatsoever that takes place in the half of the play preceding." The same critic

[37] Boas, p. 502.
[38] John W. Draper, "The Theme of 'Timon of Athens,'" *MLR*, xxix (1934), 30; E. C. Pettet, "Timon of *Athens*: The Disruption of Feudal Morality," *RES*, XXIII (1947), 336.

was worried by the appearance of Alcibiades at the end of the play as "a kind of Fortinbras in the drama, fighting out the wrongs at which Timon can only curse"; Hardin Craig spoke of "the rather inconsistent Alcibiades" who "appears as a restorer of normal social life—a sort of Richmond or Octavius"; and E. K. Chambers could not make up his mind whether Alcibiades was intended to contrast with Timon or was "merely Timon over again, in a weaker and less motived version of the disillusioned child of fortune."[39]

The Alcibiades subplot parallels the Timon plot, for commercial Athens, thinking only of money, is ungrateful to both, but Alcibiades is not merely a weaker Timon. Timon is not, as Pettet says: ". . . a portrait of the ideal feudal lord living up to the full obligation of bounty and housekeeping" (p. 324); he is rather an idealization of the new Tudor aristocracy, which practiced old-time hospitality as one of the feudal traditions it assimilated, spent money freely in maintaining its position and acted as the patron of literature. In his lavish bounty to poet, painter and jeweler Timon is a man of the Renaissance, not of the feudal Middle Ages. Alcibiades, however, is representative of a surviving feudal militarism unmodified by humanism. He comes in with a troop of horsemen in the midst of Timon's banquet, and the trumpet which announces his arrival sounds just as Apemantus is saying to the merchant (I. i. 247): "Traffic's thy god; and thy god confound thee!" It is as if the trumpet's harsh, brazen note signals a warning to an effete commercial society. At the banquet table he sits silent as the wealthy lords flatter Timon and inveigle money out of him. Timon banteringly tells him that his heart does not share in the sociality of the banquet, that sociality which is in Shakespeare so frequently sym-

[39] *Timon of Athens*, ed. H. J. Oliver (London 1959: "Arden ed."), p. xv.

bolic of fraternity, harmony and love, but is yearning for the battle-field (I. ii. 75–79): "Captain Alcibiades, your heart's in the field now. . . . You had rather be at a breakfast of enemies than a dinner of friends." Alcibiades with rough humor replies by using a cannibalistic image that suggests a comparison between him and a ravenous god of war: "So they were bleeding new, my lord, there's no meat like 'em" (I. ii. 80). Like Coriolanus, he is a man of war in some ways deficient in human feeling.[40]

Just as, however, Coriolanus' loftiness of spirit and commitment to a principle, even though it be mistaken, make him superior to the temporizing patricians and the sly, crafty tribunes, so Alcibiades is superior to the flattering lords and the mean senators. The values of Alcibiades and those of the senators are opposed to each other. Alcibiades is concerned only with honor, they with money. His defense before the senate of his friend, who he states killed a man in a duel only after having been greatly provoked and in hot blood, has merit according to Christian humanist theory, but it reveals the touchiness of the adherent of the neo-chivalric cult of honor in its praise of the "noble fury and fair spirit" with which his friend, "seeing his reputation touched to death," (III. v. 18–19) opposed his foe. The governing senators are, however, hardhearted practicers of usury who stick to the letter of the law with the puritanical rigor of Shylock and Angelo. One of the senators pushes the doctrine of Christian forbearance ("To revenge is no valor, but to bear") even beyond the point of Bryskett, who says that "a man of magnanimitie" will "shake off" an injury "because the excellencie

---

[40] Cannibalistic images are also used in relation to Coriolanus. Cf. I. i. 202–204; I. ix. 10–11; IV. v. 198–201, 230–233.

of his virtue is greater then any iniury that can be done vnto him" but permits one who is not so secure in his honor that he can be above any affront to react violently.[41] But the senator's words, like Shylock's boasts of how he bears his injuries with a "patient shrug," (I. iii. 110) are only pharasaical self-righteousness; the senate itself knows no forbearance or charity. The same senator, speaking in the vein of Angelo, says of Alcibiades' friend: " 'Tis necessary he should die./ Nothing emboldens sin so much as mercy" (III. v. 2–3).

It is this lack of either charity or gratitude, a lack expressed in terms of insistence on the payment of a debt, which links the scene of Alcibiades' banishment with the previous scene in which Timon is beset by his creditors. The victories which his friend won for Athens, says Alcibiades, "might purchase his own time/ And be in debt to none"(III. v. 77–78)—that is, they should be regarded as having paid in full for his pardon. He offers to pledge his honor for his friend's future behavior, using the language of usury of the senators as one which they can understand but with underlying satiric meaning: "And, for I know your reverend ages love/ Security, I'll pawn my victories, all/ My honours to you upon his good returns" (III. v. 80–82). Finally, he urges the senate to permit his friend to pay his debt to society by another means than execution, through service in war: "If by this crime he owes the law his life,/ Why, let the war receive 't in valiant gore" (III. v. 84–85). But, just as the plea of Timon's steward that Timon is ill is met with the hardhearted reply (III. iv. 76–77), "Methinks he should the sooner pay his debts/ And make a clear way to the gods," so the senators insist that Alcibiades' friend pay his debt with his death in the manner prescribed by law. "We are for law," says the First Senator (III. v. 86), as Shylock had said (IV. i. 142): "I stand here for

---

[41] Bryskett, pp. 77–78.

law."[42] The principle of the bond,[43] the business contract, which has no provision for mercy and exalts the cash nexus above every tie of human feeling, governs the members of the senate who exact the payment of his life from Alcibiades' friend and push Timon into bankruptcy by demanding payment of his loans from them.

Carried away by anger like Coriolanus, Alcibiades is, like him, banished, and he rages at the slight he has received, affirming his intention to avenge himself on his native country for the sake of his honor: "'Tis honour with most lands to be at odds;/ Soldiers should brook as little wrong as gods" (III. v. 116–117). When he appears before Timon's cave preceded by fife and drum, in military accoutrements and accompanied by two whores, he is a god-like incarnation of the devastation of war and rapine.[44] As such Timon addresses him:

> Follow thy drum;
> With man's blood paint the ground, gules, gules!

[42] Cf. also the comparison between Timon's creditors and Shylock, p. 54 above.

[43] Shakespeare plays upon the word "bond." "'Tis a bond in men," a social obligation for gentlemen to help each other as brothers, says Timon (I. i. 144), as he gives a fortune to a gentleman of his household that he may marry the daughter of an avaricious old Athenian. Later, as his creditors press into his presence before his noble friends, he exclaims in amazement:

> How goes the world that I am thus encount'red
> With clamorous demands of date-broke bonds,
> And the detention of long-since-due debts,
> Against my honour? (II. ii. 37–40)

In the new world of the cash nexus, in which "bonds" means financial contracts and not social ties, usury takes no account of honor and forecloses the mortgage on nobility.

[44] For other associations between the destruction wrought by war and by lust, cf. Thersites' "Lechery, lechery! Still wars and lechery!" (V. ii. 196) and the clown's joke (IV. v. 99–104) that Bertram's wound may be a syphilitic sore rather than a battle scar.

Religious canons, civil laws are cruel;
Then what should war be? (IV. iii. 58–61)

From this figure of destruction Alcibiades is transformed at the conclusion of the play into a "noble and young" (V. iv. 13) deliverer of his country from the tyranny and injustice of its aged rulers. Critics, as we have seen, have been puzzled by the change in him. What they have not seen is that the function of Coriolanus is split between Alcibiades and Timon. Like Coriolanus, Alcibiades foregoes his intention of razing his country, but Coriolanus's scapegoat role is played by Timon, the unwitting cause of his change of mind. The tragic irony of the play is that the bitterly antisocial Timon, by acting as a terrible object-lesson of what man can suffer from his fellows and by presenting a picture of ultimate chaos in his diatribes, excites a feeling of human solidarity. After Alcibiades announces his purpose of reducing "proud Athens" to a "heap," Timon's imprecation (IV. iii. 103–104), "The gods confound them all in thy conquest;/ And thee after, when thou has conquered," shakes him. "Why me, Timon?" he asks, taken aback. Timon's answer hits home: "That, by killing of villains,/ Thou was born to conquer my country" (IV. iii. 106–107). When Timon gives him gold for his discontented soldiers and bids him spare not an old man, matron, maid or infant of Athens, drawing a graphic picture of horror, Alcibiades, dismayed, indicates that he renounces his previous intention of levelling Athens. He accepts Timon's gold but says, "I'll take the gold thou givest me;/ Not all thy counsel" (IV. iii. 129–130).[45]

---

[45] So too Timon's harangue causes the impoverished derelict soldiers who have become banditti to resolve to be loyal to the state and to restore peace to it instead of causing them to persevere in their banditry. Rapt in amazement by his vision of a cannibalistic humanity devouring itself ("You must eat men"—IV. iii. 428), they are made to look upon them-

Freed of the "general and exceptless rashness" of Timon (IV.
iii. 502) by Timon himself, he does not take the unnatural
revenge of destroying his motherland, his "Athenian cradle,"
(V. iv. 40) because of the guilt of some. Instead, he preserves
the "great towers, trophies, and schools," (V. iv. 25) the public
buildings, sculpture and academies of philosophy that are the
glory of Athens. He does not accept the one-tenth of the inhabi-
tants, to be arbitrarily selected and presented as if they were an
offering to a cannibalistic god, with which one of the senators
wishes to appease him: "By decimation and a tithed death,/ If
thy revenges hunger for that food/ Which nature loathes, take
thou the destin'd tenth" (V. iv. 31–33). Instead, he promises
to punish only those designated as guilty by the senate itself,
which has purged itself of its wrongdoers, and to see to it that
not a soldier will "offend the stream/ Of regular justice" (V. iv.
60–61). No longer a ruthless destroyer, he is now a soldier-
statesman who will toughen the fibre of Athens after it has gone
soft through a prolonged peace but will not bleed it to death
in a lengthy war.

> Bring me into your city,
> And I will use the olive with my sword,
> Make war breed peace, make peace stint war, make each
> Prescribe to other as each other's leech.
> Let our drums strike. (V. iv. 81–85)[46]

selves and give up their cut-throat profession. His "Love not yourselves.
Away,/ Rob one another" (IV. iii. 447–448) ironically results in a retieing
of the bonds between men.

[46] So too Fortinbras, who, in a cannibalistic image, is said to have
"sharked up a list of lawless resolutes," (I. i. 98) threatens Denmark at
the beginning of *Hamlet*. He later is seen as a military commander leading an army against Poland, chasing "a fantasy and trick of fame," (IV.
iv. 61) the will o' wisp of personal honor. At the end of the play, however, the cannon roar signals his coming as a king who, tested and ma-
tured, will regenerate a corrupt Denmark.

Fusing the humanistic virtues with the chivalric military virtues which have been his, he has become capable of regenerating Athens, strengthening her in foreign war, as Henry V did England, while nourishing the arts and promoting internal order. To do so, however, he has had to reject the dictates of the neo-chivalric cult of honor which here, as in the other four plays, could only bring destruction.

Shakespearean Comedy and the

Elizabethan Compromise

I.

In the preface to *Shakespearean Tragedy and the Elizabethan Compromise*, where I summarized the book, I stated:

Its thesis, briefly and all too schematically stated, is that the Elizabethan social order was based on a social, political, and religious compromise dependent on the fact that the old pre-Tudor aristocracy, the new Tudor aristocracy, and the bourgeoisie balanced one another in strength and that the continuation of this compromise was rendered impossible when the bourgeosie grew in power after the defeat of the Spanish Armada. The destruction of the Elizabethan compromise brought with it questionings of the Christian humanist world view, a rationalization of the social position of the new aristocracy that dominated the thought of the time. Shakespearean tragedy expresses this world view and the philosophical and emotional reverberations caused by the breaking up of its material basis.[1]

What I wish to do here is to examine the development of Shakespearean comedy in relation to the Elizabethan compromise and its dissolution. Comparatively few critics have asked about Shakespeare's comedies the question corresponding to Bradley's question about the tragedies, a question which many others continued to ask after him: "What is the nature of the tragic aspect of life as represented by Shakespeare?" I found that Bradley was a necessary starting point for a discussion of the tragedies but that a study of the Christian humanist basis of the tragedies made it necessary to modify him. For the comedies, however, although such a critic as Northrop Frye is highly suggestive in his remarks,[2] we have no such starting point. Shakespearean comedy lacks its Bradley, just as the theory of comedy lacks its Aristotle. We can only proceed as best we can, using our own powers of generalization and the insights gained from these critics.

One difficulty, of course, is that, as has been realized since the time of the Victorians, there are really three different kinds of comedies: what have been called variously the romantic, gay or happy comedies; the bitter, dark, problem or satiric comedies; the romances or tragi-comedies. Once we have affixed these labels, we have made a beginning toward defining the nature of each group of comedies, but only a beginning. We are aided in the understanding of each group by seeing Shakespearean comedy as changing in response to a changing emotional envi-

---

[1] Siegel, *Shakespearean Tragedy* . . . , pp. vii-viii.

[2] *A Natural Perspective: The Development of Shakespearean Comedy and Romance* (Columbia University Press, 1965).

ronment. Behind the comedies, as behind the tragedies, is a system of ideas which is given different artistic expression as the climate of feeling changes.

II.

Shakespeare's romantic comedies appealed to his audience's appetite both for romantic love and adventure and to its hearty and ebullient sense of fun. They transported it to an enchanted land of heart's delight in which the time is fleeted carelessly in love-making and laughing. The strangeness of this land and the marvelous incidents which occur in it are derived from the ideal world of the chivalric romance, both directly and as these were assimilated in Spanish and Italian pastoral romances and novelle. The popularity of these works with middle-class readers reflected their admiration for a glamorous court and their ideological subjection to the new aristocracy. This ideal world of the chivalric romance, although such old romances as *Guy of Warwick* and *Palmerin of England* were no longer fashionable with aristocratic readers, continued to be familiar to them through those works of moral edification and delight, *Arcadia* and *The Faerie Queene*. Consequently, the mixed though predominantly middle-class audience of Shakespeare's theatre was receptive to a drama containing the characteristic features of romantic literature.

The figures which move in Shakespeare's romantic comedies, however, are not the knight and his feudal mistress of medieval chivalry but the gentleman and gentlewoman of the humanist ideal, who retained many of the chivalric manners and sentiments. Shakespeare's heroes and heroines are not merely the stock types of a literary tradition but the idealized representatives of a social class of Shakespeare's time. Thus *The Two Gentlemen of Verona* with its knightly Sir Eglamour dedicated to chastity and ready to perform the most perilous duty at a lady's call, its lions and its forest outlaws, its extravagant generosity in friendship, even to the relinquishing of one's mistress, has the conventional features of romance, but Valentine and Proteus are represented as having the humanistic interests of the Renaissance gentleman as well as chivalric qualities. In the first words uttered in the play, Valentine states it as his intention "to see the wonders of the world abroad" and not to wear out his youth in "shapeless idleness." Proteus, who is lost in love, regrets that he cannot seek honor, as his friend does, and we are told of the new opportunities and realms of experience which are open to young men: "Some to the wars, to try their fortune there;/ Some to discover islands far away;/ Some to the studious universities" (I. iii. 8–10).

The humanist scholars who were the theoreticians of the new aristocracy had changed the character of the aristocratic ideal. Far from having the old feudal contempt for the scholar, the gentleman combined the martial virtues of medieval chivalry with the learning of the scholars with whom he mingled in the universities as well as with the social graces of the court. He was to serve the prince by adapting classical studies to the use of statecraft, acting as the counselor of the prince in peace and as a military commander in war. Again and again we are told that Shakespeare's heroes are both soldiers and scholars. The witty young courtiers of *Love's Labors Lost* are described as "well fitted in arts, glorious in arms" (II. i. 45). Bassanio is said by Nerissa to be "a scholar and a soldier" (I. ii. 125). Sebastian is not only an able swordsman; he also has a humanistic desire to "feed" his "knowledge" (III. iii. 41) in his travels by observing the glorious relics of the past. "Let us satisfy our eyes," he says on his first evening in Illyria, "With the memorials and the things of fame/ That do renown this city" (III. iii. 22–24). The athletic young Orlando complains that while his brother Jaques has been sent to school his own gentility has been undermined by lack of education, but Oliver admits in soliloquy that Orlando is "gentle, never schooled, and yet learned," (I. i. 172–173) having, it seems, miraculously inherited from his father his father's learning together with his other gentlemanly qualities.

The gentlemanly qualities of the romantic hero are often all that he has in the world. Shakespearean tragedy is concerned with the fall through some tragic flaw of a king, a king's son, a great general or, at the very least, as in the instance of Romeo, a member of the high aristocracy; Shakespearean comedy is typically concerned with the rise of a simple gentleman as a result of his gentlemanly virtues, which enable him to win the hand of a great lady in a male Cinderella story that may be said to be a symbolic representation of the rise of the new Tudor aristocracy.

To refer once more to *The Two Gentlemen of Verona*, the prototype of Shakespeare's mature romantic comedies, the theme of the play might almost be summed up in a rephrasing of a line by Robert Burns: a true gentleman is the noblest work of God. When Proteus comes to court, Valentine speaks glowingly of his friend to the Duke, describing how Proteus had spent his time in studies to clothe himself in "angel-like perfection," and concluding, as praise beyond the highest he can bestow, "He is complete in feature and in mind/ With all good grace to grace a gentleman" (II. iv. 62–74). The Duke replies, although he is to forget his words when he discovers that Valentine and his daughter are in love, "Beshrew me, sir, but if he make this good,/ He is as worthy for an empress' love/ As meet to be an emperor's counsellor" (II. iv. 75–77).

So Orlando, a disinherited third son of a gentleman, wins Rosalind, a duke's daughter, and Sebastian, a shipwrecked gentleman in a strange land, wins Olivia, a countess. Olivia, in love with Sebastian's disguised twin sister, nature Puckishly erring somewhat before it brings her destined love to her, affirms as the greatest praise she can give her loved one that his appearance, speech and behavior proclaim him to be the gentleman that he says he is despite his ill fortune. Similarly the debt-laden Bassanio is not the fortune hunter that he has frequently been said to be. He has come to woo Portia not for mercenary reasons but as on a romantic quest. He wins this great lady, who, like a fairy-tale princess, has attracted princes from all over the world in spite of the perils of the suit, because his confession to her that all the wealth he has runs in his veins was in reality an indication of his worthiness: his gentle blood, which gives him the fineness of character to love truly, renders him deserving of her and her fortune.

If the romantic heroes, however, are male Cinderellas who win their ladies by their virtue, their ladies carry, as it were, the glass slippers in their pockets that will transform the heroes and set everything right. Through the all-powerful magic of their love they effect a kind of miracle, as they shed their masculine disguise or return from a mysterious disappearance or supposed death. Revealing that she had left Belmont to become the learned doctor whose wisdom saved Antonio, Portia gives him a letter she has inexplicably acquired that informs him his argosies have miraculously returned, gives Lorenzo Shylock's deed of gift and gives Bassanio the supreme gift of herself after he had thought he lost her. "Fair ladies," says the wonder-struck Lorenzo to her and Nerissa, her assistant in gift-giving, "You drop manna in the way/ Of starvèd people" (V. i. 294–295). Rosalind promises to "do strange things," having been tutored since infancy in the depths of the forest by an uncle, "a magician most profound in his art" (V. ii. 64–66). She is as good as her word, returning to the Duke his daughter, bringing to Orlando his lady and gaining for Silvius his Phoebe by appearing before them in her own feminine person.

Both *The Two Gentlemen of Verona* and *Twelfth Night* have two heroines, the faithful, distressed maiden disguised as a page of Italian romantic fiction and the great lady who is won by the simple gentleman. Here it is the discovery of the identity of the faithful, distressed maiden which sets everything magically right. Julia wakes from the swoon into which she has fallen as a result of Valentine's over-great generosity in granting Sylvia to Proteus to effect by the revelation of her selfless devotion an instantaneous conversion of Proteus from inconstancy in love to constancy, a conversion which restores Sylvia to Valentine. So too Viola, announcing that she is the twin sister of Sebastian, reclaimed from the sea, effects the coupling which nature, underneath all of the confusion, had been working to bring about. "But nature to her bias drew in that," says Sebastian (V. i. 267) of Olivia's love for the supposed Caesario: nature attracted her to Caesario as the image of the one who was her destined true love. Orsino's affection for Caesario was also, unknown to him, the work of nature, which now produces its miracle that resolves the confusion, "a natural perspective" (V. i. 224), a seeming optical illusion of nature that yet is reality: "One face, one voice, one habit, and two persons" (V. i. 223).

If, however, Shakespeare's heroines are surrounded by an aura of romance and magic, they are in addition characters so individualized that they evoked the rhapsodies of romantic and Victorian critics. Yet in spite of this individuality they bear a family resemblance to each other in their wit, grace and charm, for they all conform to the ideal of the gentlewoman, as it was notably painted by Castiglione in his *Courtier*. At the court of Urbino the gentlemen gather with the ladies in the evening in a company presided over by the gracious duchess. What gives zest to these social gatherings is the "intercourse most free and honourable"[3] between the sexes that the accomplishments of the women and their high position makes possible. A duel of wits is constantly in play, as Castiglione has the participants of his dialogue, discussing the nature of the courtier and the court lady, dramatize the concept through their own courtly behavior. Shakespeare has been thought by some scholars to be indebted to Castiglione's Lady Emilia Pia for his Beatrice, but in truth, whether or not he had read Castiglione, the ideal of the court lady who "in her talk, her laughter, her play, her jesting . . . will be very graceful" and whose "beauty, behavior, cleverness, goodness, knowledge, modesty and . . . many other worthy qualities" are "the cause of the Courtier's love for her"[4] laid its impress on all of his romantic comedy heroines.

Aspiring to the romantic heroine there is sometimes a stupid, cowardly rival of the hero, the counterpart of Cinderella's graceless sisters. This rival has great estates, his wealth contrasting with the poverty of the hero, but, although "spacious in the possession of dirt," as Hamlet says of Osric (V. ii. 90), a representative of the same social and literary type, he has nothing else. Thus the silly, cowardly Sir Thurio in *The Two Gentlemen of Verona* boasts of his lineage and of his possessions, but he is a disgrace to his ancestry and has had to lease out his land (V. ii. 18–29), as had so many of the conservative older members of the aristocracy, who were attacked in the courtesy books for their idleness and degeneracy.

Sir Andrew Aguecheek, a suitor of Olivia in *Twelfth Night*, is not a serious rival of Sebastian since his comic role is more developed than that of Sir Thurio. An ignorant fool as well as

[3] Baldessar Castiglione, *The Book of the Courtier*, trans. Leonard Eckstein Opdyke (New York, 1903), p. 11.

[4] Castiglione, pp. 226–227.

the coward that his name indicates, Sir Andrew is, as Maria tells us, a wealthy prodigal whose high living will cause his income to melt away in short order. Because of his recently acquired knighthood, Sir Andrew has been sometimes taken to be a *nouveau riche* bourgeois, but the older gentry as well as new families entered into the bidding for such honors, and Sir Andrew is probably, like Jonson's Master Kastril, a country gull. A "roaring boy" in his own effeminate way, he regards Sir Toby's roistering as the accomplishments of a true gentleman. Master Slender, a rival of Master Fenton,[5] who resembles the "thin-faced" (V. i. 213) Sir Andrew in appearance—no doubt he was played by the same actor—and in being a student of fencing and a lover of bear-baiting (I. i. 293–302), is a member

[5] Master Fenton, who courts the daughter of a wealthy citizen, not of a duke, is not the highly accomplished and courtly gentleman of the romantic comedies; he is a simple country gentleman of few possessions, but he has the freshness and graces of Chaucer's squire: "He capers, he dances, he has eyes of youth, he writes verses, he speaks holiday, he smells April and May" (III. ii. 68–71). As in Shakespeare's other farces, *The Comedy of Errors* and *The Taming of the Shrew*, love-making in *The Merry Wives of Windsor* is less important than relationships in marriage, and the milieu is bourgeois. Even in *The Taming of the Shrew*, whose characters are not labelled as merchants and burghers, Padua, where the heroine's home faces the market place, is the commercial city of the Italy of actuality, not the scene of romance of a fictional Italy, and the characters, although they are called gentlemen and gentlewomen, are not the gentlemen and gentlewomen of the humanist ideal. In this farcical version of a popular folk story, they have taken on bourgeois manners. Petruchio tames Katherine in order to get her dowry and make her "a Kate/ Conformable as other household Kates," (II. i. 279–280) and even Lucentio, the young lover of the slight romantic underplot in this comedy of the market place, is, although esteemed a young gentleman come to study at the university, the son of a grave citizen, "a merchant of great traffic through the world," (I. i. 12) who seeks to "deck his fortune with his virtuous deeds" (I. i. 16) and so to establish the gentility of his father's house.

of the rural gentry. A worthy relative of the country justice of the peace Shallow, Slender, "though well landed, is an idiot" (*Merry Wives of Windsor*, IV. iv. 86).

Another foolish rival of the hero, although far different from humble Master Slender, is the conceited Prince of Arragon in *The Merchant of Venice*, French and Spanish nobles often being presented as haughty on the Elizabethan stage. He speaks contemptuously of "the fool multitude, that choose by show" and chooses the silver casket with its inscription "Who chooseth me shall get as much as he deserves," declaiming about the "low peasantry" which has undeservedly gained high place and about noble families now undeservedly living in poverty (II. ix. 26–49). He is fittingly rewarded with a picture of an idiot and the statement "Take what wife you will to bed,/ I will ever be your head" (II. ix. 70–71).

Sir Thurio, the Prince of Arragon, Master Slender, Sir Andrew Aguecheek and the other foolish rivals of the hero are members of the world of comic realism that exists in the midst of the world of romance of the romantic comedies and subserves it. This world of comic realism is composed of uncultivated feudalistic gentry, rustic country artisans, drunken retainers, aspiring puritanical stewards and affected Italianate courtiers, characters of classes other than that of the enterprising gentry and the new aristocracy. This subworld enabled the Elizabethan audience to leave the rarefied atmosphere of the world of romance occasionally for the familiar sights and smells of England. The London shopkeepers and craftsmen who found delight in a romanticized view of aristocratic life roared with laughter at the sight of their inept country cousins blundering about incongruously in it (Dekker's London shoemaker Simon Eyre knew how to speak to a king, if Bottom did not) as well as at the sight of degenerately unchivalric "carpet knights," so unlike their beloved Sidney and Essex, acting the poltroon as the hero in his world of romance was being most heroic; the gentlemen and the courtiers who listened admiringly to the witty interchanges and the poetic speeches they would have liked to utter listened amusedly to the malapropisms of the unlettered rural gentry as well as to those of the rustic artisans and village constables.

The chief inhabitant of the world of comic realism is, of course, the clown. The word "clown" meant both "rustic" and "fool," and the Shakespearean clown is of the country or, like Launcelot Gobbo, whose countryman father wreaks considerably more havoc upon language and logic than his son does, recently of the country. The clown may, like William in *As You Like It*, be utterly stupid or he may, like Launcelot Gobbo, have, despite his misuse of the language, a shrewd mother wit of his own. This shrewd mother wit, especially characteristic of the "clownish servants," links them with the court-jesters Touchstone and Feste, who are often referred to as clowns and fools.

This confusion between the court jester and the clown mirrors both the actual ambiguous position of the Renaissance court jester as one who was both the object and the source of laughter and the interchanging traditions made use of by court jesters and the clowns of the inherited folk festivals. The court jester was regarded somewhat as a tolerated child, amusing in his clever impudence but lacking in adult intelligence. Sometimes he was indeed of less than normal intelligence, and sometimes he was sharp-witted but played the part of the clown, a country innocent who was not responsible for his gibes. The clown of the folk festivals, on the other hand, was influenced by the court jester.

The growth of towns, the increasing importance of the bourgeoisie, the guild movement, the spread of education, did not leave even the folk-festivals unchanged. When a lively young clerk took the part of the traditional fool, he was not likely to rest content with an unintelligent repetition of the actions of his predecessors; on the contrary the role would afford him an admirable opportunity for dramatic experiment and satirical comment. He was a "Fool," the elected "King of Fools": very well, then, he would exercise the fool's right of free speech, and he would model himself on the ways of the court rather than of the country village; he would in fact adopt the dress, assume the role, and claim the privileges of the court-jester. And so the two divergent types of fool come to be reunited in the person of "the Lord of Misrule," "the Abbot of Unreason," "the Prince of Fools," who is none other than the traditional mock-king and clown, who has adopted the appearance and behaviour of the court-jester. . . .[6]

Court jester and clown are therefore confused in Shakespeare: Touchstone is referred to as "the clownish fool" (I. iii. 132) by Rosalind. But this is in Duke Frederick's court, where he needs a protective guise. In the Forest of Arden he delights in playing the part of the courtier in speaking to Corin and William. Feste is said by the sour Malvolio to have been bested in a wit combat by an "ordinary fool" (I. v. 91), that is, by a genuine moron, not a pretended fool. Even Puck, the court jester of Oberon in the fairy kingdom, (II. i. 44) is identified as "thou lob of spirits," (II. i. 16) a lubberly clumsy oaf, as far as fairies go, who is really Robin Goodfellow or Hobgoblin, the goblin prankster of the villages. Like Touchstone and Feste, he is a commentator on the folly about him: "Shall we their fond pageant see?/ Lord, what fools these mortals be!" (III. ii. 114–115).

Just as Hamlet, Lear and Richard II suggest that they are

[6] Enid Welsford, *The Fool, His Social and Literary History* (New York, 1961), p. 200.

mock-kings and princes of folly, so Touchstone and Feste suggest that it is their superiors who are fools. They are privileged social critics, and the willingness to listen to them is presented as evidence of the liberal spirit of a true aristocracy and its generosity and graciousness toward the lower classes.

The fool, whether really shrewd or genuinely inane, jester or clown, lends a hearty plebian spirit to Shakespearean comedy, infusing it with the festive atmosphere of the popular holidays, which supply the motifs, as C. L. Barber[7] has shown, of many of them. Feste's very name indicates that he is the spirit of mirth and festivity reigning over the revels of *Twelfth Night*. The fool is often spoken of as a "natural" and an "innocent." Both of these words mean "idiot," but they also suggest that the fool is representative of the instinctual feelings of man: he is devoid of sophisticated conventions and does what comes naturally.

Thus in a number of comedies there is the joke of the fool having had sexual relations or seeking to have sexual relations with a woman who is ill-favored but is, as he is, of the earth, earthy. Costard disobeys the king's edict by talking to the country wench Jaquenetta, knowing better than the king and his courtiers that "Such is the simplicity of man to hearken after the flesh" (*Love's Labors Lost*, I. ii. 220). Launcelot Gobbo is said to have impregnated a Moor, who is dragged into the dialogue by Lorenzo solely for the jest. Touchstone seeks to have Sir Oliver Martext marry him and his goat-maid Audrey in order that he may challenge the legality of the marriage after he has enjoyed her.

The fool, then, is the amoral representative of an elemental life-force. He harks back to the days of Merrie England. Touchstone had been loved by Rosalind's father before Duke Frederick

---

[7] *Shakespeare's Festival Comedy* (Princeton, N. J., 1959).

had usurped his place, and Feste had been loved by Olivia's father before the days of Olivia's mourning and Malvolio's assumption of the stewardship of her household. In the world of the comedies, however, the fool is confronted by the killjoy, who is hostile to gaiety and to life. The killjoy, given over to a single ruling passion, is the counterpart of the villain in the tragedies, a killer whose reason has been perverted to serve his master passion. Malvolio, "sick of self-love," (I. v. 97) cannot abide merry-making, as Richard, who "loves Richard," (*Richard III*, V. iii. 184) hates "the idle pleasures of these days" (I. i. 31). So too Don John at the beginning of *Much Ado About Nothing* avows himself a villain, as had Richard. He too is not for "this weak piping time of peace" (*Richard III*, I. i. 24) that has succeeded the recent war. Whereas such villains as Richard, Iago and Edmund have, however, a malevolent glee which causes them to chuckle to themselves as they go about their deviltry, supplying the tragedies with a mordant humor, the killjoy of the comedies is utterly without a sense of humor and is juxtaposed to those capable of joyousness.

The killjoy is a figure associated with either Puritanism or Italianism. Puritanism, the religion of the incipiently revolutionary section of the bourgeoisie, and Italianism, the fashion set by the old aristocracy at court, were frequently spoken of as twin threats to the Elizabethan order.[8] Each was attacked as subversive of the ideal of an organically integrated hierarchical society. Shylock, the Jewish usurer, is suggestive of the Puritan money lender.[9] Malvolio, the aspiring steward, representative of a class on the make, is stiff, unbending and puritanical in his conduct. His Puritanism, however, is only the hypocrisy and

[8] Cf. Siegel, *Shakespearean Tragedy* . . . , pp. 61–63.
[9] Cf. below, pp. 238–248.

176

mask for his self-seeking which Puritanism was so often charged with being, and he is ready to assume another mask whenever he has need. "Marry, sir," says Maria, drawing his character, "sometimes he is a kind of puritan. . . . The devil a puritan that he is, or any thing constantly, but a time-pleaser" (II. iii. 151–160). Duke Frederick is a usurper under whom the court has degenerated and acquired an Italianate tone. Monsieur Le Beau, a frenchified, effeminate English courtier although the scene is France, as Tybalt is an Italianate Englishman although the scene of *Romeo and Juliet* is Italy, is representative of the foreign manners which were stigmatized as decadent and broadly called Italianate. Touchstone mocks the adherence of the court to the code of the duello, the system of honor by which the Italianate courtiers were governed, and refers also to the Machiavellian treachery and vengefulness that were said to be peculiarly Italianate (V. iv. 45–49). Similarly Don John is a skulking Machiavellian plotter at an Italian court.

Jaques in *As You Like It* is another kind of killjoy. He is a jaded, listless Italianate courtier who, reacting against his previous libertinage, finds delight in the indulgence of his melancholic humor. "Farewell, Monsieur Traveller," says Rosalind to him with bright mockery (IV. i. 33–38). "Look you lisp and wear strange suits, disable all the benefits of your own country, be out of love with your nativity and almost chide God for making you the countenance you are, or I will scarce think you have swam in a gondola." In his scenes with Orlando and Rosalind, Jaques acts as their foil. His comically exaggerated antipathy to love and love-making reinforces the values of their romantic love. He delightedly patronizes Touchstone, not realizing that the fool in philosophizing on life is parodying his own folly in posing as a cynic. Unlike the other killjoys, Jaques is not a threat to gaiety, for he is like the foliage which tries to keep the sun out of the

Forest of Arden but only makes it more bright and colorful as it shines through the fantastically colored leaves.

Launcelot Gobbo runs away from Shylock's house, accompanying Bassanio to Belmont; Touchstone escapes with Rosalind and Celia to the Forest of Arden; Feste wanders off from Olivia's house, where Malvolio has usurped a place that does not belong to him and thus exceeds his proper function as steward, to the palace of Orsino, who appreciates his old-fashioned songs. The society at the beginning of a Shakespearean romantic comedy, as Northrop Frye has pointed out, is in some way restrictive. From this restrictive "normal" world, he continues, we move into a "green world," a magical forest derived from the drama of folk ritual, where characters are regenerated or a comic resolution is achieved so that we may be brought back to a reconstructed normal world.[10] In *The Two Gentlemen of Verona* and *As You Like It* there is explicit reference to Robin Hood, the outlaw of folk legend who formed a better, merrier society in the forest than the corrupt society from which he had run away. Two points should be added to Frye's valuable observation: that Shakespeare is also indebted to pastoral literature and that this free world of the forest operates on monarchical principles. Having established the presumably vital fact that Valentine knows foreign languages, the outlaws of *The Two Gentlemen of Verona*, who include men of gentle birth, make him their king. The rightful duke has his court of gentlemen seeking the simple life in the Forest of Arden, and Oberon commands his fairy court in the woods near Athens. The free world of the forest may be an expression of the popular discontent for which the Robin Hood legend was long a focus, but it is not a revolutionary idea and in fact really pictures a transformed Renaissance

---

[10] "The Argument of Comedy," pp. 60–67.

court purged of corruption by being transplanted to a natural environment.

So too the magically transfiguring worlds of Belmont and Illyria, to which Frye applies the term "green world" in an extended sense even though they are not forests, evidently derive from the dream of the ideal court of the courtesy books, not from the Robin Hood legend or folk ritual.[11] In fact, the secluded retreat from reality of Shakespeare's romantic comedies, including that of the forest comedies, probably owes something, if only indirectly, to that idealized description of a Renaissance court which Castiglione, writing at a time when Italy had become decadent and looking back with nostalgia upon the recent past, drew in his picture of Urbino.

In "the little city of Urbino," on the slope of the Apennine mountains near the Adriatic coast in a country region distinguished by its plenty and "the wholesomeness of the air," the wise and benevolent Duke Frederick built a palace, the fairest in all Italy, where a noble assembly of gentlemen and ladies dwelt. Here there was that continuous high spirits and that exhilarating atmosphere of the ideal world of romantic comedy: "Here then, gentle discussions and innocent pleasantries were heard, and on the face of everyone a jocund gaiety was seen depicted, so that the house could truly be called the very abode of mirth."[12] Never at any other place was there such delightful conversation occasioned by an amiable and loving company as there was here. In this ideal court prevailed the generosity of spirit, the friendship unto death, the loyalty to the code that made all gentlemen brothers which was part of the chivalric tradition and which found expression in Elizabethan romance and romantic drama as it had in medieval romance. For the presence

[11] Ibid., p. 67.
[12] Castiglione, pp. 8–11.

of the duchess was "a chain that held us all linked in love, so that never was concord of will or cordial love between brothers greater than that which here was between us all."[13]

The restrictive "normal" world of the beginning of the romantic comedies is sometimes shown as a society that has declined from this ideal. Thus Sir Thurio is a reminder that, although chivalric ideals are maintained by a few choice characters such as Valentine who live in a world of romance of their own, chivalry has declined. So too is Proteus' treachery a reminder of this. Valentine exclaims when he discovers it, "Thou common friend, that's without faith or love,/ For such is a friend now" and goes on to speak of the times as "most accursed" (V. iv. 62–72). In *As You Like It*, Adam—his very name is significant—embodies the virtues of the olden days which have become lost in these degenerate times of selfish ambitious striving. "O good old man," exclaims Orlando to Adam, "how well in thee appears/ The constant service of the antique world,/ When service sweat for duty, not for meed!/ Thou art not for the fashion of these times" (II. iii. 56–59). Adam in turn also contrasts the heroic young Orlando, whose name, like his character, brings back memories of ancient romance, with the degeneracy of the age: "O, what a world is this, when what is comely/ Envenoms him that bears it!" (II. iii. 14–15).

But, as we have seen in discussing the magical powers of the heroines, nature in conjunction with love brings about a metamorphosis that effects a comic resolution and a transformation of society. This metamorphosis is the result of a consciousness-expanding experience, strange, bewildering and entrancing, like an LSD trip as described by the devotees of that drug, from which one returns to a new and different normality. The world

---

[13] Ibid., p. 20.

of this experience is dream-like and unreal, but those who have been transported to it say with Sebastian "If it be thus to dream, still let me sleep!" (IV. i. 67). Their behavior is odd, as, giving themselves up to the emotion of love, they disregard external reality. The gentleman, the well-balanced personality who in his customary behavior is a contrast to the "humors" character of the kill-joy, now finds himself a prey to love and melancholy, and his behavior is as amusingly predictable as that of any "humors" character. Benedick laughs at the love-sick manner of Claudio, but, induced to fall in love, he behaves in the same ridiculous way, as does that other mocker at love, Beatrice. Love is a form of madness, but one from which, as Orlando says, the lover does not wish to be cured and one, as Rosalind says, to which everyone is susceptible. Like the madness of Lear, more-over, it brings a greater insight into reality. The King of Navarre and his courtiers, whose oath not to see ladies, to study continu-ously, to eat sparingly and sleep little for three years was a fool-ishly presumptuous flouting of human nature, a foredoomed attempt to extirpate the physical and emotional desires instead of curbing them, learn that "We cannot cross the cause why we were born" (IV. iii. 218). So too Benedick, another offender against love, comes to a new realization: "No, the world must be peopled" (II. iii. 251). Love serves the purposes of the uni-verse. Lovers emerge from their state of madness at one with each other and the world.

There is throughout the romantic comedies the suggestion of a higher power working through love and nature that Bruce Wardropper finds in the highly popular Spanish pastoral ro-mance, Montemayer's *Diana Enamorada*, which was a direct or indirect source for *The Two Gentlemen of Verona*:

As loving humanity is shown fused with a sympathetic nature, so too the natural order is shown to blend with the supernatural order. The pastoral setting would be incomplete without its Christian and pagan deities, and its nymphs hovering between the natural and supernatural worlds. . . . Belisa, a villager, and Felismena, a city-dweller, have to cross the line and come to the country in search of a happy end to their loves. Their salvation is made possible only by their acceptance of the natural order, and consequent implication in supernatural grace.[14]

The beneficent fairies of *A Midsummer Night's Dream* are only the visible expression of the supernatural order that is fitfully suggested in Shakespearean romantic comedy.

In the tragedies the supernatural order manifests itself by its retributive justice upon the undeserving even though this also entails suffering for the good; in the comedies the supernatural order manifests itself by the conferral of good fortune upon the deserving even though this also entails the instantaneous and effortless conversion of the wicked. In the tragedies the villain is struck as by a thunderbolt when he least expects it; in the comedies grace is showered as from the heavens when it seems as if the comic complications cannot be resolved. As Viola says of her seemingly hopeless love for Orsino and Olivia's seemingly hopeless love for her in her guise as Caesario, "O Time, thou must untangle this, not I;/ It is too hard a knot for me t' untie" (II. ii. 41–42). In the goodness of time, things work themselves out, guided it seems by some underlying purpose. To attain its goal this purpose is able to make use of such an unlikely tool as Dogberry:

Dogberry and his group, by their sheer consistency in blundering, help to force the story of Claudio and Hero into a comedy of renewal. As Borachio says: "What your wisdoms

[14] Bruce Wardropper, "The *Diana* of Montemayor: Revaluation and Interpretation," *SP*, XLVIII (1951), 129–130.

could not discover, these shallow fools have brought to light," reminding us of the scriptural passage about God using the foolish things of the world to confound the wise.[15]

The doctrine which lies behind the romantic comedies is that sexual love is a manifestation of God's love which permeates the universe, working against the chaos that would otherwise result from the clash of opposing elements. Love causes the species to be replenished so that the principle of plenitude—that everything conceivable in a hierarchically ordered universe has been created by the divine creative energy—is maintained.[16] The lesson that Benedick and the courtiers of *Love's Labors Lost* learn is this doctrine that love keeps the great chain of being intact.

The concept of the great chain of being is related to the concept of a series of hierarchies—cosmic, social and psychological —each of which repeats the details of the others. This concept is in turn related to the concept of the universe as constituting a harmony or being engaged in a cosmic dance.[17] "Take but degree away," says Ulysses, "untune that string,/ And hark, what discord follows" (*Troilus and Cressida*, I. iii. 109–110). Human society is not only part of the great chain of being, which it duplicates in little; it is also a musical scale, running from high to low. The pun on "base" in the sense of low on the social scale and in the sense of low on the musical scale occurs frequently in Shakespeare. Love as the governing principle of the universe reconciles the warring elements and joins them together in a cosmic dance, as it makes the stars to dance to the music

---

[15] Northrop Frye, *A Natural Perspective* . . . , p. 126.
[16] For sexual love as a manifestation of divine love, see above, pp. 91–95. For love as a chain, see the quotation from Castiglione above, pp. 179–180.
[17] See E.M.W. Tillyard's seminal *The Elizabethan World Picture* (London, 1950), pp. 94–99.

of their own turning. The cosmic dance, where "every one doth keep the bounded space,"[18] implies the same universe of order as does the great chain of being, but now it is a universe of ordered motion.

The ideas of universal harmony and the cosmic dance had their origins in classical and medieval philosophy, but, Gretchen L. Finney tells us, "they were revived in the Renaissance with extraordinary enthusiasm and credence, first on the continent and then in England. . . ."[19] They were incorporated into the Christian humanist ideology of the new aristocracy formulated by the humanist scholars. Sir Thomas Elyot instructed the tutor of his governor to "commend the perfect understanding of music, declaring how necessary it is for the better attaining to the knowledge of a Public Weal, which, as I before have said, is made of an order of estates and degrees and, by reason thereof, containeth in it a perfect harmony. . . ."[20] The courtier, moving gracefully in time to the music of existence, was to advise his prince on how to attain social harmony, a harmony which would blend with the harmony of the universe.

The music and the dancing in the romantic comedies does not merely serve the function of spectacle or atmosphere; it is expressive of the idea of a universal harmony or cosmic dance that underlies them. The madness, the ecstacy of love associated it with music: "both might draw the soul to become one with universal concord."[21] Music was therefore frequently employed "as a symbol of that proper harmony which only true love can

[18] Davies, *Orchestra*, 123.

[19] "Music: A Book of Knowledge in Renaissance England," *Studies in the Renaissance*, VI (1959), 39.

[20] *The Book Named the Governor*, ed. Arthur Turberville Eliot (London, 1834), p. 24.

[21] Laurence J. Ross, "Shakespeare's 'Dull Clown' and Symbolic Music," *SQ*, XVII (1966), 111.

bring about."[22] So it is in Shakespeare. Even the common dis-cords of love ("The course of true love never did run smooth," says Lysander [I. i. 134]) are preliminary to the final harmony which reconciles them.[23] The same harmony brings a reconcilia-tion of social discord.

Since the most explicit statement of this final harmony of love and its relation to the universal harmony is contained in the final scene of *The Merchant of Venice*, it may therefore be worth our examining it in some detail. "The moon shines bright," says Lorenzo to Jessica in the garden before Portia's house.

> In such a night as this,
> When the sweet wind did gently kiss the trees
> And they did make no noise, in such a night
> Troilus methinks mounted the Troyan walls,
> And sighed his soul toward the Grecian tents
> Where Cressid lay that night. (V. i. 1–6)

"For what," Antinous asks in Davies' "Orchestra," (11. 202–203) "are breath, speech, echoes, music, winds,/ But dancings of the air, in sundry kinds?" Gentle breezes, as G. Wilson Knight has shown,[24] are associated in Shakespeare with love and music, as the "sweet wind" is said to "gently kiss" the trees and the softly expelled breath of Troilus manifests his true love. The sound of the wind kissing the trees is not to be heard, for the universal concord is a music beyond the ears of men, and Troilus' soul is emitted from his lips to join in this concord. Jessica responds to Lorenzo's allusion to Troilus with one of her own,

---

[22] Ibid.

[23] Miss Finney (59 and n.) quotes George Wither in his book of em-blems concerning the discords of love causing a sweeter music and cul-minating in a "moving Diapason" and notes that Lyly had earlier said the same thing about friendship.

[24] *The Shakespearian Tempest* (New York, 1932), passim.

and the lovers vie with each other in a playful contest of recalling similar nights in the literature of love. Finally Jessica recalls the night of their elopement, saying with tender banter that then Lorenzo stole her soul with false oaths. Lorenzo's reply—"In such a night/ Did pretty Jessica (like a little shrow)/ Slander her love, and he forgave it her" (V. i. 17–22)—brings the succession of recalled nights down to the very moment of the loving wit-combat. The effect is to link famous lovers of the past with these two lovers of the present, suggesting a sense of timelessness: the ineffable music of love sounds through the ages, as one true lover is succeeded by another. However, the love of each of the previous lovers mentioned had ended unhappily. It is as if Troilus longing for Cressida and Dido longing for Aeneas are metamorphosed into Lorenzo and Jessica and achieve the realization of their desires in them. Lorenzo's forgiveness of Jessica is the reconciliation of their mock-quarrel, the harmony emerging from their loving competition, a reconciliation which prefigures the forgiveness of Bassanio by Portia for having given away her ring.

Lorenzo, hearing of the approach first of Portia and then of Bassanio, orders that music be played and, pointing to the stars, utters his famous words about the unheard music of the spheres to Jessica. The music of the spheres cannot be heard because, although "such harmony is in immortal souls" as answers to the music of the spheres, although there is, as the philosophers called it, a *musica humana*, a lost internal music in man which he can only in some measure regain, this *musica humana* attuned to the *harmonia mundi* is muffled in one's bodily existence so that one cannot respond to the larger harmony of the universe: "But whilst this muddy vesture of decay/ Doth grossly close it in, we cannot hear it." The "sweet harmony" of the instrumental music, however, is heard through the "soft stillness and the night."

Earthly harmony, penetrating the silence, as "the sounds of music/ Creep in our ears," recalls the heavenly harmony against which our ears are stopped up, whose sounds will, when we have divested ourselves of our bodies, penetrate what is now for us silence (V. i. 50–65).

"The man that hath no music in himself," Lorenzo goes on, "Nor is not moved with concord of sweet sounds,/ Is fit for treasons, stratagems, and spoils" (V. i. 83–85). We are reminded of the vengeful Shylock and his scornful reference to "the sound of shallow foppery," (II. v. 35) the gay music of the masquers. But now the threat of Shylock is no more. Portia appears and comments on how the music gains in effectiveness by contrast with the silence of the night. In the same way the candle shining from indoors penetrates the darkness of the night, being all the more clearly seen because of that darkness. To Nerissa's comment "When the moon shone we did not see the candle," Portia replies:

> So doth the greater glory dim the less.
> A substitute shines brightly as a king
> Until a king be by; and then his state
> Empties itself, as doth an inland brook
> Into the main of waters. (V. i. 92–97)

She herself, "the mistress of the house," has just returned to resume her place, dimming her substitute Jessica, whose radiance merges into hers, as the harmony of the well-ordered person and the well-ordered state merges into the harmony of the universe. It is such a harmony, in which *musica instrumentalis* and *musica humana* join together in *harmonia mundi*, that is heard at the conclusion of *The Merchant of Venice*.

Although other romantic comedies do not present the doctrine of the harmony of love as part of the universal harmony in such detail, it is implicit in them. In *A Midsummer Night's Dream* the reconciliation of Oberon and Titania, which signalizes the concord in which the two pairs of lovers are to awake, is celebrated by their joining in dance to the sound of fairy music, of which the lovers sleeping by them on the ground are to retain, it seems, a confused recollection. Their dance concluded and day about to break, they leave to follow the night to the other end of the globe, the sounding of Theseus' hunting horn announcing the coming of the day as they vanish. The fairies, associated with weddings in Elizabethan folklore, have wrought their work: the marriage of Theseus and Hippolyta is to be a multiple wedding. Bringing true loves together who had been separated by arbitrary barriers or irrational infatuations, the fairies fulfill the purposes of nature, and their music, unheard or only dimly heard by human beings, suggests the universal harmony beyond the hearing of man.

As Theseus and Hippolyta take the place of the vanished fairy king and queen, night having given way to day, they too talk of music, but it is the music of daytime, the music of the baying of a pack of hunting dogs, "matched in mouth like bells,/ Each under each," (IV. i. 125–126) chosen so that their cries of varying pitch may blend together in harmony. "My love," says Theseus (IV. i. 110), "shall hear the music of my hounds," and Hippolyta recalls having once before heard such a music:

> Never did I hear
> Such gallant chiding; for, besides the groves,
> The skies, the fountains, every region near
> Seemed all one mutual cry. I never heard
> So musical a discord, such sweet thunder. (IV. i. 117–121)

The whole of nature seemed to echo with the sound—and echoes, Davies' *Antinous* had said, are "dancings of the air"—

as if overflowing with the harmony. It is, however, a harmony that is paradoxically a discord, a "musical confusion/ Of hounds and echo in conjunction," (IV. i. 113–114) a man-made imitation of the harmony of the universe, beautiful but only faintly resembling it.

Seeing the couples sleeping on the ground, Theseus has them wakened by the sound of the horns. He regards the erstwhile rivals with surprise and benevolent humor: "How comes this gentle concord in the world?" He does not know that this concord is the work of the beneficent fairy king, who has promised to come to his wedding to dance in festive procession with his fairy court and bless it with all good fortune. And so, Bottom's play and rustic dance having been concluded, the fairies do come to sing and dance, their song and dance being a benediction that "all the couples three/ Ever true in loving be."

At the conclusion of *As You Like It*, Rosalind appears before the company in her own person as if by enchantment, together with the second bride, Celia, led by Hymen, the god of marriage, to the accompaniment of soft music. This may be a little masque that Rosalind has got up, but Hymen, it is suggested, is not merely an allegorical character in a spectacle but in some sense a presiding spirit. His words, "Then is there mirth in heaven/When earthly things made even/ Atone together," (V. iv. 114–116) with their New Testament echo, are an invocation that conjures up a picture of the joy of heaven when human beings, reconciled and brought together in harmony, are at one with each other and repeat heaven's concord on earth. The wedding song in praise of Hymen (V. iv. 149)—"'Tis Hymen peoples every town"—is a celebration not only of the wedding and its promise of the renewal of life but a celebration of the return of the Duke's courtiers to a regenerated court and its ladies after having had their holiday game of playing at being the merry followers of Robin Hood. The "rustic revelry" (V. iv. 183) of their dance is their last fling before they return.[25]

The romantic comedies, therefore, whose dominant story, the myth of the male Cinderella, is, as we have seen, symbolic of the rise of the new aristocracy, convey the sense of a natural law which causes life constantly to renew itself and society constantly to reconstruct itself. They are expressive of this aristocracy's faith in itself and its ideology and of the acceptance of that ideology by the members of Shakespeare's audience.

III.

With the dissolution of the Elizabethan compromise, there developed among young intellectuals of the late 1590's a sense of disillusionment with humanist ideals. This took the form of a satirical inveighing against the degeneracy of the age. The formal verse satires, obscure, full of topical allusions and classical in form, were an avant-garde literature addressed primarily to the students at the inns of court and the universities, and satiric comedy was most popular at the private theatres. However, the comedies of the public theatres, including those of Shakespeare, were influenced by this trend.

With their foreign locales, their devoted, long-suffering, gentle-born maidens, their unrealistic plots derived from folk material and their happy marriage endings, *All's Well That Ends Well* and *Measure for Measure*, written for Globe audiences, have romantic characteristics, but the spirit which animates them is largely satiric. This satiric spirit is, however, not incompatible with the romantic and folk elements of these plays. The happy endings are not inappropriately imposed, for Shakespeare is

[25] For the dance pattern of *Much Ado About Nothing* and its relation to the doctrine of universal harmony, see below, pp. 212–226.

drawing not only upon the contemporary drama of "comicall satire," with its concluding derisive exposure and ejection of its gulls, but, as critics have failed to realize, upon an older satiric tradition, that of popular religious satire inherited from medieval times.[26]

Medieval religious satire, apparently written by lower members of the clergy close to the peasantry, was an expression of the social protest that accompanied the disintegration of the social structure. Like the Elizabethan verse satirists, medieval satirists pointed to the difference between the ideal and reality, but they spoke as zealous reformers seeking to correct abuses by recalling the religious ideal rather than, as did the Elizabethan verse satirists, as scornful critics flaying vice with savage pleasure. The emblem of the medieval religious satirist is the steel glass enabling the sinner to see himself; the emblem of the Renaissance satirist is the whip.

The tradition of medieval religious satire persisted throughout the sixteenth and early seventeenth century. Thus in *A Looking-glass for London and England*, a play by Greene and Lodge about Nineveh, the prophet Oseas periodically acts as a commentator calling upon London to repent before it is too late. At the end of the play Nineveh is saved as a result of the contrition of the king and his nobles, and London is urged to do likewise lest the prayers and virtues of Elizabeth do not avail to ward off the plague and lest the fires of civil wars in neighboring countries sweep over England.

---

[26] For medieval religious satire, see John Peter, *Complaint and Satire in Early English Literature* (New York, 1959), pp. 1–103 and Alvin Kernan, *The Cankered Muse: Satire of the English Renaissance* (New Haven, 1959), pp. 40–54. *Troilus and Cressida*, whether or not we accept the argument of Peter Alexander and Oscar James Campbell that it was written for an Inns of Court audience, is written in the sophisticatedly cynical vein enjoyed by this audience. See above, pp. 138–144.

So too Nashe's *Christ's Tears over Jerusalem* and Dekker's *The Seven Deadly Sins of London* present other cities that fell in their pride as images of London while holding forth hope of redemption. In *Christ's Tears over Jerusalem,* the city of the ancient Israelites, which was destroyed as a result of its wickedness, is a mirror for London, and the pamphlet ends with a plea to God to exercise His mercy instead of justice, for "more praise shalt Thou reap by preserving than by killing, since it is the only praise to preserve where Thou mayest kill."[27] *The Seven Deadly Sins of London* finds a lesson for London which has already received warning through the visitation of the plague, in the destruction of Sodom, Gomorrah and Jerusalem and, in more recent times, in the fall of Antwerp, the spoliation of the cities of the Netherlands and the ruination of the cities of France through civil war. If London, however, will only perceive the ugliness of its sins, the pamphlet promises, it will be "the happiest and most renowned of cities."[28]

The existence of these works, with their castigation of sin but their hope for salvation, enables us to understand better *Measure for Measure* and *All's Well That Ends Well. Measure for Measure,* which has received more attention than *All's Well That Ends Well,* has been regarded by some critics as a Christian parable and by others as a "comicall satire." Each group of critics has focussed on different elements of the play so that it has

[27] *Works,* ed. R. B. McKerrow (London, 1910), II, 174.

[28] *The Non-Dramatic Works of Thomas Dekker,* ed. Alexander B. Grosart (London, 1885), II, 15. Dekker in his induction describes the fear of civil war during the year of Elizabeth's death, the jubilation on the peaceful accession to the throne of James and the return of a feeling some time later that London was bound to suffer the wrath of God. The fact that *A Looking Glass for London and England,* first printed in 1594, was reprinted in 1602 and 1617, also indicates a continued uneasiness and fear of disaster upon the part of the solid citizen.

almost seemed as if they were talking about two different plays. But the themes and techniques of "comicall satire" such as the presence of two commentators, the sturdy moral teacher and the scurrilous buffoon, are combined in *Measure for Measure*, as in *All's Well That Ends Well*, with the tradition of religious satire. The consequence is a satiric comedy with religious overtones in which a central figure, representative of a widespread social corruption, degenerates steadily, only to be finally saved by the intervention of a ruler acting as an agent of heaven who confers mercy after the sinner's shame and suffering on the exposure of his vices to himself and others have made him repent. This intervention of providence, more direct than in the romantic comedies, is effected, as in the romantic comedies, by heroines who return from apparent death, from an isolated moated grange or from a secluded convent. These heroines, representative of love and forgiveness, intercede with the ruler, the deputy of God, for the sinning protagonist. This conclusion of the satiric comedies, as Robert Grams Hunter has shown, is in the tradition of the Renaissance "comedies of forgiveness," which were secularized continuations of medieval miracle plays of sinners who repented and were forgiven by God.[29] But this denouement of forgiveness is made possible by the spirit of religious satire, which castigates but holds forth hope of salvation.

"Every man with his affects is born," says Berowne in *Love's Labors Lost* (I. i. 152–153), "Not by might mastered, but by special grace." He is speaking half-jokingly of the power of love, which is later seen to serve the divine purpose. In the satiric comedies, however, the driving force is lust, not love, and man truly stands in need of God's grace to combat this passion. "Now, God delay our rebellion! As we are ourselves, what things

---

[29] *Shakespeare and the Comedy of Forgiveness* (New York, 1965).

are we!" exclaims the Second Lord (IV. iii. 23–24) when he hears of Bertram's supposed seduction of Diana. Man, who is naturally depraved, needs God's grace to hold him back from rebelling against His law. "All sects, all ages smack of this vice," says the provost in Measure for Measure (II. ii. 5). Lucio and Pompey say the same thing in their own ways, and although the good-humored toleration of vice of the libertine and pimp, their attitude of "sin and let sin," is certainly not the attitude projected by the play, their view of the proneness of man to sin is presented as the truth. Even the chaste Isabella assumes that if Angelo will look in his heart in all honesty he will find there a "natural guiltiness" (II. ii. 139) such as her brother's. It is a natural guiltiness because natural, unregenerate man without the help of God's grace is subject to the temptations of the flesh. Christian charity, knowing the weakness of man, forgives the repentant sinner without tolerating sinfulness. Although man can go wrong and societies can become corrupt, there remains the hope of redemption.

The degenerate society which is present at the beginning of some of the romantic comedies is present in All's Well and Measure for Measure until their conclusions. These two comedies have no green worlds, and there is a notable lack of music. The fools in them are the amoral clowns of the romantic comedies, but with a difference. Lavache, like Touchstone, seeks to get married because "I am driven on by the flesh, and he must needs go that the Devil drives" (I. iii. 30–32). He is, however, described (IV. v. 66–71) as a bitter and unlucky knave who remains in the household as a consequence of having enjoyed the favor of Bertram's dead father but who in his present bitterness exercises no restraint on his tongue. Similarly, the pimp Pompey does not escape to a Forest of Arden but is consigned to prison. He is, to be sure, an amiable clown with whom we sympathize even as we laugh at the unabashed manner in which he acknowledges that he will do anything, no matter how shameful, to satisfy his natural wants. "Truly, sir, I am a poor fellow that would live," he replies to Escalus' questioning about his occupation (II. i. 235), and he readily accepts the ignoble position of hangman's assistant in order to have his sentence commuted.[30]

The essential difference between *All's Well* and *Measure for Measure* on the one hand and of the romantic comedies on the other is summed up in the difference in the basic story. Whereas in the romantic comedies we have the myth of the male Cinderella, the simple gentleman who marries a great lady, in these two comedies we have the myth of the rejected maiden, the worthy gentlewoman whom a proud lord deserts. The myth of the rejected maiden may be said to be a symbolic expression of the dissolution of the Elizabethan compromise.

Just as Bertram represents the nobility corrupted by Italianism,[31] one of the two principal threats to the Elizabethan order, so Angelo represents the state animated by the spirit of Puritanism, the other principal threat to that order. Angelo is not an ordinary stage-Puritan, a caricature of a sect or social type; rather he represents a way of living, an approach to life. That this approach to life would have been recognized as that of the Puritan has been amply shown by Donald J. McGinn.[32] "Lord

---

[30] The commutation of his sentence in return for his becoming hangman's assistant is at once poetic justice and mercy. For the combination of poetic justice and mercy as constituting the pattern of the play, see Paul N. Siegel, "*Measure for Measure*: The Significance of the Title," *SQ*, IV (1953), 317–320.

[31] See above, pp. 146–147.

[32] "The Precise Angelo," *Joseph Quincy Adams Memorial Studies*, ed. James G. McManaway *et al.* (Washington, D. C., 1948), pp. 129–139.

Angelo is precise," says the Duke, using the Elizabethan vernacular for "puritanical,"

> Stands at a guard with envy; scarce confesses
> That his blood flows, or that his appetite
> Is more to bread than stone: hence shall we see,
> If power change purpose, what our seemers be. (I. iii. 50–54)

Partly to correct corruption by a temporary leaning to an extreme of severity, partly to test the puritanical Angelo, the Duke appoints him his deputy. The outcome of the experiment is that Angelo is shown to have, waiting to be unloosed from beneath the gravity of his bearing, a predatory passion which must cause him to act tyrannically upon assuming power. Puritanism, it is implied, is a cure worse than the ills of a sick state.

Angelo does not know himself. Thinking himself immune to temptation, he has no sympathy for people in their frailties and wishes to enforce in all its severity an ancient, dead-letter law which, like the Mosaic code that the Puritans wanted to revive, prescribes the death penalty for adultery. But "this outward-sainted deputy," as Isabella says (III. i. 89–94), making the conventional charge in the conventional phraseology that satirists made against the Puritans, "is yet a devil;/ His filth within being cast, he would appear/ A pond as deep as hell." His assurance of his righteousness destroyed by his discovery of lust within himself, he recoils, like a too tightly wound spring, from his previous asceticism and gives himself up to the tyrannical fulfillment of his passions.

Lacking humility, the puritanical Angelo has not felt the need of God's grace. When he discovers that, as he says (II. iv. 121), "We are all frail"—even he—he uses the idea "It's only natural" to attempt to persuade Isabella to submit to him. "Be that you are,/ That is, a woman. If you be more, you're none" (II. iv.

134–135). It is the kind of argument that Bertram employed. The extremes of Puritanism and Italianism meet as the puritan turning away from his asceticism speaks the language of seduction of the libertine.

Like Bertram, Angelo is forced to pile lie upon lie at the conclusion. He regards marriage as a business contract which, unmoved by love or compassion, he, like Shylock with his bond, insists be observed to the letter, but he casts off his betrothed on the pretense that "her reputation was disvalued in levity" (V. i. 221–222) rather than admitting his meanness in jilting her for the loss of her dowry. Becoming a tyrant, he uses his reputation for austerity as a means of satisfying his appetite and sentences a man to death for a sin which he thinks he himself has committed. He is indeed exposed as a "seemer" whose "power" has changed his "purpose." "We of the clergy would be the best judges," had ironically said Bishop Whitgift, addressing himself to the Puritan preachers, whom he charged with seeking a theocracy, "and they must require the law at our hands."[33] In the kind of justice dispensed by the pharisaical Angelo could be seen, as in a glass, what would happen if, as Isabella says, "every pelting, petty officer" could "thunder/ As Jove himself does" (II. ii. 112, 110–111).

The "little brief authority" in which Angelo is "dress'd" (II. ii. 118–123) is brief not only in that he, like all rulers, is a deputy of God to whom he will have to make his accounting after his death, but in that he is a deputy of the all-seeing Duke, who, the audience is constantly aware, is, "like power divine," (V. i. 374) watching his actions, waiting for the time when he will pass judgment upon him. This judgment restores her husband

[33] *The Works of John Whitgift, D. D.*, ed. John Ayre (Parker Society, 1851), III, 273.

to Mariana, but it is a husband who has been regenerated, purged of the spirit of Puritanism, as Bertram is purged of the spirit of Italianism.

Thus the rejected maiden triumphs in each of the two satiric comedies, and her triumph marks the restoration of a healthy social order. The corruption of the proud lord who rejects her indicates, however, the dangers rising from the dissolution of the Elizabethan compromise.

IV.

Shakespeare's tragi-comedies mark a further stage in this dissolution. The tone of the court, which had already deteriorated in the last years of Elizabeth, worsened under James. This court was beginning to gain that dominance over the theatre which was to be characteristic of the Caroline period. Shakespeare's own company now received the patronage of the king, assumed his livery and was known as the King's Company. It acquired the comfortable indoor accommodations of the Blackfriars' Theatre for the winter season, and Shakespeare's tragi-comedies were written not only for the Globe audiences but for the exclusively aristocratic audiences of the Blackfriars' Theatre as well.

To satisfy the tastes of both these audiences, Shakespeare and the two new young aristocratic playwrights, Beaumont and Fletcher, devised the tragi-comedy. Which of them took the lead it is impossible to tell, but Fletcher in his preface to *The Faithful Shepherdess* showed that he was well aware that tragi-comedy was a new, distinct form. What went into this form that attempted to reconcile the conflicting tastes of two different audiences varied with the dramatist. Beaumont and Fletcher, closer to the Blackfriars audience, wrote one kind of tragi-comedy; Shakespeare, closer to the Globe audience, wrote another kind.

The tragi-comedy of Beaumont and Fletcher is diverting rather than profoundly stirring. It presents a world which, although its aristocratic characters have the manners and speech of the world of its audience, is remote from reality; it seeks not to give a heightened impression of life but to give a striking demonstration of theatrical virtuosity. The plot is full of swift turns, the characters are continually faced with sensational situations that arouse in them conflicting emotions, and often they surprise the audience by doing the unexpected. The scene is generally a corrupt court, and there are passages of delicate obscenity as well as touches of satiric comedy. Beautiful sentiments and noble conduct seem unreal in this setting. The conflicts between different views of kingship, honor, friendship and love are jugglings with fashionable ideas and occasions for emotional displays, the frivolous use of serious issues without any underlying deep conviction.

Quite different are the tragi-comedies which Shakespeare wrote. With their remoteness of atmosphere, their striking theatrical effects at the expense of probability, their spectacle, their swift changes of character, their tyrants and corrupt courts, they are similar to the tragi-comedies of Beaumont and Fletcher in form. There is also a new insistence on the mystique of royalty such as is present in their plays. The royal blood of Guiderius and Arviragus, as of Perdita, miraculously manifests itself in their rude surroundings. We have a sense not so much of the divinity that hedges a king as of the semi-divinity that is a king. Lear, when he is stripped of everything, learns what Henry V knew—that a king, although greater than other men, has the frailties of mortality; the princes and princesses of the tragi-comedies learn that the light which shines from them in their mountaineers' garb and the shepherdess' weeds, giving them the aspect of gods and godesses, is a sign of their royalty.

But if Shakespeare's tragi-comedies are similar to the tragi-comedies of Beaumont and Fletcher in form, they differ essentially from them in spirit. They have decadent courts, but an atmosphere of corruption does not permeate the plays. Characters undergo sudden change, but a change signifying a giving way to evil or a repentance and conversion, not a change solely for the purpose of creating or prolonging an exciting situation that weakens the idea of moral responsibility. The lack of reality is not that of frankly theatrical contrivance, avowedly artificial in its ingenuity and with its sole purpose to entertain, but that of myth, which has a surface improbability but legendary significance.

The basic myth of Shakespeare's last plays may be said to be that of the lost royal child recovered. A new royal generation, which has been brought up away from court in a fresh, renewing natural environment, after having passed through a period of helpless exposure to danger, returns as if from death, miraculously restoring the harmony destroyed by members of the older generation. In this final harmony there is general reconciliation and forgiveness. The mythical character of this theme is illustrated by the unusually large number of character-names with symbolic meaning: Marina ("born at sea"), Posthumous Leonatus ("lion's whelp born after death"), Fidele ("faithful one"), Perdita ("lost one"), Miranda ("wonder-inspiring"), Prospero ("make happy").

The recurring theme of royalty recovered through a new generation may be a reflection of popular feeling for Prince Henry and Princess Elizabeth and the strength of the hopes for the future attached to them during the years the tragi-comedies were written. The godson of Elizabeth, Henry, created the Prince of Wales at the age of eighteen in 1610, "bred hopes that he would restore Elizabethan days that, now distant, seemed

great and glorious."[34] "Never in the long history of England,"
writes the foremost historian of James' reign, "had an heir to
throne given rise to such hopes. . . ."[35] His boyhood was spent in
the highlands of Scotland, as that of Guiderius and Arviragus
was spent in the mountain fastnesses of Wales, and he was said
by poets to be descended from "Cadwalader, the last king of
British blood," and was called the "sweet flower of Wales, the
hope of Britain great."[36] In his eager spirits and his dreams of
heroic exploits he also resembled Shakespeare's two young mountain eagles: "His thoughts, even in his childhood, had been
filled with images which presaged a stirring life. . . . When he
first came to England, he talked of imitating the Plantagenets
when he should be a man, and of leading armies to the conquest
of France. These dreams passed away, and he threw himself
heart and soul into the tales of maritime adventure which were
so rife in England."[37] His Nonsuch household was a much
praised seat of learning and of courtly exercises. "A school of
taste and manners that contrasted with the coarseness and fri-
volity of much that went on at James' court, it was as well a
stimulus to literary men."[38] He was hailed as the champion of
aggressive Protestantism and of a strong navy in the Elizabethan
tradition of Sidney and Raleigh, and when he died in Novem-
ber, 1612, popular grief was so intense that it was widely alleged
that he had been poisoned by Rochester or Northampton or even
by James.[39]

[34] Elkin Calhoun Wilson, *Prince Henry and English Literature* (Ithaca,
N. Y., 1946), p. 173.
[35] Samuel R. Gardiner, *History of England from the Accession of
James I to the Outbreak of the Civil War* (London, 1889), II, 158.
[36] Wilson, pp. 26 and 36n.
[37] Gardiner, II, 73.
[38] Wilson, p. 53.
[39] Wilson, pp. 171–173; Gardiner, II, 158.

Elizabeth was similarly beloved. Brought up apart from the court like Perdita and Miranda, she was, like them, lauded for her grace and dignity. "The Lady Elizabeth had grown up far from the frivolities and dissipations of the Court, at Combe Abbey, under the watchful care of Lord and Lady Harrington. No better school could have been found for her than a country house, presided over by a master and mistress who gained the respect and love of all who knew them. . . . In the spring of 1611, she had not completed her fifteenth year, but she was already noted for a grace and discretion beyond her years."[40] The deep affection of Henry for Elizabeth, perhaps the conscious or unconscious inspiration of the brotherly attraction of Guiderius and Arviragus to Fidele, was celebrated.[41] In January, 1611, Elizabeth's marriage to Ferdinand, the Elector Palatinate, was first proposed by his mother, the widow of the man who formed the Protestant Union of the German princes and the daughter of the great William of Orange, and by her brother-in-law, the Duke of Bouillon, a French Protestant leader. The match, which Henry vigorously supported and Northampton and the Queen opposed, was finally agreed upon after a good deal of hesitation by James. The arrival of the young Elector in England in 1612 was an occasion of great popular rejoicing.

> The enthusiasm in London was unbounded. As his barge passed up the river to Whitehall, he was welcomed by the thousands who had come out to see him arrive. . . . The impression which he made upon all who conversed with him was favorable, and even those who, before his arrival, had spoken slightingly of the match, were obliged to confess that, as far as his personal appearance went, he was worthy of Elizabeth herself.[42]

[40] Gardiner, II, 136.
[41] Wilson, pp. 56–57; Gardiner, II, 136.
[42] Gardiner, II, 152–153.

At the marriage *The Tempest* was shown as part of the wedding festivities, perhaps with the fertility masque which Prospero provides for the betrothed Ferdinand and Miranda interpolated for the entertainment of the bridal couple looking on as Ferdinand and Miranda were looking on in the play.

The myth of the lost royal child recovered may, then, be a reflection of popular feeling toward James' own children. In any event, the renewal of life and the regeneration of society which accompanies this recovery is the expression of Shakespeare's faith in the restoration of the conditions of the Elizabethan compromise. Instrumental in this renewal of life is the humanistic scholar who takes the part of the "medicine man," the man versed in the mysteries of nature who cures seeming death in the festival folk plays that are related to the distant origins of Shakespeare's last plays.[43]

In *Pericles*, Thaisa, pronounced dead and thrown into sea in a sealed chest, is restored to life by the "secret art" (III. ii. 32) of Lord Cerimon, who, although a nobleman, holds to the humanist belief that virtue and learning are superior to nobility and riches, which can be sullied and wasted by dissolute heirs. Humanist knowledge releases royalty from its trance.

Similarly in *Cymbeline*, Belarius, a banished lord, having acquired a natural piety, paying "more pious debts to heaven" (III. iii. 72) during his twenty years living in a mountain cave than in all of his previous life, teaches Guiderius and Arviragus "t' adore the heavens" (III. iii. 3). In addition he teaches them to be contemptuous of "the art o' th' court," (III. iii. 46) which, under the influence of the queen, who, with her interest in perfumes and poisons resembles Catherine de Medici, the Florentine queen mother of France held responsible for St. Bar-

---

[43] Cf. Richard Wincor, "Shakespeare's Festival Plays," *SQ*, I (1950), 219–240.

tholomew's Eve, has become increasingly corrupt. Inspired by Belarius' tales of his martial feats, they are to bring back to it its ancient British virtue.

In *The Winter's Tale*, Camillo is a humanistic counselor of Leontes, a gentleman who has been raised because of his "clerk-like" attainments from "meaner form" to a position of the highest authority and dignity (I. ii. 313–314, 391–394). He has served not merely as Leontes' adviser on matters of state but as his spiritual guide. "Priest-like," he has "cleansed" Leontes' "bosom" (I. ii. 237–238). Having fled from Leontes' tyranny rather than perform the crime of regicide Leontes has commanded, he has in like manner served Polixenes. Florizel speaks of him as "the medicine of our house" (IV. iv. 598). It is Camillo who advises Florizel to go to Sicily with Perdita and who promises, he does not say how, to reconcile Florizel to his father in spite of the marriage. "How Camillo," asks Florizel (IV. iv. 544–545), "May this, almost a miracle, be done?"—but he takes the promise on faith, not pursuing the question. The near-miracle is accomplished when Camillo, questioning the shepherd, discovers the secret of Perdita's birth, revealing that Florizel's natural impulse, directed by heaven, has guided him to the best of all possible marriages. Camillo has thus not only found a lost son and daughter for Leontes but also a lost son for Polixenes, who had complained that having a son who has not turned out well is as bad as losing a good one.

In *The Tempest*, it is Prospero himself, who had given "all my study" to "the liberal arts" (I. ii. 73–74), who possesses humanistic knowledge and is the mentor of Miranda. From the Duke of Milan he has become the "master of a full poor cell" on the island, but here he has developed his character and his learning, as was required by the practitioner of natural magic. When his magic has accomplished its purpose of putting his enemies in his power and he has proved himself able to forego revenge, he gives it up to return ennobled to the world of men. Describing how Antonio transformed his court, raising new men to power, cutting down some old courtiers and corrupting others, he traces a process of degeneration similar to that after the accession of James:[44]

> Being once perfected how to grant suits,
> How to deny them, who to advance and who
> To trash for over-topping, new created
> The creatures that were mine, I say, or changed 'em,
> Or else new form'd 'em; having both the key
> Of officer and office, set all hearts i' the state
> To what tune pleased his ear. (I. ii. 79–85)

But if man can degenerate, he can be regenerated; if Antonio can "new create," so can Prospero on being restored to his dukedom.

Social regeneration takes place in the tragi-comedies after a sojourn by some of its characters in a green world. This green world, however, is somewhat different than that of the romantic comedies. It is not a place for love-making but rather for the growing up of royal children. The marriage of Imogen, the king's daughter, and Posthumous Leonatus, "a poor but worthy gentleman" (*Cymbeline*, I. i. 7) like the heroes of the romantic comedies, takes place at court before the beginning of the play, not here. Rather they are temporarily separated as Imogen joins her brothers in the green world while Posthumous goes to Italy, where he is deceived by the "Italian brain" (V. v. 196) of the accomplished Italianate courtier Iachimo into adopting Italianate cynicism toward women as his own, being regenerated only after he divests himself of his "Italian weeds" (V. i. 23) and

---

[44] Cf. Siegel, *Shakespearean Tragedy* . . . , pp. 37–40.

goes to fight for Britain dressed as a simple British peasant, "a very drudge of Nature's" (V. ii. 5). Florizel meets Perdita in the green world, but Shakespeare is too concerned with having them play their parts as fertility figures to have them engage in the delightfully irrational behavior that is love in the romantic comedies. Miranda indulges in some of this in offering to carry logs for Ferdinand, but our prime concern is with Prospero and the workings of his plan in which Ferdinand and Miranda have a place.

The dreamworld of the tragi-comic romances is not like that of the romantic comedies, a world that is strangely aberrant, to which one submits feeling that he would not have it otherwise and from which one wakes to solid reality. It is a world of intense suffering from which one wakes to find that it has suddenly dissolved to be replaced by a reality that itself seems strangely dream-like. The awakening takes place to the accompaniment of music, not the harmony of wedding music but a music as of another world, and the dreamer is so overcome by wonder that he blesses the gods.

"You had a bastard by Polixenes," Leontes had told Hermione with savage irony, "And I but dreamed it" (III. ii. 84–85). He had indeed been shaken by the nightmare terror of the wraiths of his own imagination. At the end of sixteen years of penitence his suffering is still sharp, but the chorus Time asks the spectators of the drama to imagine themselves as having slept through this sixteen-year interval between the third and fourth acts. Those sixteen years are indeed as a dream, as Paulina, calling upon Leontes to have faith when they are in the chapel in which she acts as a priestess, brings Hermione to life to the sound of solemn music.

Just as Leontes becomes convinced that Hermione is not a statue but alive, so the repentant Alonso, looking upon Prospero, who has appeared to the sound of music, exclaims (V. i. 113–114) "Thy pulse/ Beats, as of flesh and blood" and finds himself emerging from the "madness" that "held" him. So too Pericles, stretched out in sackcloth on a couch, is as a figure of death, over which bends Marina, who in her quiet, serene endurance seems the allegorical figure of Patience sculpted on tombs. But the sculpted figure moves and the figure of death revives. Pericles awakes to Marina's singing to find that the daughter whose supposed death had brought him to a state of inanition is alive. And so too Thaisa emerges from her faint to find her husband alive before her as in a dream.

> O, my lord,
> Are you not Pericles? Like him you spoke,
> Like him you are! Did you not name a tempest,
> A birth, and death? (V. iii. 31–34)

Birth, death, life's storms are dim and distant. The present consummation is everything.

Man is born to suffer in order that he may experience a greater joy. There is an ultimately beneficent purpose to the suffering of the good. "No more, you gods!" exclaims the enraptured Pericles (V. iii. 40–41). "Your present kindness/ Makes my past miseries sports." Posthumous, cast into prison to be executed, has a vision while asleep. The ghosts of his father, mother and two brothers appear and beseech Jupiter, in words reminiscent of Gloucester's comparison of the gods to wanton boys, no more to show his spite on "mortal flies" (V. iv. 31). Jupiter descends and, in an echo of the Biblical (Heb. 12:6) "For whom the Lord loves, he chasteneth," asserts, "Whom best I love I cross" (V. iv. 101). He concludes by promising that he will raise Posthumous from his fall to a greater happiness: "Your low-laid son our godhead will uplift. . . . He shall be lord of Lady

Imogen,/ And happier much by his affliction made" (V. iv. 102–108). And so it is to be. The "secret purposes" (V. i. 36) of the gods in *The Winter's Tale*, working themselves out, prove to be good, for Leontes' "saint-like sorrow" (V. i. 2) redeems his tyrannical actions. Prospero, a seemingly irascible father and harsh taskmaster, is in reality animated by paternal benevolence. The purpose of his affliction of the good is to test and confirm them in their love: "All thy vexations/ Were but my trials of thy love," he tells Ferdinand (IV. i. 5–6). The purpose of the affliction of the bad is to purge them as they are being punished and to bring them to repentance and regeneration: "They being penitent,/ The sole drift of my purpose doth extend/ Not a frown further" (V. i. 28–30).

The miraculousness of the happy ending is insisted upon. Three times in the last act of *The Winter's Tale* are the happenings said to be so wonderful by those witnessing them that they are like those of an old tale, whose marvels do not seem as if they could ever actually have happened. They have the qualities of a folk-story told over a peasant hearth to regale a winter night. Indeed, what seems to the characters of the drama to be like an old tale is so in fact to the spectators of the drama, for *The Winter's Tale* is an old story of the dim pagan past, as are *Pericles* and *Cymbeline*.

The oldness of the stories of the tragi-comic romances is recalled by the use of choric narrators, who by their observations contribute a sense of remoteness and also of providential control. In *Pericles* the strange and varied adventures of the hero are presented for us by the ancient poet Gower. His spirit has assumed flesh to conjure up this fiction, which, we are told by him (I. i. 1–10), was old before his time and which, related through the ages on festive occasions and read by generations of lords and ladies for its ever-working refreshment, seems to have a precious timeless and universal significance. Gower creates the story anew, bringing it to life again, as he has been brought to life to do. He is the maker, the shaper, who keeps returning to remind us that what we are seeing is coming to us through his magic revivification and who, by so doing, invests it with a strange remoteness: "Like motes and shadows see them move a while;/ Your ears unto your eyes I'll reconcile" (IV. iv. 21–22). But, although the magic of the long dead poet calls up the characters of Greek romance, he cannot manipulate them as he will. He is bound to make them reenact the recorded legendary events: "What shall be next,/ Pardon old Gower,—this longs the text" (Prologue, II. 39–40). The experiences of Pericles are not merely extraordinary happenings; they are, we are made to feel, directed and controlled, and we are urged to await their ending without repining at his bad lot: "Be quiet then as men should be,/ Till he hath pass'd necessity" (Prologue, II. 5–6).

We are likewise reminded of the oldness of *The Winter's Tale* by Time, who comes to tell us that, just as he has always changed things since before the dawn of civilization while himself remaining unchanged, so will he "make stale/ The glistering of this present, as my tale/Now seems to it" (IV. i. 13–15). Speaking of Perdita, grown to wondrous young womanhood in the sixteen-year interval, Time, hinting of a coming event already known to him but to be known to human beings only after it has emerged from the womb of history, says: "What of her ensues/ I list not prophesy, but let Time's news/ Be known when 'tis brought forth" (IV. i. 25–27).

Prospero is the author of *The Tempest* in almost the same sense that Gower is of *Pericles* and that Time the Chorus is of *The Winter's Tale*. He recalls to Miranda her life as a three-year-old princess, which she remembers dimly as a dream, relates what happened to have brought them to the island, spins the threads of the plot and ties everything together in the end. Always aware of what each of the groups on the island is doing, he is in full control of their action. And it is he who brings to us, in his comments to the young people, so charmingly concerned with themselves and their coming nuptials, the dream-like transcience and unsubstantiality of the human scene, which he compares to the masque that he creates.

Dream-like and unsubstantial as life appears to be when it is viewed from one vantage-point, from another angle it is seen as solidly enduring through the ages. What Charles Barber well describes as present in *The Winter's Tale* is present also in the other tragi-comic romances:

> Another theme of the play is the continuity of human history, the way life goes on generation after generation despite all conflicts and disturbances. This is suggested by the seasonal imagery itself, for the seasons are cyclical. It is also suggested by the images given more than once in the play of generations of man stretching backwards and forwards in time. . . . Another example comes in the scene where Perdita's recognition is described; it is said that Leontes
>
> > thanks the old shepherd, which stands by like a
> > weather-bitten conduit of many kings' reign.
> > (V. ii. 54–5)
>
> The shepherd here becomes a type of the continuity of rural life, with its toughness ('weather-bitten'), its lifegiving qualities, and its channeling of tradition (both suggested by *conduit*, which presumably carries water). This life continues whatever goes on at court: 'of many kings' reigns' not only evokes the perspective of history, but also suggests a fabric of local life which is tough and enduring through the vicissitudes of political history: kings may come and go, but the conduit and the old shepherd remain.[45]

[45] Charles Barber, "*The Winter's Tale* and Jacobean Society," *Shakespeare in a Changing World*, ed. Arnold Kettle (New York, 1964), pp. 248–249.

Not only do they endure but they are the sources of regeneration, as are the creatures and elements of the green world in the other romances: the little unspoiled society of good fishermen who take in Pericles and enable him to reassume his kingly heritage by bringing up his ancestral armor from the sea, the invigorating mountain air of the dwelling of Guiderius and Arviragus, the magic island of Prospero.

The faith in the workings of time to regenerate the decadent society of the present as it regenerated decadent societies of the past lies behind all of the romances. "It is in my pow'r," says Time, "To o'erthrow law, and in one self-born hour/ To plant and o'erwhelm custom" (IV. i. 7–9). This expression of the idea of concomitant destruction and creation repeats what had been said by the shepherd immediately before on his finding the infant Perdita while his son witnessed the devouring of Antigonus by the bear: "Thou mettest with things dying, I with things new born" (III. iii. 16–17). Death and birth are interlinked throughout the romances. This linkage signifies the reconciliation gained from the perception that one's children are a rebirth of one's self in another form, from the faith that a new society will be born as an old one dies, from the faith that rebirth in this world is the analogue of a new life in another world after death. In the comedies, as in the tragedies, it is not our adherence to Shakespeare's system of ideas that gives them significance for us, but our entering into the experience they provide for us. We need not accept either faith in an afterlife or faith in the automatic workings of history to respond to Shakespeare's acceptance of life.

VII

The Turns of the Dance: An Essay on
Much Ado About Nothing

Much Ado About Nothing is like a formal dance in which couples successively part, make parallel movements and then are reunited. Although some of the figures performed in this dance have been noted, the dance as a whole, with its various advances, retreats, turns and counter-turns, has not been described.[1]

As the music strikes up in the dance scene of the second act, Beatrice says to Benedick, "We must follow the leaders," but

[1] Much Ado About Nothing has not been fortunate in its critics, who, failing to see its pattern, have for the most part found the main plot to be melodramatic and only tenuously connected with the subplot, Claudio to be an unfeeling and unworthy hero, and the play itself to exist solely for the wit of Benedick and Beatrice. The best discussion of the structure of the play is Francis Fergusson's introduction to the Laurel edition (New York, 1960), to which I am indebted on some points.

she adds, "Nay, if they lead to any ill, I will leave them at the next turning" (II. i. 157–160). Beatrice and Benedick repeat the steps of Hero and Claudio in the dance of love which Beatrice describes with light-hearted gaiety (II. i. 72–84), but with variations of their own. Don Pedro not only presides over the dance and directs it, but he also offers to woo Hero for Claudio and suggests the stratagem to make Beatrice and Benedick fall in love with each other. If they succeed in this stratagem, he says, "we are the only love-gods" (II. i. 403). His brother Don John, however, is an opposing force which seeks to get in the way of the dancers and to disturb the harmony of the dance. As Don Pedro leaves the stage, telling Leonato, Claudio and Hero how he will bring about the match between Benedick and Beatrice, Don John, sick with hatred in the presence of the happiness of Claudio and Hero, about to be married, enters and says to his tool Borachio, "Any bar, any cross, any impediment will be medicinable to me. . . . How canst thou cross this marriage?" (II. ii. 4–8). Although both Don Pedro and Don John use the language of plotters—they will "practice on" Benedick, says Don Pedro to his confederates (II. i. 399), and Don John tells Borachio (II. ii. 53–54) "Be cunning in the working this"—Don Pedro's plot is benevolent while Don John's is malevolent.

Each succeeds, but there is a greater force at work which reunites Claudio and Hero in a strengthened unity at the conclusion of the play, when they join Benedick and Beatrice—ironically brought together by Don John's plot as well as by Don Pedro's—in the dance that signalizes the close. Don John's plot not only fools Don Pedro and Claudio but almost causes bloodshed when Leonato and Benedick disregard Friar Francis' wise advice. Instead of letting time and remorse work on Claudio, as this man of God suggests, they challenge him; it is not until foolish Dogberry exposes Don John and his accomplices that they realize their error. In setting right their blunders, Dogberry furthers the purpose of nature, which is itself animated by love —the love of God pervading creation—and which is engaged in a cosmic dance.

Benedick and Beatrice have followed in the steps of Claudio and Hero in falling in love, but in their preliminary estrangement they have also set a pattern. The "skirmish of wit" (I. i. 64) in which they engage in the masked dance scene causes some real wounds. Probably since Hero, informed of Don Pedro's intention to woo her, knew him despite his mask and since Ursula recognized Antonio as well, Margaret and Beatrice, in keeping with the method of repetition so noticeably employed in the play, should also be portrayed as recognizing the masked gentlemen speaking to them in much the same way that the queen and her ladies are aware of the identities of the masked gentlemen in a similar scene in *Love's Labor's Lost*. When Beatrice is informed by Benedick that a gentleman whom he refuses to name has charged her with being disdainful and with having borrowed her wit from a collection of humorous tales, she surmises that the unnamed gentleman is Benedick. When her interlocutor professes not to know Benedick, she replies, it would seem with veiled irony, "I am sure you know him well enough" (II. i. 138) and charges Benedick in turn with being the Prince's fool, with his only gift consisting of "devising impossible slanders" (II. i. 142–143). This gift of devising impossible slanders seems to be an allusion to what he has just said about her. So Benedick also tells himself a little later that her statement that he is the Prince's fool is a slander emanating from "the base (though bitter) disposition of Beatrice" (II. i. 214–215). In the fencing match between them, that is, the sword dance which is a feature of this masque, each is wounded by an identical thrust.

Jest as Benedick may, he has been hurt: "She speaks poniards, and every word stabs" (II. i. 255–256). The hurt inflicted by the words of each is a prefiguration of the much more grievous hurt inflicted by Claudio, who "killed" Hero "with his breath" (V. i. 272). "Sweet Hero, she is wronged, she is slander'd, she is undone," bitterly exclaims Beatrice (IV. i. 314–315), bidding Benedick fight her "enemy." So Don Pedro tells Benedick after the dance, "The Lady Beatrice hath a quarrel to you. The gentleman that danced with her told her she is much wronged by you" (II. i. 243–245). Benedick is later to act as Beatrice's champion in her quarrel with Claudio, but now he announces, "I would not marry her though she were endowed with all that Adam had left him before he transgressed" (II. i. 260–262). So Claudio publicly refuses to marry Hero, the heiress of her wealthy father, returning to Leonato what he calls with bitter irony the "rich and precious gift" (IV. i. 27) he has received from him. Following the suggestion of Don John that "it would better fit your honor to change your mind" (III. ii. 118–119), Claudio is revenging himself by this public disgrace of Hero; similarly Benedick, ruminating over Beatrice's slur upon him, had exclaimed, "Well, I'll be revenged as I may" (II. i. 217–218).

Claudio's misapprehension that Hero has been unfaithful to him has been prefigured by his misapprehension that the Prince has deceived him by wooing Hero for himself; both false appearances and the instigation of Don John have misled him in each instance. His first misapprehension comes in the masked dance scene, his brief separation from his partner coinciding with the disengagement of Benedick and Beatrice. Benedick jests at the sulking of the jealous Claudio—"Alas, poor hurt fowl! Now will he creep in sedges" (II. i. 209–210)—but immediately reveals his own hurt: "But, that my Lady Beatrice should know me, and not know me! The Prince's fool! Ha!"

When Claudio, however, rejoins Hero after his brief separation from her, Benedick and Beatrice remain apart. "Come, lady, come," says Don Pedro (II. i. 285–286), as Benedick leaves upon Beatrice's entrance, "you have lost the heart of Signior Benedick." "Indeed, my lord," replies Beatrice, "he lent it me awhile, and I gave him use for it, a double heart for a single one. Marry, once before he won it of me with false dice; therefore your Grace may well say I have lost it" (II. i. 287–291). Her words have been mystifying to the commentators. Is she saying that Benedick had once wooed her and gained her heart? This would be contrary to everything we learn of the two of them in the play, for the whole point of Don Pedro's efforts to make a match between them is that it seems impossible that they fall in love with each other. Is she merely speaking "all mirth and no matter" (II. i. 344)? It would appear that her joking must have some subject. Perhaps the suggestion that she is referring to a game played with cards and dice is the most acceptable.

In any event it is significant that her reference to a previous exchange of hearts, however lightly uttered, parallels Claudio's recital of how taken he was by Hero before he went to war and is echoed immediately afterwards in Claudio's statement that Hero has whispered to him that he is "in her heart" and in his words to her, "Lady, as you are mine, I am yours. I give away myself for you and dote upon the exchange" (II. i. 319–320). The repetition of motifs is continued in the conversation which follows. When Beatrice, looking at the happy couple, gayly exclaims, "Good Lord, for alliance! Thus goes everyone in the world but I, and I am sunburnt. I may sit in a corner and cry 'Heigh-ho for a husband!'" Don Pedro responds in the same vein, "Lady Beatrice, I will get you one." So had he got Hero a husband. When Beatrice turns his statement around with "I would rather have one of your father's getting. Hath your Grace ne'er a brother like you?" Don Pedro replies, "Will you have me, lady" (II. i. 330–338)? His question, laughingly asked to minister to her wit, repeats his wooing of Hero on behalf of Claudio, which had been mistaken for a wooing for himself.

Don Pedro does get Beatrice a husband. Benedick and Beatrice go as goes everyone in the world, more specifically as Claudio and Hero have gone. In response to Benedick's question in the opening scene "But I hope you have no intent to turn husband, have you?" Claudio had replied, "I would scarce trust myself, though I had sworn the contrary, if Hero would be my wife" (I. i. 197–198). Benedick retorted with a scoff at those who give up their bachelorhood, but he himself, although he indeed swore the contrary, came to do the same. In his very scorn for Claudio's blindness, he revealed the inclination which, like Claudio, he had felt before going to the wars, but which he is resisting: "There's her cousin, and she were not possessed with a fury, exceeds her in beauty as the first of May doth the last of December" (I. i. 192–195).

The comedy lies in Benedick's repeating Claudio's behavior immediately after he laughs at it. "I do much wonder," he says (as we await with gleeful expectation the plot against him) "that one man, seeing how much another man is a fool when he dedicates his behaviors to love, will, after he hath laughed at such shallow follies in others, become the argument of his own scorn by falling in love; and such a man is Claudio" (II. iii. 7–12). Undoubtedly, he is to make a marked pause after the phrase "falling in love" so that the audience may mentally supply his name before he applies his observation to Claudio. He mocks at Claudio, who had previously enjoyed only martial music, for being entranced by the music of the lute—"Is it not strange that sheep's guts should hale souls out of men's bodies?" (II. iii. 59–60)—but he himself will soon yield to the sweet harmony of love, composing songs, albeit, since he was "not born under a rhyming planet," (V. ii. 40–41) halting ones. So too he follows Claudio's behavior in paying new attention to his personal appearance and in mooning about in the melancholy induced by love.

Repetitive as their behavior is, however, there is variation. Claudio is the tongue-tied, timid lover who needs the Prince to do his wooing for him. There are no love scenes between him and the demure Hero. Each can speak well enough with others, Claudio engaging in repartee with Benedick and Hero joining in the fun at the expense of Beatrice, but in each other's presence they are mute. When Don Pedro informs Claudio that he has won Hero for him, Claudio can only say "Silence is the perfectest herald of joy. I were but little happy if I could say how much" (II. i. 318–319). Beatrice pushes the overwhelmed Claudio and the modest Hero into their proper positions. "Speak, Count, 'tis your cue," she tells Claudio and then, having elicited from him his few fervent words of love, she turns to Hero, saying, "Speak, cousin; or (if you cannot) stop his mouth with a kiss and let not him speak neither" (II. i. 316, 321–323).

Benedick and Beatrice, a highly loquacious pair, do not love in this fashion. Benedick, who, after having been taken in by Don Pedro's plot, resolved "I will be horribly in love with her," (II. iii. 244) is as extravagant in his professions of love as he had been in his professions of misogyny. Beatrice, for her part, is as witty as ever, although now she fences with a buttoned foil. Her progress of love parallels his. As he had revealed an inclination toward her, she had revealed an inclination toward him in her eagerness to make him the subject of conversation and in her Freudian slip in the dance scene, "I am sure he is in the fleet; I would he had boarded me" (II. i. 148–149): "board" not only means "accost," with the implication that she would have repulsed him, but is also capable of a sexual significance. She, as he did, eavesdrops on a conversation whose participants tell each other gleefully in asides that the plot is working and make use of the same figures of the trapped bird and the hooked fish. With comic repetition, each, formerly high-spirited, becomes woebegone in the pangs of love, he pretending to the Prince and Claudio that he has a toothache, she pretending to Hero and Margaret that she has a cold. "I shall see thee, ere I die," Don Pedro had said to Benedick, "look pale with love" (I. i. 249–250). It was more true than Leonato's "You will never run mad, niece" after Beatrice had said of Benedick, "He is sooner caught than the pestilence, and the taker runs presently mad" (I. i. 87–88). "No, not till a hot January," had replied Beatrice. She might better have said not till the springtime, the season for the madness of love, that "ecstacy" (II. iii. 157) from which Leonato is to state she is suffering.

Beatrice duplicates not only Benedick's behavior. Just as Benedick repeats Claudio's actions, she repeats those of Hero, who, lessoned by her father, had replied to Don Pedro's wooing in proper decorous fashion, making light of it, as a lady should, only to accept the suit he had pressed on behalf of Claudio. So Beatrice, after keeping up her defenses, permits herself to be won, although protesting to the end that she is unwounded and unyielding. Margaret, it may be said, takes Beatrice's place in the dance. Struck by Margaret's jests, flying thick as arrows, Beatrice asks her caustically how long it has been that she has professed herself a wit. "Ever since you left it," retorts Margaret. "Doth not my wit become me rarely?" (III. iv. 69–70). Thus the dance of love is an unending succession of dancers in which the erstwhile jester becomes the subject of fresh jests by one who is as yet heart-whole and able to cavort gaily around the disconsolate lover.

As Beatrice is in the dumps, Hero is getting dressed for the marriage ceremony. Unexpectedly, however, Beatrice has the company of Hero in her melancholy, as Benedick had found himself hurt at the same time as Claudio. "God give me joy to wear it," says Hero of her wedding gown, "for my heart is exceeding heavy" (III. iv. 24–25). Her heaviness of spirits is a premonition, such as is Antonio's melancholy at the beginning of *The Merchant of Venice* and Hamlet's misgivings before the duel, of the blow she is about to receive. Unknown to her, Don John's plot has succeeded, just as, unknown to Beatrice, Don Pedro's plot has succeeded.

There are a number of echoes from one plot to the other. "I pray God his bad voice bode no mischief," says Benedick sourly of Balthasar's song, which has just won Don Pedro's commendation (II. iii. 82–84). "I had as live have heard the night raven, come what plague could have come after it." Mischief is indeed afoot, for Don Pedro and Claudio are about to practice their deception on him. We are reminded, however, of the kind of genuine disaster supposed to be presaged by the raven's cry that is to be brought about by another enacted deception when Don Pedro says immediately after, "Dost thou hear, Balthasar? I pray thee get us some excellent music; for tomorrow night we would have it at the Lady Hero's chamber window" (II. iii. 86–89). Benedick, wondering if he has been tricked, is dissuaded of it by the gravity of Leonato's demeanor: "Knavery cannot, sure, hide himself in such reverence" (II. iii. 24–25). "Knavery" is a word that is more readily applied to the other plot. The deception of Benedick successful, Don Pedro and Claudio congratulate themselves and eagerly await the outcome of the deception of Beatrice. "Hero and Margaret have by this played their parts with Beatrice," says Claudio (III. ii. 78–79)—and just then

Don John, who is using Margaret to play another part, enters to tell him that his Hero is "every man's Hero," that she has been playing a part with him. And when Margaret is teasing Beatrice as Hero is preparing for the wedding, she remarks on Beatrice's observation that she cannot smell Hero's perfumed gloves because she is "stuffed," that is, has a head cold, "A maid, and stuffed! There's goodly catching of cold" (III. iv. 64–66). The jesting allegation contained in the double entendre "stuffed" is shortly to be made with deadly earnestness about Hero.

With the marriage ceremony disrupted, it is now Benedick and Beatrice who are united and Claudio and Hero who are separated. Benedick and Beatrice, on overhearing how their pride was condemned, had learned their lessons and sacrificed their egoism to give themselves to each other. As Benedick said "Happy are they that hear their detractions and can put them to mending" (II. iii. 237–238). So Claudio does "penance" for his "sin" (V. i. 282–283). It is a venial sin, for he sinned only in "mistaking." Yet, in not trusting to the heart's promptings but to the false knowledge of the senses, he has sinned against love. Beatrice, strong and loyal in her friendship, trusts despite all evidence to what her heart tells her: "O, on my soul, my cousin is belied!" (IV. i. 147). To Benedick's question "Think you in your soul the Count Claudio hath wronged Hero?" she replies, "Yea, as sure as I have a thought or a soul" (IV. i. 331–334). Beatrice's heart-felt conviction is sufficient for Benedick, believing in her as he does. Claudio, however, has to learn how to give himself wholeheartedly without regard to the impressions of the senses.

This he does in the final scene, when he atones for the wrong he had done Hero by keeping his contract with Leonato and marrying her supposed cousin without seeing her face.[2] The final scene, which may be regarded as a highly patterned wedding masque, is a repetition of the previous marriage scene, to which Claudio and Don Pedro came pretending that they were in earnest before they threw off the mask to unmask, as they thought, the guilty Hero. So Leontes and Antonio come to the second marriage ceremony "with confirmed countenance," (V. iv. 17) with steady faces in pretended earnest, as they play out their little fiction that the disguised Hero is Antonio's daughter. When his bride removes her mask, Claudio finds to his joy that she is Hero herself—or rather, "another Hero," (V. iv. 62) the Hero of his false imaginings, "every man's Hero," having died. So too Beatrice, in response to Benedick's "Which is Beatrice?"—an echo of Claudio's "Which is the lady I must seize upon?—removes her mask to reveal herself. In this masquerade, unlike the dance scene of the second act, which the scene recalls, every one finds his true love.

Before the happy union of both couples is completed, however, there is a final turn by Benedick and Beatrice which repeats in a lighter, quicker tempo the previous turn by Claudio and Hero: it seems for a moment as if the marriage between them that was about to have taken place is not going to take place after all, as the two continue their fencing until the end, with each thrust being parried and met by an answering thrust.

> *Benedick.* Do you not love me?
> *Beatrice.*   Why, no; no more than reason.
> *Benedick.* Why, then your uncle, and the Prince, and Claudio
>   Have been deceived—they swore you did.

[2] Far from displaying the lightness of his love, Claudio's determination to make amends—"I'll hold my mind, were she an Ethiope" (V. iv. 38)—shows the deepness of his penitence.

Beatrice.   Do not you love me?
Benedick.   Troth, no; no more than reason.
Beatrice.   Why, then my cousin, Margaret, and Ursula
             Are much deceived; for they did swear you did.
Benedick.   They swore that you were almost sick for me.
Beatrice.   They swore that you were well-nigh dead for me.
Benedick.   'Tis no such matter. Then you do not love me?
Beatrice.   No, truly, but in friendly recompense.

                                              (V. iv. 77–83)

The revelations that have just taken place are here lightly glanced
at: Leonato and the Prince and Claudio, says Benedick, were
deceived in believing that Beatrice loved Benedick (just as they
were deceived in believing that Hero did not love Claudio); it
was given out, says Beatrice, that Benedick was well-nigh dead
(just as it was given out that Hero was indeed dead). From this
it seems that, having been talked into love, Benedick and Beatrice may talk themselves out of it although their repartee may
also be taken as the teasing of two people who are sure of each
other. However, Claudio produces a love sonnet that Benedick
has written and Hero produces a love sonnet that Beatrice has
written. "A miracle!" exclaims Benedick. "Here's our own hands
against our hearts" (V. iv. 91–93). It is a miracle rather less
wonderful than the resurrection of Hero. The near-rejection of
Beatrice is linked with the repudiation of Hero when, Benedick
stating to Claudio that he had thought to have beaten him
but, since they are about to become kinsmen, will let him live
unbruised, Claudio retorts, "I had well hoped thou wouldst
have denied Beatrice, that I might have cudgeled thee out of
thy single life . . ." (V. iv. 114–118).

Here we have an amusing turn-about: Benedick had acted
as Hero's champion out of love for Beatrice and Claudio now
would act as Beatrice's out of love for Hero. Just as in the
concluding fencing between Benedick and Beatrice, there is a

moment in the final scene when it seems as if the exchange between Benedick and Claudio may become serious. Claudio having made a jest about the prospect of horns for Benedick, Benedick replies with a taunt about the horns of Claudio's father implying that Claudio is both a calf and a bastard. Claudio's "For this I owe you" (V. iv. 51)—that is, I will repay you for this—is an echo of Benedick's statement immediately before expressing pleasure that he will not have "to call young Claudio to a reckoning" (V. iv. 9). But the proposed duel turns into an exchange of wit, and the threats become pleasant banter. In the final harmony love and friendship are reconciled. "Come, come, we are friends," says Benedick.

Beatrice at the beginning of the play had said of Benedick, "He hath every month a new sworn brother. . . . He wears his faith but as the fashion of his hat; it ever changes with the next block" (I. i. 73–77). Ironically, Benedick is to quarrel with his friend Claudio as a result of his love for Beatrice. Benedick's calling Claudio a villain is the counterpart of Claudio's calling Hero a wanton. Benedick's inconstancy in friendship illustrates the truth of the conclusion to which he comes in justifying his change of mind about marriage: "man is a giddy thing" (V. iv. 107–108). To be sure, this inconstancy is the result of his admirable wholeheartedness in love, but his initial recoil in dismay after his lover's offer to do any thing at all for Beatrice is answered by her curt "Kill Claudio" and his plaintive entreaty "Beatrice," (IV. ii. 291–315) five times overborne by Beatrice's furious tirade (the last time he is not even allowed to complete the second syllable), have their comic aspect as an exhibition of the power of love. The vagaries of love induce the most ridiculously inconsistent behavior; men are, as Balthasar sings just before Benedick is made to turn to Beatrice and Claudio is about to be made to turn away from Hero, "One foot in sea, and one on shore,/ To one thing constant never" (II. iii. 66–67).

When Benedick challenges Claudio, neither Claudio nor Don Pedro believe that he can be serious but at length perceive that he is really in earnest: "As I am an honest man, he looks pale. Art thou sick, or angry?" (V. i. 130–131). Early in the play in response to Don Pedro's "I shall see thee, ere I die, look pale with love," Benedick stated: "With anger, with sickness, or with hunger, my lord, not with love" (I. i. 251–252). Don Pedro did indeed live to see the merry Benedick look pale, first with love-melancholy and then with anger, but, as Claudio says (V. i. 199), "for the love of Beatrice" in each case.

Benedick's challenge came just after Claudio had been challenged, first by Leonato and then by his rather comically irate brother Antonio, who, after having counseled patience to Leonato, outdid him in his fury. Wearied by the effort he had made to exercise forbearance with the two fuming old men and dejected by this sequel to his repudiation of Hero, Claudio welcomed Benedick, thinking that his wit would raise his spirits. Instead, he was greeted with another display of anger and another challenge. The scene falls within the pattern formed by a number of scenes in which Benedick mocks Claudio first when he is lovelorn and then when he is jealous and next Claudio in turn mocks Benedick when Benedick himself becomes lovelorn. When one's spirits are low, the other's are high. In the challenge scene, although Claudio is shaken up by his encounter with Leonato and Antonio, he is determined to be merry and meets Benedick's equally determined quarrelsomeness with sallies of wit.[3] It is only at the end that they are in tune with each other,

---

[3] Shakespeare takes care to have Claudio say (V. i. 123) "We are high-proof melancholy." Claudio jokes to maintain the pattern, but we are assured that he is not heartless.

each happy in his approaching marriage. The turns have been completed, each couple is united and the two couples are joined together in love and friendship, as the pipers strike up the music for the dance that precedes their joint marriage.

VIII

A Midsummer Night's Dream
and the Wedding Guests*

The manner in which the marriage of Theseus and Hippolyta is made the setting of A *Midsummer Night's Dream*, the music, dancing and spectacle with which it is filled, and the virtual epithalamium at the conclusion testify, it is generally agreed, that the play was written as part of the festivities of some aristocratic wedding. "Can anyone read the opening scene, or the closing speech of Theseus, and doubt that the occasion was a wedding?" ask the editors of the New Cambridge Shakespeare (p. x); and they add, "Be it remembered, moreover, how the fairies dominate the play; and how constantly and intimately fairies were associated with weddings by our Elizabethan ances-

* Reprinted with permission from *Shakespeare Quarterly*, vol. IV, 1953.

tors, their genial favours invoked, their possible malign caprices prayed against." In the back of the minds of the wedding guests who composed the first audience of *A Midsummer Night's Dream* was at all times the awareness that the stage-performance which they were witnessing was a part of the wedding celebration in which they were engaged. Shakespeare, writing not only for all time but for the occasion, played upon this awareness, exploiting to the full the theatrical potentialities of a situation in which the audience saw on the stage an enactment of the circumstances in which it was at the same time participating in life. By reading the play with the occasion constantly in our minds, by becoming the wedding guests in our imagination, we can recapture something of the total aesthetic experience of its first-performance audience, an experience which adds to the experience of the audiences of all ages a teasing piquancy of its own.

"Now, fair Hippolyta," says Theseus in the first words of the play, which immediately set the background and tone, "our nuptial hour/ Draws on apace" (I. i. 1–2). In rich, stately music he expresses to her his longing for the marriage night which is to come after four days and then turns to his master of revels and commands him to "stir up the Athenian youth to merriments" and "awake the pert and nimble spirit of mirth" (I. i. 12–13). For this wedding of the Duke of Athens is a public festivity to be celebrated "with pomp, with triumph, and with revelling" (I. i. 19). The wedding guests could not miss the flattering similarity between the Elizabethan bridal couple and the gracious, exalted pair of legendary antiquity. In the revels of this famous wedding they saw an historical analogy with the revels of the present wedding, a feature of which was this very play, which was to stir them, the choicest of English aristocratic youth, to merriment.

No sooner are the words of Theseus spoken than Egeus, Hermia, Lysander and Demetrius come on the stage, as if in answer to the summons to merriment. The two pairs of lovers are like puppets in the hands of a puppet-master, now jerked this way, now that, now chasing after, now running away from, in an amusing exhibition of the vagaries of love and the absurdities to which it impels its victims. Their "fond pageant" (III. ii. 114) is ideally suited for a wedding entertainment, for with what could a wedding play deal if not with love, and, since it must be written in the "pert and nimble spirit of mirth," how could love be presented if not as a pixilation which seizes young folk, from which they awake, as from a dream, to find themselves happy in their approaching marriage? Such must be the fate of the aristocratic young unmarried guests (although, to be sure, the happy consummation was dependent on their finding their true loves); such was the fate of their elders. While the love of ordinary aristocrats such as those who were on the stage and those who were viewing the play is thus presented sportively, the love of Theseus and Hippolyta, and by implication that of the august bridegroom and bride whose wedding was being celebrated, is decorously presented on a different level. About to be married, Theseus is free of the sighs, the silences, the variable humors of the lover of romance who has not yet won his mistress. His passion is controlled, his love dignified and elevated.

From his serene height Theseus looks down with humorous condescension and benevolent tolerance upon the lovers and their moon-struck madness. Finding them asleep in the woods (now entirely different in the early daylight from the moonlit grove in whose shadows the mischievous Puck had caused them to chase madly about) where he has come to hunt, he tells his huntsmen to wake them with their horns. It is as if this spectacle, in which what had been discord is resolved into harmonious concord, takes the place of the sound from afar of the baying of his hounds, their cries of varied pitch blending together, to which he had invited Hippolyta to listen: "We will, fair queen, up to the mountain's top/ And mark the musical confusion/ Of hounds and echo in conjunction" (IV. i. 113–115).

At the sound of the horns the lovers open their eyes to a new world. The fantastic story they have to tell is regarded skeptically by Theseus.

> I never may believe
> These antique fables, nor these fairy toys.
> Lovers and madmen have such seething brains,
> Such shaping fantasies, that apprehend
> More than cool reason ever comprehends.
> The lunatic, the lover, and the poet
> Are of imagination all compact. (V. i. 2–8)

Although an exalted figure, Theseus is an earthborn mortal and hence can only deem the lovers' story the product of their imaginations. But the audience witnessing the play had seen the "fairy toys" whose existence he does not believe in, and it knew better. It knew that they were unseen powers in the lives of human beings in innumerable ways, crossing them, bemusing them, giving them good luck, and that disturbances in the fairy kingdom were reflected in disturbances in human affairs (although, to be sure, fairies being fairies and not gods or planets, these disturbances were nothing more serious than unusually bad weather). It knew that they looked with amusement upon the "fond pageant" of human beings working at cross-purposes, changing their minds, not knowing themselves and unaware of the fairy influences affecting their lives. It knew that great Theseus himself was under the special protection of the fairy queen and his fair bride under the protection of the fairy king.

But did it really know? How sure can one be, even though one has seen them, of the existence of beings so small that they can hide in an acorn and so elusively fleet that they can girdle the earth in forty minutes? Those fairy forms which had disappeared as Theseus' horns were heard sounding in the distance— were they real or a dream that the audience had shared with an ass? "I have had a dream, past the wit of man to say what dream it was. Man is but an ass, if he go about to expound this dream" (IV. i. 209–212).

But although by the exercise of its imagination an audience may lose itself in a dramatic universe which a dramatist has created, it can never entirely forget, if it is beyond the most primitive level of response, that this dramatic universe is in fact a dramatic universe and not the world of reality—and the aristocratic wedding guests were not at all unsophisticated. As Theseus continued to speak of the imagination of the poet, he made them more sharply aware that this perplexing dream, this evanescent reality which they witnessed, was itself but part of a dramatic illusion.

> As imagination bodies forth
> The forms of things unknown, the poet's pen
> Turns them to shapes and gives to airy nothing
> A local habitation and a name. (V. i. 14–17)

The creatures of the fairy world, things unknown, had indeed been given shape, habitation ("a bank where the wild thyme blows,/Where oxlips and the nodding violet grows," II. i. 249– 250); and names, names which Bottom had soon come to use with incongruous courtly familiarity ("Mounsieur Cobweb," "Mounsieur Mustardseed," IV. i. 7–18) as he had addressed the members of the fairy court waiting upon him. And not only the creatures of the fairy world. Did not the speaker, Duke Theseus, himself have existence only in "antique fables," and was not the Duke Theseus before the audience but a poor player who passed his hour upon the stage and then was heard no more and who could as fittingly as Oberon be called a "king of shadows" (III. ii. 347)? Some perception of this paradox must have made the keener members of Shakespeare's courtly audience sense an irony in the large assurance with which Theseus spoke of the lovers' story of "fairy toys" and of the fantasies of the poet, whose eye, "in a fine frenzy rolling,/ Doth glance from heaven to earth, from earth to heaven" (V. i. 12–13). Perhaps, as Hippolyta replied, there was something to the lovers' story, after all. Perhaps—on a different level—it is true that the imaginative intuition of the poet can actually apprehend more essential truth than "cool reason," that there are more things in heaven and earth than the Duke dreamt of.

But "these things seem small and undistinguishable,/ Like far-off mountains turned into clouds" (IV. i. 190–191). When, as Hippolyta finished speaking, Lysander and Hermia, Demetrius and Helena came on the stage and Theseus broke off the discussion with the remark "Here come the lovers, full of joy and mirth" (V. i. 28), the wedding guests were brought back from such thoughts to the solid world of human society, of which marriage is the base. "Come now," they heard Theseus exclaim,

> what masques, what dances shall we have,
> To wear away this long age of three hours
> Between our after-supper and bed-time?
> Where is our usual manager of mirth?
> What revels are in hand? Is there no play
> To ease the anguish of a torturing hour? (V. i. 32–37)

The four days before the marriage ceremony was to be performed, to which he had referred at the beginning of the play, had passed, and the time was now close at hand. As the wedding guests realized this, they realized also that the play which they

themselves were witnessing was, with the approach of the consummation of the marriage of its chief characters, coming to an
end. Very likely this play too was a play of three hours between
after-supper and bedtime, a presentation on a midsummer night
which was the final part of the wedding revels. If so, the audience must have felt piqued at seeing the same situation dupli-
cated upon the stage. With the enactment of the play which the
stage-audience was watching, the time of the consummation of
the stage-marriage and the time of the consummation of the
actual marriage, which at first had been far apart, were becoming more and more closely synchronized: at the conclusion
of the play-within-the-play the play itself would end, and both
stage-marriage and actual marriage would be consummated. The
perception of this and the fulfillment of the expectancy roused
by the comical rehearsals of Bottom and his mates would have
added relish to the wedding audience's enjoyment of the play-
within-the-play as burlesque and would also have impressed on
it the neatness of the play's conclusion.

The play put on by the rude country artisans for the Duke,
moreover, is not merely a burlesque of the performances put on
by such groups during Elizabeth's progresses; it is a kind of comment on *A Midsummer Night's Dream* itself which gives added
significance to the manner in which it completes it. The story of
Pyramus and Thisbe of the play-within-the-play is, like that of
A Midsummer Night's Dream, an illustration that "true lovers
have been ever crossed" (I. i. 150) and that "the course of
true love never did run smooth" (I. i. 134). Like Lysander and
Hermia, Pyramus and Thisbe are forbidden by their parents to
love. As with them, there is unfortunate misunderstanding and
confusion, and Pyramus believes Thisbe to be dead, as for a time
Hermia thought Lysander to have been slain by Demetrius.
Indeed, if we are to define categories as Polonius did, the story

of Lysander and Hermia might more properly than that of Pyramus and Thisbe have been called "very tragical mirth" (V. i. 57), while the story of Pyramus and Thisbe might have been better called "very mirthful tragedy." The play-within-the-play might be said to be a presentation in little of *A Midsummer Night's Dream* as it would be seen through a distorting medium. "This is the silliest stuff that ever I heard" (V. i. 212), says Hippolyta of it. The same might have been said of *A Midsummer Night's Dream* by a hardheaded businesslike man of affairs who would have no truck with fairies and such. In fact, it was said. "It is the most insipid ridiculous play that ever I saw in my life," wrote Mr. Samuel Pepys in his diary after having seen a Restoration performance of Shakespeare's airily fanciful comedy. Through the Pyramus-Thisbe play Shakespeare was subtly asking his aristocratic audience to regard his play with imaginative understanding and sympathy. "The best in this kind are but shadows," replies Theseus to Hippolyta, "and the worst are no worse, if imagination amend them" (V. i. 214–215). This is lordly graciousness, to which Shakespeare was appealing and which he was at the same time flattering: the aristocratic spectator would remedy in his own mind the defects of the piece being presented before him. "Our sport shall be to take what they mistake;/ And what poor duty cannot do, noble respect/ Takes it in might, not merit" (V. i. 90–92).

While asking his audience, however, to aid him with its imagination, Shakespeare was, with the assurance of genius, displaying his mastery of his art. Although the imaginative cooperation of an audience is necessary for the success of a play, the Pyramus-Thisbe scene shows that, despite the Duke's words of gracious condescension, not all of an audience's good will and tolerant receptivity can make rant moving. "This passion, and the death of a dear friend, would go near to make a man sad" (V. i. 293–294). The contrast between the crude literalism of a man with a lantern representing moonshine of the Pyramus-Thisbe scene and the poetic magic of the moon-drenched imagery of A *Midsummer Night's Dream* itself, between the inept explanatory comments that the play is but a play and not real life ("When lion rough in wildest rage doth roar,/ Then know that I, as Snug the jointer, am/ A lion fell," V. i. 225–227) and the delicate suggestion that the play, while only reflecting life, may be a kind of enchanted mirror displaying unseen truths—this contrast is a daring virtuosity calling attention to itself at the close of its performance.

With the conclusion of the rustic dance that follows the artisans' play, the clock strikes, and the Duke announces: "The iron tongue of midnight hath told twelve./ Lovers, to bed; 'tis almost fairy time" (V. i. 370–371). Perhaps the actor who delivered these lines addressed himself to the bridal couple as well as to the two pairs of stage-lovers. At any rate, the wedding audience knew that the play was at an end and, if the play was indeed the conclusion of the revels, that it was time to go bedward.

But all was not yet over. As the Duke, his bride, and their court left, the torches illuminating the hall where the play was being performed were extinguished one after the other, and, with the chamber silent and, except for the flickering light from the hearth, dark, suddenly Puck appeared. For, as he proclaimed, now when "the wasted brands do glow" (V. i. 382), it was again time for the frolicsome fairies, "following darkness like a dream" (V. i. 393). After him came tripping Oberon, Titania and the members of the fairy court, taking the stage left vacant by the members of the Athenian court, with crowns of lighted tapers on their heads making them appear as dancing circles of

235

light.[1] They were here to bless the wedding of the noble pair under their protection, and, as they sang and danced, their song and dance, performed with fairy grace, contrasted with the rustic dance that had preceded it, masque following anti-masque, as was fit and proper. Their song, in which they were led by Oberon, is a song of benediction preliminary to their scattering through the great house to hallow all of its rooms and to bless it and its noble owners for all time:

> Now, until the break of day,
> Through this house each fairy stray.
> To the best bride-bed will we,
> Which by us shall blessed be;
> And the issue there create
> Ever shall be fortunate . . .
> With this field-dew consecrate,
> Every fairy take his gait,
> And each several chamber bless,
> Through this palace, with sweet peace;
> And the owner of it blest
> Ever shall in safety rest.
> Trip away; make no stay;
> Meet me all by break of day. (V. i. 408–429)

And, as the fairies vanished from the stage with their "glimmering light" (V. i. 398), the wedding guests dispersed, leaving the bridal couple to themselves and the house to darkness—and, as the more imaginative ones may have half-believed, to the beneficent fairies.

---

[1] This description of the fairies crowned with lighted tapers is suggested by the editors of the New Cambridge Shakespeare (p. 151), who point out that it is not only indicated by the text but that this scene resembles closely the one in *The Merry Wives of Windsor* in which the fairies, "with rounds of waxen tapers on their heads" (IV. iv. 51), are instructed by the Fairy Queen to bless Windsor Castle.

IX

Shylock, the Elizabethan Puritan and Our Own World[*]

I.

What can Shylock mean for us in the twentieth century, with the inexpugnable memory of Auschwitz in our minds? The historical scholarship of E. E. Stoll and Edgar Rosenberg has demonstrated that Shylock conforms to the medieval stereotype of the diabolical Jew.[1] To be sure, the sentimentalized version of Shylock of nineteenth-century humanitarianism is still pre-

---

[*] Earlier versions of this essay appeared in *Studies in Shakespeare*, eds. Arthur D. Matthews and Clark M. Emery (University of Miami Press, 1953) and *Columbia University Forum*. Reprinted by permission.

[1] E. E. Stoll, *Shakespeare Studies* (New York, 1927), pp. 255–336 and Edgar Rosenberg, *From Shylock to Svengali: Jewish Stereotypes in English Fiction* (Stanford, 1960).

sented on the stage, where, by dint of judicious cutting and unwarranted pieces of stage business, it is imposed on the text. In the Joseph Schildkraut production of some years ago, for instance, a giggling Portia draped herself about the neck of every man within arm's reach, turning Shakespeare's Renaissance lady into an empty-headed floozy in order to set off the dignified Jewish patriarch. But a maltreated text invariably takes its revenge on the production: how can a sympathetic Shylock be made credible in the trial scene, where, sharpening his knife on his shoe, he is adamant in his resolution to cut a man's heart out in cold blood? Unfortunately for the interpretation of a sympathetic Shylock, however, the trial scene cannot be omitted.

However, historical criticism can show us how we can come to terms with the play. While it is true that Shylock was for the Elizabethans the Jew of medieval legend, he was not merely that; he also had contemporary significance. It is through an understanding of Shylock's meaning for the Elizabethans that I believe we can come to an understanding of his meaning for our own time.

II.

Shylock, as we shall see, must have strongly reminded the Elizabethans of the Puritans in their midst, for these early Puritans were a minority of outsiders who were sharply attacked and derided. They were, of course, the fathers of our own Pilgrim fathers. Shylock is not only the ancestor, then, of the American Jews whose grandparents came to this country from European ghettos but, in a sense, of the Americans who proudly trace their family line to the Mayflower passengers. The Old World, New York Jew of Harry Golden's story, who came to the South, and, on being followed by a crowd of urchins fascinated by his earlocks, his beard and his long, black coat, turned upon them, exclaiming, "Vot's de mattah? Hevn't you ever seen a Yenkee?" was not so far off the mark after all.

The connection between the villainous Jewish moneylender of folk tradition, whom Shakespeare made a richly colorful figure, the member of an alien, exotic race, and the Elizabethan Puritan usurer is not pointed up by any direct allusion in the play. However, a contemporary audience, alive to the issues of its own time, does not need the pointers that posterity does. Neither Maxwell Anderson's *Barefoot in Athens* nor Arthur Miller's *The Crucible*, written during the McCarthy era, have a sentence alluding to McCarthyism, but no one failed to see the parallels. There are many expressions of Elizabethan opinion that indicate that Puritanism was a similar generally current concern and that Judaism, Puritanism and usury were so connected in the popular mind that many of Shylock's traits would have reminded Shakespeare's audience of the Puritan usurers of its own time. In the romantic world of *The Merchant of Venice* the audience could catch piquant resemblances to the world with which it was familiar.

Usury was a burning social issue of the day. Always excoriated, the moneylender was a man of increasing importance during this period of nascent capitalism, squeezing landowners impoverished by fixed rents at a time of rising prices and squeezing craftsmen no longer producing for a local market but for a complex commercial organization and in need of credit to maintain production. The moneylender appeared an arrant individualist, who for his own selfish purposes disrupted the traditional relationships of a hierarchical society founded upon the laws of man's nature.

The association of usury and Puritanism appears as early as 1572 in Thomas Wilson's *Discourse Upon Usury*. The contem-

porary usurer, Wilson repeats several times, is worse than the
Jewish moneylender, who no longer existed in England since
Judaism was outlawed. The Jewish moneylender, Wilson observes, had at least followed his own creed and did not pretend
to be a member of the Christian commonwealth. And the typical
contemporary usurer is the Puritan. "[The 'dissembling gospel-
ler'] under the colour of religion overthroweth all religion, and
bearing good men in hande that he loveth playnesse, useth
covertlie all deceypte that may bee, and for pryvate gayne undo-
eth the common welfare of man. And touching thys sinne of
usurie, none doe more openly offende in thys behalfe than do
these counterfeite professours of thys pure religion."[2] So too
Marston describes a "seeming saint" who "with his bait of
usury/ He bit me in deepest usury./ No Jew, no Turk, would
use a Christian/ So inhumanely as this Puritan."[3]

Indeed the Puritans, because of their emphasis on Old Testament law, had from the start of the religious controversy been
charged with returning to Judaism. Bishop Whitgift, arguing
with Thomas Cartwright, told him that he did "Judaizare, 'play
the Jew.'"[4] It was a charge that was frequently made, as we can
infer from Zeal-of-the-land Busy's excuse for attending the fair
(Jonson's work was written after The Merchant of Venice, but
the quotation, like other such quotations I shall use, seems to

[2] Thomas Wilson, A Discourse Upon Usury, ed. R. H. Tawney (New
York, 1925), p. 178.

[3] John Marston, Works, ed. A. H. Bullen (London, 1887), III, 271. Cf.
Robert Greene's picture of Gorinius, the Machiavellian usurer (The Life
and Complete Works, ed. Alexander B. Grosart, London, 1881–1883,
XII, 104): "He was religious too, neuer without a booke at his belt, and
a bolt in his mouth, ready to shoote through his sinfull neighbor." See
R. H. Tawney, Religion and the Rise of Capitalism (New York, 1926),
pp. 232–233, for later identifications of usury and Puritanism.

[4] The Works of John Whitgift, I, 271.

imply a long-standing attitude): "There may be a good vse made of it, too, now I think on't: by the publike eating of Swines flesh, to profess our hate, and loathing of Iudaisme, whereof the brethren stand taxed."[5] The extreme Puritan sects such as the Family of Love, which was being attacked as early as the 1590's, seem indeed, in their adherence to Old Testament law, to have adopted religious observances usually regarded as peculiarly Jewish. "I am a Puritan," says one of the characters in Davenport's New Trick to Cheat the Devil (IV. i):

> One that will eat no pork,
> Doth use to shut his shop on Saturdays,
> And open them on Sundays; a Familist
> And one of the arch limbs of Belzebub
> A Jewish Christian and a Christian Jew.

From their close and continued reading of the Old Testament, Puritans became saturated with its diction. Many, as we can see from Middleton's The Family of Love and Jonson's The Alchemist, assumed Hebrew names[6] and zealously studied Hebrew.[7] Like the Old Testament Jews, they thought of themselves as a chosen people, looking upon the Anglican Church as idolatrous. They in turn were regarded as a minority of foreigners, having imported their religion from Geneva and adopted a strange attire and strange manners, such as talking through their noses. These similarities between the Puritans and the Jews must have given point to the identification of Puritanism and Judaism. They made it possible for Shakespeare to suggest that Jewish moneylenders and Puritan usurers were kindred spirits in their villainy and in their comically outlandish grotesqueness.

[5] Bartholomew Fair, I. vi. 93–96.
[6] Cf. The Family of Love, III. iii. 59.
[7] Cf. The Alchemist, II. v. 334.

The common accusation made by the satirists and dramatists against the Puritans was that they were hypocrites. Thus Nashe includes under hypocrisy "all Machiavilisme, puritanisme, and outward gloasing with a mans enemie."[8] Critics who have sought to soften Shakespeare's picture of Shylock have failed to notice his consummate hypocrisy; they accept his statement that his proposal of a pound of flesh as surety is a "merry sport" (I. iii. 146) and find that he only desires payment after his thirst for revenge has been aroused by the elopement of Jessica. But Shylock is not a man for "merry sport."

As soon as Antonio enters, Shylock expresses in soliloquy his profound hatred for him as a Christian who brings down the rate of interest by lending gratis in "low simplicity" (the audience would have understood it to be in Christian charity) and concludes "Cursèd be my tribe,/ If I forgive him" (I. iii. 43–53). When Bassanio interrupts his evil meditations with "Shylock, do you hear?" he pretends to have been mentally casting up his accounts to see if he can make up the sum required by Bassanio. To Antonio he addresses himself courteously: "Rest you fair, good signior;/ Your worship was the last man in our mouths" (I. iii. 60–61). Antonio had indeed been spoken of just before he entered, but not in the affable manner which Shylock implies. As Antonio had appeared, Shylock in fact was rejecting with fierce contempt for the eaters of pork an invitation to dine with him.

Now, when Antonio impatiently asks if he will grant the loan, as he is characteristically delaying his answer in Levantine bargaining fashion, Shylock reveals in a flash of indignation his rancor and inquires with bitter irony if, in return for Antonio's

---

[8] I, 220. See also, for instance, Wilson, Marston and Greene, quoted above.

insults, he should "bend low and in a bondsman's key" (I. iii. 125) offer to lend him money now that Antonio needs his financial aid. When Antonio, however, does not act the suppliant but forthrightly says that he will insult him again and when he tells Shylock that if he wishes to lend him money, he should do so as an enemy, for friendship would not permit the taking of interest, he changes his tone, cringing obsequiously:

> Why, look you, how you storm!
> I would be friends with you and have your love,
> Forget the shames that you have stain'd me with,
> Supply your present wants and take no doit
> Of usance for my moneys, and you'll not hear me:
> This is kind I offer. (I. iii. 138–143)

This is indeed spoken "in a bondsman's key." Shylock acts like the cur he has been called by Antonio and snaps viciously when he thinks he can do so with impunity but immediately returns to bootlicking when he is met with a show of strength.

His refusal to make an open and aboveboard deal as an avowed enemy, as Antonio proposes, his profession of friendship after his momentary revelation of the hatred concealed beneath his "patient shrug," his offer to lend without interest after his defense of usury—all stamp him as a hypocrite of the worst sort. The audience, which has already heard Shylock tell what he will do if he catches Antonio "once upon the hip" (I. iii. 47), is not permitted to be in doubt about his intention in proposing the bond. "I like not fair terms and a villain's mind," (I. iii. 180) warns Bassanio, concluding a couplet at the close of the scene, but he is overridden by the devoted Antonio, who does not fear to incur any dangers which would enable him to help his friend.

Until Shylock announces his desire for revenge in a burst of rage, he continues to be hypocritical. In spite of his previously declared religious scruples at dining with Christians, he accepts Bassanio's invitation to join him in the fellowship of the banquet-table, but he goes "in hate, to feed upon/ The prodigal Christian" (II. v. 14–15). So too does he recommend Launcelot Gobbo to Bassanio, not out of friendliness to either, but with the design of ridding himself of a heavy-eating, inefficient servant and fastening him as an added expense upon Bassanio.

Puritan hypocrisy was generally portrayed as taking the form of a pretence of being better than other men, and the Puritan was presented as stiff-necked rather than obsequious, but he could be made on occasion to be self-abasing if it served his need. Thus Tribulation in *The Alchemist* submits to humiliating conditions involving denials of his religious principles in order that Subtle might counterfeit money for him, just as Shylock goes to dine at Bassanio's in order to help ruin him. Shylock, on the other hand, can be as self-righteous as any Puritan. "O father Abram," he exclaims, "what these Christians are,/ Whose own hard dealings teaches them suspect/ The thoughts of others!" (I. iii. 161–163). He thinks of himself as belonging to a "sacred nation" (I. iii. 49) and affirms "sufferance is the badge of all our tribe," (I. iii. 111) just as Tribulation says, "These chastisements are common to the *Saints*,/ And such rebukes we of the *Separation*/ Must beare with willing shoulder, as the trialls/ Sent forth, to tempt our frailties" (*The Alchemist*, III. i. 1–4).

Shylock's pharisaism, like that of the Puritans, takes the form of contempt for merrymaking and revelry. "What, are there masques?" he exclaims in the very accents of the Puritan.

> Hear you me, Jessica:
> Lock up my doors; and when you hear the drum
> And the vile squealing of the wry-necked fife,
> Clamber not you up to the casements then,

> Nor thrust your head into the public street
> To gaze on Christian fools with varnish'd faces,
> But stop my house's ears, I mean my casements:
> Let not the sound of shallow foppery enter
> My sober house. (II. v. 28–36)

His narrow, ungenerous mind, meanly restricted to money-making, renders him incapable of unbending to laughter; it is the antithesis of the well-rounded personality of the Renaissance gentleman Bassanio.

Like the morally rigid Puritans, Shylock is intolerant of others and attributes to them his own spiritual defects. Immediately after Launcelot has pointed up for us the contrast between Bassanio's munificence and Shylock's miserliness, Shylock tells Launcelot that Bassanio will not allow him to eat and sleep all day long as he did. When the princely merchant Antonio enters, he comments to himself, "How like a fawning publican he looks," (I. iii. 42) and unwittingly echoes the Pharisee's words about the Publican in the parable,[9] although he himself immediately fawns upon Antonio. And, after having said with hypocritical humility that "sufferance," patient endurance, is the badge of all his tribe, he justifies his lust for revenge by saying that he has learned it from the Christians. "If a Christian wrong a Jew, what should his sufferance be by Christian example? Why, revenge" (III. i. 73–75). But the future is to show the difference between Christian mercy and the ferocious vengefulness which he has hidden under his "sufferance."

Shylock's malevolence is presented as diabolically inhuman. Medieval literature had given the story of man's redemption in the symbolic form of his being freed by the "ransom" of Christ from a bond to the Devil, an unrelenting creditor with the char-

---

[9] Luke, 18:10–14.

acteristics of a usurer.[10] The Jew had also been portrayed as a devil serving Satan.[11] By having Shylock referred to as a devil again and again,[12] Shakespeare continued this tradition. But Puritans as well as Jews were called devils in Shakespeare's time. Certain that they were on the side of the angels, Anglicans regarded all those not of their party as being of the devil's party and made "the Devil is a Puritan" a cant phrase.[13] The pious exterior of the Puritan, it was charged, concealed the spirit of the Devil. Those who owed money to a Puritan usurer found that they had the devil to pay. "Do you call us devils?" exclaims a creditor in Middleton's *A Trick to Catch the Old One* (IV. iv. 322). "You shall find us puritans—Bear him away; let 'em talk as they go." The Devil in the guise of a Puritan was more relentlessly cruel than ever.

With the bibliolatry of the Puritans it was inevitable that the saying about the Devil citing scripture be applied to them. In *A Merry Knack to Know a Knave* (1592), when a beggar asks a Puritan preacher for alms, the preacher twists Scripture to justify a refusal: "And in good time, look in the blessed Proverb of Solomon, which is Good deeds do not justify a man; therefore, I count it sin to give thee anything."[14] "The answer," observes Holden, "is a piece of theological web-spinning typical of the stage Puritan when he would get himself out of moral difficulties."[15] Thus too does Shylock cite Jacob's acumen in his business

[10] See above, p. 54.
[11] Stoll, pp. 270–271.
[12] I. iii. 99; II. ii. 23–26; II. iii. 2; III. i. 22–24; III. ii. 35; IV. i. 217.
[13] William P. Holden, "The Religious Controversy and Anti-Puritan Satire, 1572–1642," Harvard doctoral thesis, p. 266. Dr. Holden's thesis, since the time I made use of it, was published by Yale University Press. I am grateful to him for having loaned me his personal copy of his thesis and for his scholarly courtesy in volunteering information.
[14] Dodsley, *Old Plays*, VI (1875), 580. Quoted by Holden, p. 265.
[15] P. 265.

gamble with his brother to justify the taking of interest, a citation whose fallacy is exposed when, in reply to Antonio's pointed question, "Did he take interest," Shylock has to hem and haw: "No, not take interest, not, as you would say,/ Directly interest" (I. iii. 76–78).[16] Antonio's comment on Shylock's sophistry is like Honesty's comment on the sophistry of the Puritan preacher in *A Merry Knack to Know a Knave:* "See how he can turn and wind scripture to his own use." "Mark you this, Bassanio," says Antonio, (I. iii. 98–103). "The devil can cite Scripture for his purpose."

In the trial scene "this cruel devil," as Bassanio calls him (IV. i. 217), who has cited Scripture and whose language is full of Old Testament allusions and phraseology, insists on his pound of flesh, holding to the strict letter of the law. Similarly the Puritans had demanded undeviating adherence to the Mosaic code. Bishop Whitgift, contending that the teachings of the New Testament had superseded the Mosaic code, had pointed out that the Puritan demand would rigorously enforce a small body of laws without the least modification or exception and that the sovereign would "be abridged of that prerogative which she hath

---

[16] Shylock's talmudical manner of citing Scripture, with its repetitions and involutions and its show of learning, is similar to Puritan biblical exegesis. Compare Shylock's turn of speech with Zeal-of-the-Land Busy's.

Shylock. When Jacob grazed his uncle Laban's sheep—
This Jacob from our holy Abram was,
As his wise mother wrought in his behalf,
The third possessor: ay, he was the third—(I. iii. 72–75).
Busy. Verily, for the disease of longing, it is a disease, a carnall disease, or appetite, incident to women: and as it is carnall, and incident, it is naturall, very naturall: Now Pigge, it is a meat, and a meat that is nourishing, and may be long'd for, and so consequently eaten: but in the Fayre, and as a *Bartholomew*-pig, it cannot be eaten for the very calling it a *Bartholomew*-pigge, and to eat it so, is a spice of Idolatry. (I. vi. 48–55)

in pardoning such as by the law be condemned to die."[17] This defense of the power of the Queen to render mercy was really a defense of the powers of the Queen in general, for, as Whitgift was aware (he accused the Puritans of seeking a theocracy in which the presbyters would be supreme),[18] behind the religious dispute lay the question of political power, toward which the advanced Puritan section of the bourgeoisie was groping. Shylock, in his stubborn insistence ("I stand here for law"), is dramatizing the doctrinal inflexibility of the Puritans, which, Whitgift charged, would infringe upon the Queen's power and deprive her of the means to exercise the mercy for which Portia pleads.

III.

The Elizabethan satire of Puritanism does not, of course, present the whole truth about it, just as the medieval stereotype that Shakespeare borrowed does not tell the truth about Jews of the time. No doubt both Elizabethan Puritans and medieval Jews did exhibit traits that were the result of their social and economic positions, but these traits were caricatured by hostile observers. Fifty years after the first performance of *The Merchant of Venice*, the Puritan forces that accomplished a great social revolution favoring both science and industry were made up of a variety of classes, from enterprising gentry to craftsmen; they included not only people like Ben Jonson's distasteful Zeal-of-the-Land Busy but John Milton as well. Outsiders, nonconformists in more than matters of church doctrine, the Puritans were able to take a revolutionary view of things, just as the Jews, remaining half-strangers and therefore able to look upon society and culture from the outside, have produced revolutionary

[17] I, 273.
[18] Ibid., III, 273.

thinkers from Spinoza to Freud. The achievements through history of both Puritans and Jews could not have been predicted from the stereotypes available to Shakespeare.

But if neither stereotype has validity today, why does Shylock still hold our attention? I suggest that, accurately understood, he is both comic and frightening because he portrays the worst side of the new capitalist individualism born in Shakespeare's time. He is the spirit of that economic self-seeking which is indifferent to the welfare of others, stultifying those whom it possesses and oppressing the rest of humanity. Jewishness, Puritanism, usury are only incidental; this spirit is what is universal in him. One does not need to be hostile toward Jews to laugh at his comic rigidity and shudder at his ferocious hatred of all those who oppose his purposes.

Shylock's comic rigidity indicates the way in which the ethos of Puritanism, while freeing men from the restrictions of the old order, also brought about a mechanization of personality. Bergson found that this mechanization of personality had produced, in the words of his commentator, Wylie Sypher, the modern comic type—"the professional man who acts with rigidity."

> He thinks with the automatism of his business code. . . .
> This comic figure is identified by his "professional callousness," his inelasticity—which is a mode of pride. The automatic responses of this egoist make him appear, when we look at him attentively, like a ready-made product standardized for the market.[19]

It is not ethnic outlandishness founded on transitory differences but the automatism of the "type," responding to only one or two emotions, which gives Shylock his abiding comic quality. As Tubal alternately tells him of Antonio's losses and of Jessica's

---

[19] *Comedy* (New York, 1956), pp. x-xi.

spending, and as he responds first with exultation and then with dismay, Shylock is like a marionette being jerked this way and that. The scene has been prepared for by a description of him running through the streets calling for his jewels, his daughter and his ducats; each is only a lost possession whose competing claim with the others for his grief drives him to comic distraction. In his frenzy he resembles a mechanism controlled by two push-buttons, whirling crazily when both buttons are pressed at once. All of the previous suffering of his race is as nothing compared with his present suffering over monetary losses; he wishes his daughter dead if he might recover his jewels: "The curse never fell upon our nation till now, I never felt it till now —two thousand ducats in that, and other precious, precious jewels. I would my daughter were dead at my foot, and the jewels in her ear" (III. i. 89–93). With Jessica safely away, Shylock's bizarre, inhuman behavior becomes comical.

This element of the comical remains as the time for settling accounts approaches, although the element of the sinister now predominates. Shylock displays that "professional callousness" which is "a mode of pride." "Gaoler, look to him," he exclaims. "Tell me not of mercy,/ This is the fool that lent out money gratis" (III. iii. 1–3). Those like Antonio, who are not governed by his business code, he looks upon as fools. He himself can think no other way. "I'll have my bond," (III. iii. 4) he vows, in comic repetition. The bond, the sacred business contract, is all. When Portia suggests that a doctor stand by to prevent Antonio from bleeding to death in discharging his debt, Shylock replies, "I cannot find it, 'tis not in the bond" (IV. i. 262). If compassion is not written into the contract, then one is not under any obligation to feel it or act by it.

Ironically, Shylock, the typical Jew for the anti-Semites, is like

the hate-filled racist. Inflexibly insisting on committing his sense-
less cruelty, he states:

> You'll ask me, why I rather choose to have
> A weight of carrion flesh, than to receive
> Three thousand ducats. I'll not answer that,
> But say it is my humour; is it answered?
> What if my house be troubled with a rat,
> And I be pleased to give ten thousand ducats
> To have it ban'd. What, are you answered yet? . . .
> So I can give no reason, nor I will not,
> More than a lodg'd hate, and a certain loathing
> I bear Antonio. (IV. i. 40–61)

To Bassanio's "Do all men kill the things they do not love?" he
retorts, "Hates any man the thing he would not kill?" (IV. i.
66–67). These words, in their avowal of an irrational hatred
that will be satisfied only by killing, in their comparison of men
with rats to be similarly exterminated, breathe forth the spirit of
the gas chambers. If he does not understand now the reasons for
his hatred, he had earlier revealed the underlying spring that
impels him to action:

> I hate him for he is a Christian
> But more, for that in low simplicity
> He lends out money gratis, and brings down
> The rate of usance here with us in Venice. (I. iii. 43–47)

Antonio, an outsider, has intruded upon Shylock's business, does
not play according to the rules of the business game and is making things difficult for him. Shylock's feeling is the sort that a
middle-class anti-Semite today might voice concerning a Jewish
business competitor.

Although Shylock has the psychology of the racist, he has
the external features of the medieval stereotype of the Jew—a

stereotype which, by the way, resembles the contemporary racist stereotype of the Negro: each is presented as bogeyman, beast and buffoon; the image of the Negro with the razor is the counterpart of the image of the Jew with the knife. The cannibalistic images, associated with Shylock throughout the play, are suggestive of the medieval legend, continuing through the Renaissance, that Jews delighted in secretly feasting on the flesh of murdered Christians. That Shylock, despite his possessing characteristics of the Jew of medieval legend, is not *merely* a fairy-tale monster is due to Shakespeare's having breathed life into the stereotype by giving him the spirit of the contemporary *homo economicus*.

IV.

Shylock's defeat at the hands of Portia is the joyous triumph of the harmonious society over the disturbing force which threatens it, the triumph of the healthy, balanced person over mechanical codes (the law of Venice is on Shylock's side), the triumph of life over death. The successive escapes of the irrepressible Launcelot Gobbo, who is representative of the life-force, and of the charming, witty Jessica from the gloomy household of the humorless Shylock prefigure this triumph. *The Merchant of Venice* is indeed what Susanne Langer calls comedy: "an image of human vitality holding its own in the world."[20] It is not a problem play.

To be sure, the identification of aristocratic largess with Christian charity produces ironies for us now, ironies unintended by Shakespeare. Thus Shylock says at one point in the trial scene:

What judgement shall I dread, doing no wrong?
You have among you many a purchased slave . . .
   Shall I say to you,

[20] *Feeling and Form* (New York, 1953), p. 330.

Let them be free, marry them to your heirs? . . .
  You will answer
"The slaves are ours": so do I answer you:
The pound of flesh which I demand of him,
Is dearly bought; 'tis mine and I will have it. (IV. i. 89–100)

This is not, as some critics have alleged, a home-thrust by Shylock at his opponents. He is not saying, as we might think, "You are just as bad as I am"; he is saying, "I am right in demanding what is my own, the pound of flesh which I paid for with the money that was never returned to me; just as right as you are in keeping what is your own, your slaves." We must remember, as Stoll points out, that this was the time when "Sir John Hawkins, who initiated the slave-trade, with the Earls of Pembroke and Leicester and the Queen herself for partners, bore on the arms which were granted him for his exploits a demi-Moor, proper, in chains" (p. 267). The aristocratic view of society, accepted in general by the shopkeepers and craftsmen of Shakespeare's audience, may be terribly blind to oppression. The careless generosity of the aristocrat can become a cavalier disregard for the lower classes, just as the dogmatism and self-righteousness of the Puritan can become a fervent zeal for social justice, as is to be seen in the American Civil War, our own version of the conflict between Cavalier and Puritan.

So, too, there is unintended irony in the sentence imposed on Shylock, with its command that he convert to Christianity presented as gracious mercy. How Shakespeare's contemporaries regarded what we think of as enforcement of conscience is indicated by the Elizabethan mariner who laughed at the forcibly baptized Moors turning toward Mecca in the evening to pray; the poor fools, he said, did not realize that they were now Christians. Antonio's condition, that Shylock become a Christian, would have been regarded by the Elizabethan audience as a mercy, in that it offered him the possibility of achieving salvation. Of course, this submission also would have given the audience a sense of satisfaction as well as a glow of moral superiority. Comic justice is rendered and at the same time the resolution of comedy, in which enmity is dissolved in laughter, is effected. But when we ponder this enforced conversion, not in terms of the play but of history, we can only reflect ruefully on the mercies of authoritarian regimes convinced that they possess the sole truth.

The awareness of such historical ironies comes, however, from the intellectual contemplation of *The Merchant of Venice*, not from partaking of the aesthetic experience which it affords. This aesthetic experience, as I have indicated, is a vitalizing one: it makes us more richly aware of the potentialities of life. Its giving us this awareness makes *The Merchant of Venice* the masterpiece that it is.

Index

DATE DUE

DEC 2 2 72			
MAY 24 78			
MAY 0 3 1999			
GAYLORD			PRINTED IN U.S A.